DATE DUE

UNDERSTANDING
HEINRICH BÖLL

UNDERSTANDING MODERN EUROPEAN and LATIN AMERICAN LITERATURE

James Hardin, *Series Editor*

ADVISORY BOARD

Understanding
HEINRICH
BÖLL

ROBERT C. CONARD

UNIVERSITY OF SOUTH CAROLINA PRESS

·Copyright © 1992 University of South Carolina

Published in Columbia, South Carolina, by the
University of South Carolina Press

Manufactured in the United States of America

Library of Congress Cataloging-in-Publication Data

Conard, Robert C., 1933–
    Understanding Heinrich Böll / Robert C. Conard.
        p. cm.—(Understanding modern European and Latin American
    literature.)
    Includes bibliographical references and index.
    ISBN 0–87249–779–8
    1. Böll, Heinrich, 1917–   —Criticism and interpretation.
I. Title. II. Series.
PT2603.0394Z597 1991
833'.914—dc20   91-25072

To

RALPH LEY

CONTENTS

EDITOR'S PREFACE

Understanding Modern European and Latin American Literature has been planned for undergraduate and graduate students and nonacademic readers. The aim of the books is to provide an introduction to the life and writings of prominent modern authors and to explicate their most important works.

Modern literature makes special demands, and this is particularly true of foreign literature, in which the reader must contend not only with unfamiliar, often arcane artistic conventions and philosophical concepts, but also with the handicap of reading the literature in translation. It is a truism that the nuances of one language can be rendered in another only imperfectly (and this problem is especially acute in fiction), but the fact that the works of European and Latin American writers are situated in a historical and cultural setting quite different from our own can be as great a hindrance to the understanding of these works as the linguistic barrier. For this reason, the UMELL series will emphasize the sociological and historical background of writers treated. The peculiar philosophical and cultural traditions of a given culture may be particularly important for an understanding of certain authors, and these will be taken up in the introductory chapter and also in the discussion of those works to which this information is relevant. Beyond this, the books will treat the specifically literary aspects of the author under discussion and attempt to explain the complexities of contemporary literature lucidly. The books are conceived as introductions to the authors covered, not as comprehensive analyses. They do not provide detailed summaries of plot since they are meant to be used in conjunction with the books they treat, not as a substitute for the study of the original works. The purpose of the books is to provide information and judicious literary assessment of the major works in compact, readable form. It is our hope that the UMELL series will help to increase knowledge and understanding of the European and Latin American cultures and will serve to make the literature of those cultures more accessible.

Robert C. Conard's *Understanding Heinrich Böll* is the first comprehensive work to be published in America treating Böll's entire oeuvre. It is a thorough and objective evaluation, but Conard's profound admiration for Böll, which goes far beyond scholarly respect for literary achievement, infuses the book with a special enthusiasm that infects the reader. It is no easy task to provide a tautly written analysis of such a prolific novelist (a historical-critical edition of Böll's work is planned for twenty-five volumes without including any of his seventy thousand letters), but in my view Conard has provided an informative, authoritative work that furthers our understanding not only of the novelist, but also of the man.

PREFACE

This book was completed before German unification. It surprises me that what I have written about Böll's work in placing it in the forty years of West German history has required so little modification. The reason, however, seems obvious enough. Although the "October Revolution" of 1989 ended the period of a Germany separated into East and West, it is West Germany's economic and political system that continues. Unified Germany is in large measure West Germany in a larger format. That Böll did not live to see this historic change is a sad fact, for he would have welcomed it, although with some reservations.

In May of 1990, I asked Böll's wife and his nephew Victor Böll, director of the Böll Archive, what they thought Böll's attitude would have been to unification. His wife and nephew both said they were not sure enough to offer an answer but were certain that he would have been both for and against it. "Pleased and saddened" is a reasonable summary of their responses: pleased that there is more freedom in the East—to speak, to travel, to criticize, and to express political opinions—saddened that the momentary possible better socialist alternative to Stalinism that glowed so brightly in the East for a few weeks in the fall and winter of 1989–1990 died so suddenly with the announcement of a currency union and the changing cry of "We are the people" to "We are one people," saddened that the word *unification* became thereafter a euphemism for the reality of annexation without official self-determination, even if unity was desired by the majority in East and West.

We will never know for sure what Böll's writing in these months would have been, although surely he would have expressed himself on this national issue as he had expressed himself on all important West German events from 1949 to 1985. I believe the essence of Böll's work that would have manifested itself in his concern with unification was his compassion, his desire for fairness, his belief that people need to be ministered to, never administrated, that all people have dignity, and that human dignity—despite proclamations of its inviolability by the West German constitution—is too often abused in the management of politics and economics. Böll's artistic talent lay specifically in his ability to show the ways in which powerless people are often violated in the normal administration of public affairs.

Böll's artistic gift was in showing the transgressions against human dignity in the details of everyday life. To him, injustice was never abstract but always concrete. In following his own principles, he did not fear to approach the artistic danger zone of sentimentality. He was never ambivalent in his concern for his fictional characters or for the real citizens of this world. His work and life were distinguished by a moral force that thrived in the aesthetic space between moral conviction and righteousness. Few writers are able to inhabit this exceptional artistic realm. It is not that Böll never knew the protective instincts that caution one about too much commitment, but he was always willing to take the personal and artistic risks that went along with his compulsion to write and his need to avoid passivity in the face of injustice—the error, he felt, that had permitted fascism to conquer Germany. His choices were not all felicitous, but his life and work as a whole succeeded. To him the bright life of the Federal Republic always had its dark side. He was critically aware of West Germany's shortcomings and its unfulfilled potential, its too eager willingness to sacrifice historical memory to comfortable prosperity and to take a short view of the future without a long view of the past. Applying Böll's personal aesthetic to unification, I have the strong feeling that he would see the terrible neglect of memory that characterized postwar West Germany in its rush to a "better" life to be an historic mistake about to be made once again, this time with the repression of the Stasi past competing with the forgetting of the Nazi past, but he would never fail to point out that heaps of files are not the same as piles of bodies.

ACKNOWLEDGMENTS

It is with pleasure and a sense of gratitude that I express my thanks to Ralph Ley of Rutgers University for his carerful reading of several sections of this book and for his valuable suggestions for improvement. I also thank James Hardin of the University of South Carolina for his editorial advice, patience, and unwavering support.

I acknowledge also my debt to Viktor Böll, director of the Böll Archive in Cologne, for his help in procuring valuable materials and for granting access to the archive itself. Without the rich holdings of the Böll Archive this book would be poorer in many ways.

In addition I wish to thank the University of Dayton Research Council for a summer research grant that helped me to complete this book, and I thank also the National Endowment for the Humanities for making possible a summer seminar at the University of Southern California where I was able, under the guidance of John Elliott, to pursue my research on Marxism, the study of which is reflected on several pages of this book.

Finally, I acknowledge all those people whose names do not appear here who have helped, supported, and encouraged me as I wrote this book.

A NOTE ON TRANSLATIONS

Unless otherwise cited in the notes, all translations from Böll's works are my own. The title of Böll's books are given first in German, followed by the date of German publication. If a work has appeared in English translation, the title of the translation is indicated in parentheses. For example, *Und sagte kein einziges Wort*, 1953 (*And Never said a Word*). Subsequent citations of the title will be in English. Works that have not appeared in translation will be cited first by German title followed by publication date and my translation of the title in parentheses. For example, *Frankfurter Vorlesungen*, 1966 (Frankfurt Lectures). The German title will be used for subsequent references to untranslated works.

ABBREVIATIONS

Works by Böll cited in the text have been abbreviated as follows. The full citations for these editions are in the bibliography.

EZ	*Ein- und Zusprüche: Schriften, Reden und Prosa 1981–1983*
Fähigkeit	*Die Fähigkeit zu trauern: Schriften und Reden 1983–1985*
FB	*Fürsorgliche Belagerung*
FF	*Frauen vor Flußlandschaft*
Q	*Querschnitte aus Interviews, Aufsätze und Reden*
Rom	*Rom auf den ersten Blick: Reisen, Städte, Landschaften*
V	*Das Vermächtnis*
VG	*Vermintes Gelände: Essayistische Schriften 1977–1981*
WESR	*Werke: Essayistische Schriften und Reden 1–3*
WHTDG	*Werke: Hörspiele, Theaterstücke, Drehbücher, Gedichte 1*
WI	*Werke: Interviews 1*
Wir	*Wir kommen weit her: Gedichte*
WRE	*Werke: Romane und Erzählungen 1–5*

CHRONOLOGY

1917	Born in Cologne 21 December, the sixth child of Viktor and Maria Böll.
1921	Family moves to Cologne suburb of Raderberg.
1924–1928	School years in Cologne Raderthal.
1928	Begins secondary education at the Kaiser Wilhelm Gymnasium in Cologne.
1929	Great Depression causes his father's cabinet- and furniture-making business to go bankrupt.
1933	Nazis come to power; illegal meetings of Catholic youth groups in the Böll family apartment.
1936	Begins writing short stories and poems as revealed by manuscripts in the Böll Archive.
1937	Finishes Gymnasium and starts an apprenticeship with a book dealer in Bonn.
1938	Called to do compulsory work service.
1939	Begins studies at the University of Cologne; drafted into the army.
1939–1945	Military service in France, Poland, Soviet Union, Romania, Hungary, and Germany; writes daily letters to family and future wife, Annemarie Cech.
1942	Marries Annemarie Cech.
1944	Death of mother from a heart attack caused by the bombing of Cologne.

1945	Birth and death of first son, Christoph; interned as POW; returns to Cologne; begins writing novels and short stories about the war (all unpublished).
1947	Publication of first short story, "Aus der Vorzeit" (From Prehistoric Times); birth of second son, Raimund.
1948	Birth of third son, René.
1949	Considers giving up writing because of lack of success and the financial condition of the family; lives from his wife's teaching; publication of the novella *Der Zug war pünktlich* (*The Train Was on Time*).
1950	Birth of fourth son, Vincent; publication of selected short stories, *Wanderer, kommst du nach Spa . . .* (Stranger Bear Word to the Spartans We . . . ; included in *The Stories of Heinrich Böll*).
1951	Prize of Group 47 for the short story "Die schwarzen Schafe" ("Black Sheep"); publication of first novel, *Wo warst du, Adam?* (*Adam, Where Art Thou?*).
1952	René Schickele Prize for *Adam, Where Art Thou?*
1953	The novel *Und Sagte kein einziges Wort* (*And Never Said a Word*), his first financial success; henceforth lives from his income as a writer.
1954	The novel *Haus ohne Hüter* (*The Unguarded House*); first trip to Ireland; prize of *Tribune de Paris* for *And Never Said a Word*.
1955	The novella *Das Brot der frühen Jahre* (*The Bread of Those Early Years*); French Publishers' Prize for *The Unguarded House*.
1956	First trip to the socialist East, Poland.
1957	*Irisches Tagebuch* (*Irish Journal*), stories; Eduard von der Heydt Prize of the city of Wuppertal; prize of the Bavarian Academy of Fine Arts.
1958	*Doktor Murkes gesammeltes Schweigen und andere Satiren* (Doctor Murke's Collected Sciences; most pieces translated in *The Stories of Heinrich Böll*).

1959   The novel *Billard um halbzehn* (*Billards at Half-past Nine*).

1960   Death of father in Cologne.

1961   *Erzählungen, Hörspiele, Aufsätze* (Stories, Radio Plays, Essays), includes first collected essays.

1962   First trip to the Soviet Union.

1963   The novel *Ansichten eines Clowns* (*The Clown*).

1964   The story *Entfernung von der Truppe* (*Absent without Leave*).

1966   The novel *Ende einer Dienstfahrt* (*End of a Mission*); second trip to the Soviet Union; *Frankfurter Vorlesungen* (Frankfurt Lectures), published version of lectures delivered at the University of Frankfurt during the summer of 1964.

1967   Georg Büchner Prize of the German Academy of Language and Literature; *Aufsätze, Kritiken, Reden* (Essays, Reviews, Speeches), essays.

1968   In Czechoslovakia at the time of the Warsaw Pact invasion.

1969   Refuses, along with his wife, to pay church taxes; elected president of West German PEN.

1971   The novel *Gruppenbild mit Dame* (*Group Portrait with Lady*); elected president of the international PEN.

1972   Nobel Prize for Literature; campaigns for Willy Brandt's *Ostpolitik;* publishes controversial article on Ulrike Meinhof; first volume of poetry, *Gedichte* (Poems).

1974   The novel *Die verlorene Ehre der Katharina Blum* (*The Lost Honor of Katharina Blum*); chosen honorary member of the American Academy of Arts and Letters; Carl von Ossietzky Medal of the League of Human Rights; Solzhenitsyn's first refuge in the West after his expulsion from the Soviet Union is with Böll at his home in the Eifel.

1976	Forced, along with his wife, to leave the Catholic church for refusal to pay church taxes, remains in his words in the "community of faithful."
1977	*Werke: Romane und Erzählungen 1–5* (1947–1977) (Works: Novels and Stories), 5 vols.; *Einmischung erwünscht: Schriften zur Zeit* (Involvement Desirable: Essays on Contemporary Issues).
1979	*Werke: Essayistische Schriften und Reden 1–3* (1952–1978) (Works: Essays and Speeches), 3 vols. *Werke: Interviews 1* (1961–1978); *Werke: Hörspiele, Theaterstücke, Drehbücher, Gedichte 1* (1952–1978) (Works: Radio Plays, Plays, Filmscripts), 1 vol; the novel *Fürsorgliche Belagerung* (*The Safety Net*); the short stories *Du fährst zu oft nach Heidelberg* (You Are Going to Heidelberg Too Often; most are in *The Stories of Heinrich Böll*).
1981	*Was soll aus dem Jungen bloß werden? Oder: Irgendwas mit Büchern* (*What's to Become of the Boy? Or, Something to Do with Books*), longest autobiographical piece; participates, along with his wife, in peace demonstrations.
1982	Death of son Raimund; the story *Das Vermächtnis* (*A Soldier's Legacy*); honorary citizenship of the city of Cologne and honorary professorship of the state of North-Rhein-Westphalia; *Vermintes Gelände: Essayistische Schriften 1977–1981* (Minefields: Essays 1977–1981).
1983	Campaigns for the Greens; participates in a peace demonstration that blockades an American base; *Die Verwundung und andere frühe Erzählungen* (*The Casualty*), a collection of previously unpublished early short stories
1984	City of Cologne acquires the Böll Archive; made commander in the Ordre des arts et des lettres by the French ministry of education; *Bild, Bonn, Boenisch*, analysis of the political writings of Chancellor Helmut Kohl's press secretary; *Ein- und Zusprüche: Schriften, Reden, und Prosa 1981–1983* (Statement of Protest and Support: Speeches and Prose Fiction, 1981–1983).

1985   Dies at his home in Langenbroich in the Eifel; buried in
            the Catholic church; the novel *Frauen vor Flußlandschaft*
            (*Women in a River Landscape*).

1986   *Die Fähigkeit zu trauen: Schriften und Reden 1983–1985*
            (The Ability to Mourn: Essays and Speeches, 1983–
            1985); *Wir kommen weit her* (We Come From Far Away),
            collected poetry.

1987   *Rom auf den ersten Blick: Reisen, Städte, Landschaften*
            (Rome at First Glance: Travels, Cities, Landscapes), es-
            says. Founding of the Heinrich-Böll-Stiftung to promote
            the arts, the study of social problems and the Third
            World, and to publish a historical-critical edition of
            Böll's works.

UNDERSTANDING
HEINRICH BÖLL

CHAPTER ONE

Biography

''My biography politicized me, forcibly, sometimes almost against my will'' (Hoffman 222). When Böll wrote these words, he was thinking in part that he was born in the empire of Wilhelm II, grew up in the Weimar Republic, spent his teens under fascism, his early adulthood in World War II, lived after the war under Allied occupation, and experienced before the age of thirty-two the founding of the Federal Republic. The key to understanding Böll lies in knowing his history.

He was born 21 December 1917 in Cologne. He claimed his first memory was of being held in his mother's arms, looking out the window of their Cologne apartment, watching the troops of General von Hindenburg's defeated army march home (*WESR* 1: 285). Böll would have been two at the time. The defeat in World War I was traumatic for Germany, and incomprehensible. Germans found it difficult to accept defeat because they believed the reports of victories at the front, rejoiced in the defeat of Russia, and had no foreign armies on their soil. The people were taken by surprise in November 1918 when the Kaiser fled the country, and General Ludendorff, Hindenburg's chief of staff, proclaimed a republic in order to mollify the conquering Allies. The truth of events at the front had actually been known only to the Kaiser, a few ministers, and the military. Even members of the government believed Germany was winning the war. It was a defeat that the historian Fritz Stern characterized as ''more apparent in its political consequences than its military causes'' (xiii). The proclamation of the republic shocked a nation unprepared for democracy and produced a deep suspicion of politics and politicians.

The new Weimar Republic was never on firm ground. The people had not been educated to think politically or to take part in the democratic process but to leave political decisions to the head of state and his ministers.

In their distrust of democracy, Germans were like the peoples of several other nations of Western Europe (Italy, Spain, Portugal, Greece) that experimented with republicanism between the world wars. In none of these countries did democracy survive the economic, political, and cultural pressures of the postwar era. The Weimar Republic, in fact, lasted longer than most of the other democratic experiments, and when it eventually succumbed, it was not to a coup but to the weight of accumulated weaknesses exploited by a fascist mass movement that developed into the nation's largest political party.

The German antipathy to parliamentarianism, as the political philosopher Ernst Fraenkel points out, was rooted in the institutions created by Bismarck: a strong civil-service bureaucracy and a tough military caste, each insistent on preserving its power against democracy (19–31). Parliament belonged to that whole complex of institutions and attitudes thought modern and un-German, even hostile to the essence of the German spirit that needed a strong leader. The anti-democrats argued that German philosophical and cultural tradition was incompatible with democracy. Defeat in World War I and the subsequent imposition of the harsh terms of the Versailles peace treaty did not weaken Germany's belief in the need for authoritarian leadership but actually intensified it by increasing dislike for the victorious democratic Western allies.

When the Social Democratic party took power in November 1918, it concentrated on preserving national unity rather than on encouraging economic reform. Although the Social Democrats passed legislation granting suffrage to women, creating the eight-hour work day, strengthening the unions, and introducing unemployment insurance, they in no way attempted to alter the foundations of society. Fritz Stern claims their efforts went into changing the "form of the state, not the structure of society" (xiv). The result was that their working-class constituency suffered most from the social structures they maintained. The inflation of the 1920s and the depression of the 1930s hit the working class hardest.

In 1923, under conditions brought on by the defeat in World War I and the resulting burden of large reparation payments to the Allies, the German economy faltered, and the worst inflation in German history ensued. Money became practically worthless, and German society was reduced to a near barter economy. The value of the Reichsmark fell so drastically that workers were paid twice a day. After a new monetary policy finally brought the inflation under control, and a period of prosperity followed in the late 1920s, the stock market crash of 1929 again sent the economy into a tailspin. The depression of the 1930s that followed, which rendered one-third of the work force unemployed, was the final economic blow for the republic. The depression caused both the right and the left to intensify their attacks on the government. The fascists believed the lack of a strong leader made democracy unworkable, and the communists believed only proletarian dictatorship could produce a just social order.

The *Freikorps*, the semi-military troops recruited from returning soldiers and sailors, employed first by the right to put down communist uprisings, were now used to overthrow the government itself. These same veterans also became the backbone of the SA (*Sturmabteilungen,* or storm troops), the private army of the National Socialists. This militia, with its hooliganism and terror, cleared the streets of opposition and led the attack against Jews and opponents of Nazism. Although opponents of the National Socialists existed in large numbers, were in every party and class, in the churches and trade unions, they never united into a single force. The conservative Catholic Center party could not work with the communists. The communists could not work with the Social Democrats, whom they considered traitors to the proletarian cause. The Social Democrats could not work with the various nationalist parties because they did not trust their commitment to democracy. Mutual distrust and suspicion of one party for the other prevailed. Hitler came to power without ever having won a majority of the vote. Even in the last election on March 1933, after he had already become chancellor and while the SA controlled the streets and terrorizd the opposition, his National Socialist party could still not achieve an absolute majority. With 43.9 percent of the votes, however, Hitler was able to end the Weimar Republic and proclaim the Third Reich.

These were the political conditions under which Böll grew up. From them he learned the need for a strong commitment to democracy and the necessity of a well-informed public capable of effective criticism and involvement. The Hitler years only intensified these convictions. The dangers of political alternatives to democracy frightened him. History and personal experience produced in him a thorough aversion for dictatorships of the right or left. He believed in a citizen's duty to take an active part in the democratic process, not just as a voter, but as a writer, not just as an essayist, but as a novelist, poet, and dramatist. Böll made no distinction in purpose between the genres. All were means to the same end—involvement in the social and political life of the nation. In 1959, when he received the literary award of the city of Wuppertal, Böll entitled his acceptance speech ''Die Sprache als Hort der Freiheit'' (Language as the Bulwark of Freedom). The word *conscience* (a word often associated with Böll) was prominent in the speech. "There are terrible ways," Böll said, "of robbing a person of his dignity: beatings and torture are but two ways to the mills of death—but the worst I can imagine, like a creeping disease of the spirit, is something that would force me to say or write a sentence that could not stand before the court that I have mentioned: the conscience of a free writer" (*WESR* 1: 304–5). And in 1978, when growing urban terrorism caused the West German government to restrict constitutionally guaranteed freedoms, Böll attacked the government so fiercely that he was accused of being a terrorist himself. His response in an open letter admitted that he may at times have gone to extremes in defending freedom but that he believed democracy requires permanent scrutiny of the condition of the world, of society, and of oneself (Hoffman 244). For Böll writing was a political act, writing just for the sake of art did not exist. However, political writing could and should also be art, he believed. In 1983 when he accepted honorary citizenship of the city of Cologne, he made this point clear, "What I have never understood . . . was the attempt to separate me as novelist from the person who also occasionally wrote essays, criticism, and whom one heard occasionally give a speech; the fact is that essays, criticism, and speeches are literature too" (*EZ* 85).

Böll recalled in an autobiographical essay that as a child his first spending money was a million-mark note to buy a piece of candy. At the time, Böll's father, a self-employed furniture maker with a small shop, could not pay his employees. When the business failed, the Bölls nearly lost their family house that two years earlier Böll's father Viktor had purchased in Raderberg, a suburb of Cologne. At that time in 1921 Viktor Böll had been thinking of a better life for himself, his wife, and six children. But the disastrous inflation caused him not only to lose his business and all his savings but also forced him to borrow heavily to start again. In the next years, the booming economy justified the expression "roaring twenties," but the stock market crash in New York at the end of the decade produced a depression in Germany greater even than the one in the United States. By 1933 six million of about eighteen million German workers were unemployed. The German economy was again in distress. This time Viktor Böll fared even worse than a decade earlier. Unable to repay his loans, he lost the family home. By this time Viktor Böll, who was born in 1870, was in his sixties, and his finances were in ruins.

Böll recalled how his father stopped opening the mail to avoid seeing the bills he could not pay and how he lived in dread of the bailiff's knock at his door. He also recalled these hard years as a time with a certain excitement. Within the family a sense of bohemian anarchy ruled, manifested by disrepect for authority and a disregard for the strict letter of the law. He said it expressed itself in the way the family dressed, talked, and acted, and in the way they all lived. In the midst of this economic uncertainty, there was the freedom of not being bound by social convention because society had failed. This taste for anarchic freedom was sweet to young Böll. He learned that one could not trust the capitalist economy to serve the public good. He discovered that the invisible hand, which Adam Smith claimed created social wealth, also produced social misery. In these years he developed an enormous distrust of the capitalist system. Within a decade, during peacetime, his father and mother's way of life, their savings, and their security had twice been destroyed. Although in a technical sense his father was never unemployed because he was self-employed, Böll realized that a hardworking, conscientious man, through no fault of his own, could be reduced to penury. He saw that his social skills and desire to work were wasted by an uncaring economic system that produced riches for the few and misery for the many. Böll recognized that, even during the depression, fortunes were being made from cheap labor and that the needs of the people were exploited. He realized that the many who suffered were helpless victims of an unstable economy. Later Böll was to say, "I do not believe it was the war that motivated me to become a writer, but the daily social misery of the twenties and thirties: that was what was decisive" (Wintzen 81).

The German middle class at this time was divided into three groups, the largest of which was the old middle estate, which consisted of peasant proprietors, artisans, and small businessmen, people mainly in preindustrial occupations.[1] This middle estate specifies perfectly the class to which Viktor Böll belonged. He was not only an artisan as a skilled craftsman and a wood sculptor but also a small businessman with his shop. In the economic crises between 1914 and 1933, this group discovered that it could not compete with larger economic units that could succeed with a smaller margin of profit. In 1923 and in 1930 these artisan businessmen suffered more than their larger competitors.

These early experiences of the twenties and the thirties lay at the heart of Böll's suspicion of functioning capitalism. Even after World War II, at the time of the currency reform of 1948 and in the middle of the economic miracle of the fifties and sixties, Böll never lost his fear of a system that might at any time fail and that was at all times essentially unjust. In the early seventies, when the German economy began to slow down and unemployment became again a factor in German life, his concern was for the social victims, the unemployed, the foreign workers who first felt the weight of the stagnant economy, and the young who were unable to find work. He expressed these concerns in a way that implied that a solution to the problems of social justice lay in a new democratic socialism, in a third way, which integrated the security of a socialized economy with the dynamism of liberal democracy.

Böll was born into a Roman Catholic family, one whose roots in German Catholicism went back to English ancestors who came to the Rhineland to avoid the state religion of Henry VIII. Böll's family was Catholic on both sides for many generations. While his family was strict in religious belief, it was relaxed and free in its practice. Although his father went to daily mass and was for religious reasons a staunch supporter of the Catholic Center party, he and the family, nonetheless, stood by Heinrich when at the age of fourteen he rebelled against attendance at mass and the reception of the sacraments (*WESR* 1: 539). Heinrich's parents gave their children freedom in religious matters while raising their family as practicing Catholics.

As Heinrich grew up in the twenties in Raderberg, a new suburb of the city with a mixed-class structure of workers, entrepreneurs, lawyers, and architects, he choose his own friends primarily from the working class. They were, he said, freer, with fewer parental restrictions. This freedom to choose his friends as he wished, even from among the children of communists, was an unusual form of liberation for children of his social class. Most of his schoolmates were limited in their choice of friends by their parents' desire to see them associate with respectable people. This democratic freedom that Heinrich enjoyed was inspired mostly by his mother, Maria Böll, who, though without formal education, was, as Böll recognized, "a real and true Catholic leftist in comparison to whom all other Catholic leftists paled" ("Interview mit mir selbst" in Beckel 10–11). She also demonstrated for him a natural radicalism and a spontaneously critical mind. He wrote of her, "She united elements seldom united: intelligence, naiveté, liveliness, instinct, and wit" (Hoffmann 36). She remained the most decisive influence in his childhood. She always showed a socialist sympathy for the poor and disadvantaged in society and was always able to express her positions with simple eloquence. She maintained one inflexible rule of family charity: no one was ever turned away from their door. No matter how bad circumstances were within the family, there was always a cup of coffee for whoever knocked. Böll claimed she would have offered coffee even to a Nazi if one had come to the door.

Böll remained a critical Catholic in the mold of his mother all his life. Even in 1976, when he and his wife officially left the Catholic church as a protest against paying church taxes,[2] he and his wife expressly said that they remained members of the community of the faithful.

Catholicism and the Catholic church play an important role in Böll's writing. Most of his characters are Catholic, and religion is one of his dominant themes. In an interview in 1967 with the prominent critic Marcel Reich-Ranicki, Böll stated, "As an author actually only two themes interest me: love and religion" (*WI* 1: 68). What Böll's statement neglects to mention is that he always places his characters in circumstances that make political acts of their decisions concerning love and religion, and it fails to make clear that these acts reveal their moral positions.

In 1928, after four years at a Catholic school in Cologne-Raderthal, Böll began his secondary education at the humanistic Kaiser Wilhelm Gymnasium in Cologne. He liked school and was a good student but did not work very hard, often skipped school, especially after Hitler came to power, and made only average grades. After the family moved back to the city in 1930, Böll could once again walk the streets of Cologne—so frequently mentioned in his stories—on his way to and from school. These school years for Böll, 1924 to 1937, were hard times for the Böll family. Money was scarce, and the Nazis had come to power. Although the moral institutions of church and state were failing in their opposition to anti-Semitism and fascism, the Bölls themselves immunized one another against these political diseases. Böll's father and mother, as well as the children, not only clearly saw the political evils of the thirties but also showed how practiced solidarity could protect the family against social and moral dangers.

When Hitler came to power in January 1933, Heinrich's mother recognized immediately that it meant war (Hoffmann 29). Later, during the war, her remarks against Hitler made in an air-raid shelter nearly cost her her life. Although she was reported to the authorities, she escaped prosecution because a Nazi party member who knew her refused to pursue the matter. After the war this minor official was de-Nazified according to Allied policy, but the person who reported Maria Böll, who was a nonparty member with a "clean" political past, made a successful political career in the CDU (Christian Democratic party). Such morally ambiguous characters appear frequently in Böll's stories about the prewar, war, and postwar eras.

Within the circle of family and friends, there was cautious but open discussion. Heinrich's parents enjoyed having the children's friends meet in their apartment. Sometimes groups of twenty to thirty people between seventeen and twenty years of age gathered in the Bölls' apartment to discuss politics, literature, and current events. They sat on the floor and stood against the wall. Most came from Catholic youth groups in which Heinrich's brothers and sisters were active. Heinrich, as the youngest in the family, was usually the youngest person present, but from these discussions with older people he learned to express himself and defend his positions. These young people did not all think alike or agree politically, but they shared an aversion to Hitler and fascism.

One young woman in the group, Annemarie Cech, a friend of Heinrich's sister, later became Heinrich's wife. They married in 1942 while Böll was home on a furlough. Annemarie was born in Pilsen. Her father was a Czech lawyer, and here mother was from the Rhineland. Her parents died young and Annemarie grew up in Cologne with relatives.

Because the terror of Nazism was very real for the Bölls and their friends, the family grew closer together. In these years, Heinrich found his *Heimat* (spiritual home) within the family, where there was security and comfort during times of turmoil. This solidarity in family life sustained him especially during the war. Throughout his work the family usually appears as an institution that nourishes its members. In fact, most of his novels, especially those of the fifties, can be read as "family novels," containing abundant illustrations of loving family cohesiveness despite examples of infection by fascism and conflict of moral values (*Billard um halbzehn/Billiards at Half-past Nine*), despite dissension brought on by poverty (*Und sagte kein einziges Wort/And Never Said a Word*), and despite loss of stability caused by the death of a husband or father (*Haus ohne Hüter/The Unguarded House*). These and later works that manifest strong family ties reflect Böll's own personal experience. Only *Ansichten eines Clowns* (*The Clown*) is an exception to this pattern. The lack of a generation gap in his novels gives his work a utopian dimension. Parents and children are normally not at odds; in fact, parents usually learn from their children and strengthen them in return. Parents protect their children, and children love their parents because they know that in spite of differences their values are the same.

Böll's last four years in the Gymnasium were in the Hitler period. Again Böll was lucky in that his teachers were not sympathetic to National Socialism. His German teacher had his students read Hitler's *Mein Kampf* and rewrite passages for conciseness and clarity. In this indirect way, without overt criticism, a disdain for Hitler, his ideas, his shoddy logic, and hisentire program was communicated to the class, and, at the same time, students learned valuable writing skills. While the teacher risked no more than ironic comments, the young Böll appreciated what he was doing.

In his entire class, Böll was the only student who did not belong to the Hitler Youth, and in the entire school only two or three others refused to join. Still, there was no pressure on him from teachers or school administrators to belong to a political organization. Böll later explained his reluctance to associate with the Hitler Youth with other than political reasons, "I simply did not want to be part of it," he said, "I did not like it—independent of the political element—I hated the stupid marching and the uniforms" (Hoffmann 41–42). This aversion to marching in step and wearing uniforms has been characteristic of his independence from movements of all kinds. He has never joined a political party, although his political sympathies are clearly socialist. In 1972 he campaigned for the SPD (Social Democratic party of Germany) because he believed in Willy Brandt's *Ostpolitik* (literally, "eastern policy," Brandt's policy toward Germany's coming to terms with its eastern neighbors), and in the last years of his life he supported the Green party because he accepted its position on disarmament, the environment, and its critique of practicing capitalism. Later, Böll said he thanked his parents, brothers, sisters, and friends that he was never tempted by Nazism.

The Nazi youth program made rapid headway with German youth because it exploited sentiments and ideas already present in German society: anti-Semitism, belief in authority, the cult of past racial grandeur, a desire to flee reality and to find security in an inner realm, a preference for the country over the city, an aversion to democracy, a readiness to die for a cause, a preference for emotion over logic, the total estrangement of youth from politics, and a belief that a great leader would solve the country's problems. One year after Hitler came to power, 3.5 million people under sixteen were in the Hitler Youth, and the ranks swelled to 6 million by the end of 1936.

In the neighborhood of Cologne where the Bölls lived, the Nazi party was not organized by fanatics. The local leaders did not force Böll's father to join the party. Only when Heinrich's brother Alois took over the family workshop was it necessary for him to join the SA to continue receiving business.

Böll's independence of the Hitler Youth actually provided unique benefits. When the other students had to march and hike, Heinrich and the few other nonmembers had to stay at school and tidy the library. These hours were, for the most part, unsupervised and provided hours of free time and a chance to read. As a student in the Gymnasium, his favorite subjects were Latin, mathematics, history, and geography. In his free time he walked along the Rhine, through the streets, and visited the many museums in the city. But above all he started writing in these years. In a biographical essay he stated, "I always wanted to write. I tried it early but only found the words later" (*WESR* 1: 285). Short stories and poems in manuscript form from the year 1936 are in the Böll Archive in Cologne.

Although he completed his secondary education in 1937, Böll could not attend the university because he had not satisfied his requirement of six months' work service. Rather than voluntarily serve the government to continue his studies, he became an apprentice to a bookseller in Bonn. After a few months he gave up his apprenticeship, and in the fall of 1938 was called into the work service. After six months of unaccustomed hard physical labor—even in the Gymnasium he was excused from physical education because of poor health—he returned home exhausted and depressed. He later wrote of these six months as worse than his six years in the army. Besides military drill, it consisted of political indoctrination and debilitating labor not required of a soldier. When he returned home, he enrolled in the University of Cologne to study German and classical philology. Within a few weeks, in late summer of 1939, even before World War II had started, he was inducted into the *Wehrmacht*.

For the next six years, until his capture by American troops in April 1945, Böll was a soldier in Hitler's armies. He served in France and Russia, and as the *Wehrmacht* retreated before the Red Army, he served in other Eastern European countries as well. He was wounded in the hand in France, in the leg in the Crimea, in the head in Rumania, and in the back in Hungary. While in a field hospital in Hungary, he realized Hitler's leadership was not inevitable for Germany. Everything could have been different if the citizens of the Weimar Republic had been more politically active, if they had been more democratic, and if they had shown more civil courage. It was at this time, Böll professed, that he awoke from apathy (Hoffman 71). Upon his dismissal from the hospital in August 1944, he began his long series of attempts to escape the war by feigning sickness and forging papers. With an illegal pass he returned to Germany instead of the front.

He hid out with his family in the Rhineland and waited for the war to end. As Germany came closer to defeat, his illegal status became more dangerous than actual service. Soldiers without papers were considered deserters and summarily executed. By war's end, more than thirty thousand German soldiers had met their deaths in this manner.[3] In March 1945, again with forged papers, he joined a combat troop in the Rhineland. On 9 April 1945 he was taken prisoner by American soldiers.

For Böll this day was one of liberation from Nazi oppression. Twelve years of fascism had ended. Despite the miserable conditions in the POW camps, he never failed to thank the Allies for freeing Germany.[4] Especially important to him was the realization that others, not Germans themselves, had liberated his homeland. During the next forty years of his writing, this theme recurs with frequency. This is one aspect of his work that has made him popular abroad and, in conservative circles at home, a despised liberal.

Except for his mother, who died of heart failure in November 1944, indirectly a result of an air attack, Böll's entire family survived the war. His first child, however, born while Böll was in a POW camp, died for lack of available medicine one month after Böll's repatriation in September 1945.

Immediately upon his return to civilian life, Böll began to write full-time. He refused to seek any real employment. He helped out in the family workshop, took temporary employment with the city of Cologne to help with a postwar census, but only worked when absolutely necessary. The family lived from his wife's meager salary as a teacher of English.

Although Böll did not begin publishing until after the war, he had begun writing as a teenager and continued to do so during the war by composing more than a letter a day to his wife, family, and friends. Over one thousand letters to his wife from this period exist and will appear in the fall of 1993 in a multivolume annotated work.[5] From the fragments of this correspondence that have already been published, a clear picture of Böll's inner life during this period has already been revealed. The candidness and lack of circumspection in the letters are remarkable. In fact, the letters seem to have escaped censorship completely. In them, many themes appear that characterize Böll's life's work. In a letter of 4 April 1941 he wrote: ''I can barely recall how it was in the fairy-tale past sunk deep in time when we could walk, smoke, drink, and sleep when we wanted. That must have been a great time! May God grant us that we do not lose the memory of it from our minds, so we won't go crazy when this time comes to us again.''[6]

And again a letter of 4 June 1941 stated, "I am dying from desire for sleep and rest and peace, but I know there is no peace in this world." Here one sees clearly that the source of the primitive attachment to simple pleasures that his characters enjoy derives from his experiences of deprivation in the war. In a letter of 5 June 1941 he wrote: "Sometimes we dream of a 'real peace,' but I don't believe such a thing exists. That would be an absolute condition without struggle. For us Christians, that can only begin when we finally have abjured the cross, but we will never be able to do that. . . . [The time will come when] we will again be allowed to speak the truth, and we will have to do it with a burning heart and a glowing mouth." In a letter to his mother of 19 July 1942 he wrote, "God lives and knows what has happened to us, and we are redeemed by the cross and have a great, great hope." These excerpts acknowledge a religious understanding of life that remained with him to his death. In large measure, the whole body of his work is meeting this self-imposed obligation to "speak the truth with a burning heart and a glowing mouth." In the same letter he explained why he refused to seek promotion, "If I would become an officer just because the dirt here below is no longer good enough, it would be a betrayal of all that we have gone through and have had to suffer." And in a letter of 19 June 1944 he wrote, "I hate the war and all those who love it." Behind Böll's refusal to become an officer and his hatred of the war is his desire to maintain solidarity with human suffering, the wish not to let the experience of fear, deprivation, and longing slip from his memory. This aspect of his work—his refusal to forget the past and his constant reminding of his compatriots of their experiences and, more importantly, what they had done to Jews, gypsies, Russians, and others by following Nazism and pursuing Hitler's wars—lies at the bottom of his commitment to a morally critical literature. The tendency of some Germans to forget their recent past has often made him angry, but their attempt to repress it, furious. Böll believed amnesia was a sickness from which no nation could recover.

The war did not make Böll a writer. He had decided to be one even in his teens, but his experience of the Hitler period in all its manifestations of war and oppression, suffering and opportunism, gave him material and a perspective of the human condition that informs all his work. Böll was gifted with a memory of unusual quality. From his recollection as a two-year-old of Hindenburg's returning army to all his other experiences, Böll gave the impression nothing was ever forgotten. One might say, not only did he remember, he could not forget. Böll's work is indeed a chronicle of his time, and that quality alone makes it deserving of the status of Dickens's work in

English literature and Balzac's in France. Böll recalled not only who suffered during the war years, and how they suffered, but also upon whose suffering the Federal Republic was built. There will always be people who do not want to be reminded, but for those who want to know, Böll's work will remain forever a record of twentieth-century German reality.

When Böll returned with his wife to Cologne in September 1945, the city, which in 1939 had 800,000 inhabitants, lay eighty percent in ruins and claimed a population of only 28,000. Housing, food, and fuel were scarce. People were allowed to move into any inhabitable dwelling. The Bölls found a house suitable for repair and began life in freedom with high expectations.

In 1947 their second son was born (the first died in 1945), in 1948 their third, and in 1950 their last. The years 1945–1948 became known as the hunger years in postwar Germany. People lived as best they could from bartered goods, the black market, stolen fuel, CARE packages, and assistance from the Allies. Although these years were for Böll far from prosperous, they were very productive. He wrote as his wife worked. In 1947 his stories began to be published in various newpapers and magazines. They dealt with the war and the immediate postwar conditions. In 1949 Böll's first book appeared, *Der Zug war pünktlich* (*The Train Was on Time*), a tragic love story about a German soldier and a Polish prostitute. In 1950 a collection of twenty-five stories was published under the title *Wanderer, kommst du nach Spa . . .* / Stranger Bear Word to the Spartans We . . . (all are in *The Stories of Heinrich Böll*). These books were critically well received but did not immediately sell well. Seven years passed before *The Train Was on Time* sold three thousand copies.

In 1951 Böll was invited to read his work at the annual meeting of Group 47, an informal literary gathering organized by Hans Werner Richter and named after the year in which it was founded. The group brought together writers who were dedicated to democracy and a politically committed literature. The best writers of postwar Germany were associated with Group 47. Each year one prize was awarded to the best reading before the group. In 1951 Böll received the prize and one thousand marks for his story "Die schwarzen Schafe" ("Black Sheep" in *The Stories of Heinrich Böll*), the largest sum he had ever received for his work. It was a sorely needed income, but more importantly, it gave him recognition, and this event became a turning point in his career. His first novel, another tragic story of love and war, *Wo warst du, Adam?* (Adam, Where Art Thou?), appeared shortly thereafter. Böll always claimed this book as his favorite. At this time Böll was still working as a part-time helper in the statistical office of the city of Cologne.

These earliest books were published by Middelhauve Verlag, an old established publisher of scientific research. It attempted after the war to expand into popular literature but with little experience in the field was unable to succeed.

In 1951, after having just published what were to become some of the major works of postwar German literature, Böll lost his contract with Middelhauve, which had decided scientific publishing was what it could do best. Böll was then offered a new contract by Kiepenheuer & Witsch, who remained his major publisher until his death.

The first work published by Kiepenheuer & Witsch was the novel *Und sagte kein einziges Wort,* 1953 (*And Never Said a Word*). With thorough knowledge of the fiction industry, Kiepenheuer & Witsch knew how to market its products. Through prepublication in a major newspaper, an advertising campaign, and by sending out hundreds of free review copies, the publisher helped make *And Never Said a Word* an immediate best-seller. From that time on, Annemarie Böll gave up her teaching job, and Böll supported his family as a freelance writer for the rest of his life.

Success came quickly after 1953, as work after work appeared in a seemingly endless stream. But more surprising than the quantity was the quality of the work. Trying his hand at various literary genres—short story, novel, drama, radio play, film script, poetry, essay—Böll succeeded as no other serious postwar German writer.

In 1953 he received the Culture Prize of German Industry, the Southern German Radio Prize, and the German Critics' Prize. In 1954 he received the prize of the *Tribune de Paris,* in 1955 the French prize for the best foreign novel (*Haus ohne Hüter, The Unguarded House*), in 1958 the Eduard von der Heydt Prize of the city of Wuppertal and the prize of the Bavarian Academy of Arts, in 1959 the Great Art Prize of the State of North-Rhine-Westphalia, the Literature Prize of the City of Cologne, and he was elected to the Academy of Science and the Arts in Mainz. In 1960 be became a member of the Bavarian Academy of Fine Arts and received the Charles Veillon Prize for the novel *Billard um halbzehn* (*Billiards at Half-past Nine*). In 1967 he received Germany's most prestigious award, the Büchner Prize of the German Academy for Language and Poetry, and in 1972 was accorded worldwide recognition when he received the Nobel Prize for Literature. Besides these honors, several universities in Great Britain and Ireland presented him with honorary doctorate degrees. The American

Academy of Arts and Letters made him an honorary member in 1974, and until his death he was awarded similar honors. Some, such as the Ossietzky Medal of 1974, were for his activity for human rights and defense of human dignity. Others recognized his diplomatic skills and mediatory talents, such as his election in 1970 to the presidency of the German PEN Club and a year later in Dublin, with the support of writers in the East and West, to the presidency of the international PEN. These domestic and foreign marks of distinction, both for his writing and for his personal convictions, were only a few that he received. Still, with all his honors and prestige, Böll remained his whole life a very accessible person. He came to the aid of many people both prominent and unknown. He assisted dissidents in the Soviet Union, in Turkey, in Chile, and in Korea. He gave the major part of the Nobel Prize money to a fund for helping oppressed writers in all lands. He is credited with bringing Aleksandr Solzhenitsyn's manuscript for *The Gulag Archipelago* to the West (Hoffman 195). He helped found and finance humanitarian organizations to take medical aid around the world, to help boat people from Asia and gypsy victims of the Holocaust in Germany, and with a group of citizens from Cologne founded in 1959 Germania Judaica, the Cologne library for the history of German Jewry.

Heinrich Böll was not a man of narrow literary interests. His life's work addresses the concerns of an age with clarity, historical awareness, and moral vision. Human affairs in a broad sense concerned him. He left his mark on postwar Germany as no other writer was able to do. Nonetheless, critics often dispute the quality of his writing. Surely, their political views color the variety of opinions. But not in dispute is Böll's prominence in the literature, culture, and intellectual life of his country. In 1978 the Allenbach Institute, West German's leading foundation for demographic research, conducted a poll of recognizable personalities. The results showed the writers Böll and Günter Grass were as well known as leading political figures. Thirty-one percent of West Germans over the age of sixteen had read a book by Böll, and eighty-nine percent knew who he was. At the time, Böll took second place in public recognition only to Helmut Schmidt, the federal chancellor. A similar poll in the eighties showed Böll again second only to the new chancellor, Helmut Kohl. The conclusion is clear. Böll's impact on his time as a personality and as a cultural figure was immense. From 1960 to 1985, the year of his death, Böll was the dominant force in German intellectual public life. For this reason future literary historians may justly be able to call these twenty-five years of German literature the Age of Heinrich Böll.

NOTES

1. The other two groups making up the middle class were those people having jobs created by industrialization and professionals: lawyers, doctors, teachers, architects, civil servants, and university students.

2. West German law requires the payment of church taxes by anyone declaring church membership. This tax on the average is ten percent of the amount of tax due the federal government. Böll objected to this legal tie between the church and state and especially between the church and the economic system. As the economy grows, the church becomes wealthier. Under such an arrangement, Böll thought the church could not become a critic of capitalism. He also argued that financial support of the church should be a matter of conscience, not legal formula.

3. This figure gains significance when compared to the single U.S. soldier executed for desertion in World War II.

4. In 1989 James Bacque published *Other Losses* (Stoddard: Toronto), an exposé of the American and French treatment of German POW's after the war. According to Bacque, about one million German soldiers and sometimes civilians were placed in fields surrounded by barbed wire and given so little shelter, food, or water that within a few months hundreds of thousands died. One of the camps mentioned by Bacque where thousands died was Sinzig near Remagen on the Rhine. Böll spent part of his internment in Sinzig, but nowhere in Böll's work does he write of the "other losses" or of the American and French violations of the Geneva convention. Instead Böll emphasizes the liberation from Nazism brought by the Allies. In the novel *Gruppenbild mit Dame* (*Group Portrait with Lady*), however, Russian POW Boris Lvovic, who is mistakenly captured by the Americans as a German soldier, suffers death during internment under conditions similar to many deaths described by Bacque in *Other Losses*.

5. Shortly after Böll's death, the Heinrich-Böll-Stiftung was founded for the purpose of bringing out a historical-critical edition of the author's works, among other things. The first publication of the *Stiftung*, the correspondence between Böll and his friend Ada Kunz, which extends from September 1945 to Kunz's death, is scheduled for 1992. This volume is to be followed in 1993 by Böll's wartime letters to his wife. In total over seventy thousand letters from Böll are now collected in the Böll Archive in Cologne.

6. All quotations from Böll's letters are from Hoffman, 79–105.

CHAPTER TWO

The War Stories

In one of Böll's earliest published short stories, "Die Botschaft," 1947 ("Breaking the News"), the narrator concludes after meeting the young widow of a fellow soldier, "Then I knew, the war would never be over, never, not as long as somewhere a wound that it had caused was still bleeding" (*WRE* 1: 11). Since the statement is made in reference to a wife who suffers from her unfaithfulness to her husband, it is clear the passage refers to psychological as well as to physical wounds. All people who suffered directly or indirectly from the war are its victims. In this reality of suffering, the guilty and the innocent share. Böll's entire body of work can be read as an explication of this single quotation. But in probing the suffering of Germans in the Hitler period, Böll does not minimize German guilt and responsibility nor relativize it by mere concern for the suffering of his compatriots.

Although the stories in *Wanderer, kommst du nach Spa . . . / Stranger, Bear Word to the Spartans We . . .* (all contained in *The Stories of Heinrich Böll*) are often called war stories, actually only eleven of the twenty-five stories treat the war directly. Thirteen treat the immediate postwar era, and one is a satire of totalitarianism without a specific time or place. The twenty-two stories in *Die Verwundung* (The Wound) form more accurately a true collection of war stories. These tales, written between 1946 and 1952 and rediscovered in the Böll Archive in the eighties, were not published in book form until 1983. While all the stories in *Wanderer* are available in English, none from *Die Verwundung* has been translated.

That Böll's first writing was in the genre of the short story is no surprise, and the reasons have as much to do with sociological circumstances as with personal preference. Immediately after the war, the German language suffered from the ravages of twelve years of the Nazi plague.[1] The language had been so misused for propaganda and ideological terror that simple words had acquired strong connotative meanings associated with Nazism. *Camp, smoke, loyalty, honor, fatherland, gas, special treatment,* for example, summoned up visions, emotions, and meanings not normally connected to these words. It was difficult for both experienced and novice writers to start restoring the lost integrity of the language. Böll summed up this linguistic problem very concisely, "It was hard beginning to write in 1945, considering the depravity and untruthfulness of the German language at that time" (*WESR* 3: 340). Because of the problem of struggling with each word, writing short fiction in 1945 was easier than writing a novel.

Also, after twelve years of quarantine from foreign literature, Germans devoured literature from abroad, especially American literature. Among the most popular writers was Ernest Hemingway. His example of the American short story was widely emulated. Still another aspect of the short story led to its popularity. Of all the prose genres, it is the most concise—the form, like the poem, most capable of saying more than its literal meaning. Because of the war, many German writers, especially Böll, felt a moral compulsion to speak. The short story was at first the best form in which to do this. There was a shortage of paper; publishing a novel was materially more difficult than publishing a short story. And finally, people did not have much free time after the war. With cleaning up the rubble, building new houses and factories, finding food and fuel, and trying to catch up with reading world literature, they did not have the leisure to spend on a novel. The short story, which could be read in a few minutes, was more suitable to their economic conditions.

Böll's stories responded to all these factors. Above all, he found a simple, sober language that spoke directly to the reader. Böll's matter-of-factness did not, however, deny the reader's emotions. His laconic plainness did not prevent a simple lyricism that appealed to a spiritual longing caused by guilt and suffering. Theodore Ziolkowski described these stories perceptively as "idiomatic dialogue, a style economical to the point of understatement, first person narrative, war experiences—and the characteristic ironic twist showing the underdog in mild rebellion against 'the system' " ("Conscience and Craft" 215).

The very nature of the short story also led to its popularity. The short story does not seek to solve problems or to analyze situations as a novel might. It poses questions and leaves answers open. The short story was in this way like life after World War II: questions without answers.

Many of Böll's early war stories end in sentences with an ellipsis, suggesting ominous catastrophe to follow. "Damals in Odessa," 1950 ("That Time We Were in Odessa"), a story of soldiers waiting for a flight to the front, concludes, "And we entered the plane, suddenly we knew, that we would never return, never . . . " (*WRE* 1: 193). The title story, "Wanderer, kommst du nach Spa . . . ," 1950, translated by Leila Vennewitz as "Stranger, Bear Word to the Spartans We . . . ," tells of a young man who awakes in a field hospital a multiple amputee. He sees his embryo-like reflection in a light bulb, but he does not scream in horror or shock; instead, in recognition of his helplessness he whispers the final word, " 'Milk' . . . " (*WRE* 1: 202). In the story "Auch Kinder sind Zivilisten," 1948 ("Children Are Civilians, Too"), another wounded soldier, recuperating in a field hospital in order to return to the front, ends his story, "You have to go somewhere, even if you're wounded in a foreign, black, dreary land . . . " (*WRE* 1: 54). In these stories with an open conclusion, the only certainty is greater suffering and probable death.

Still other war stories express a religious optimism. The story "Wiedersehen mit Drüng," 1950 ("Reunion with Drüng"), also takes place in a hospital. The reunion in the title is the recognition by the dying narrator that the person dying on the next stretcher is his school friend Drüng. As both soldiers succumb to death, the narrator has a sensation of warmth and sees the room fill with brightness just as their candle burns out. At this moment of death, he sees their nurse in white come toward them as a smiling angel. The final line reads, "Our surprised eyes saw Dina's figure entering through the closed door, and we knew that we were allowed to smile, and we took her outstretched hands and followed her . . . " (*WRE* 1: 239). Here the open end suggests more than life after death; it reveals death to be a realization of a better life, free of suffering. Böll avoids sentimentality by employing a harsh realism, as in this tale when the narrator sees through the hole in his friend's stomach. With his combination of realism and romanticism, Böll met the emotional needs of his readers who survived the war. These early stories represent Böll's period of Christian existentialism, the period before he began to analyze the causes of the political conditions of his world, while he was still too close to the emotions of the war without time for historical reflection.

Of the stories that treat the immediate postwar period, "Kumpel mit dem langen Haar," 1947 ("My Pal with the Long Hair"), can stand as a model. It contains many themes and motifs typical of Böll's entire work. In

"Kumpel" the first-person narrator[2] is a wounded veteran eking out an existence as a black marketeer with no job and no permanent address. In a train station he is attracted to a pale, young girl with long black hair and "small, quiet hands" wearing a bright coat (*WRE* 1: 21). When she looks at him, the narrator immediately realizes, "That brief glance found its mark" (*WRE* 1: 21). The girl's bright coat identifies her with hope, and she appeals to the narrator because of her vulnerability and sadness, characterized here by her paleness, her small hands, and her black hair "like a curtain of mourning" (*WRE* 1: 21). The narrator follows her to the platform and onto a train. He is cold and wonders where he will spend the night. Böll gives his longing a metaphysical dimension, "Where [will I] come to rest" (*WRE* 1: 23). On the train he offers the girl one of his black market cigarettes. She hesitates, but smokes it "with deep, hungry breaths" (*WRE* 1: 23). By feigning sleep, they try to avoid paying the conductor, but a woman passenger informs on them. They get off the train in a small town, do not know where to go and end up spending the night in a haystack. The story concludes: "So we warmed ourselves with our breath and our blood. Since then we have been together—in these hard times" (*WRE* 1: 24).

The story is important because it reveals much of Böll's style: concern for people at the bottom of society, triumphant satisfaction in meeting basic human needs: warmth, love, friendship, sleep, a place to stay. Here the enjoyment of a cigarette stands for a whole complex of human prerequisites and simple pleasures.[3] Elsewhere, eating a piece of bread or drinking a cup of coffee serves the same existential function. Böll's "sacraments of the living," as they may be called, become major topoi in his writing. Also, train stations and waiting rooms appear frequently in the war and the postwar stories as people are on the move from city to city, crowded into the waiting rooms on their way to unknown places, seeking physical and human warmth. In "Kumpel," these two anonymous heroes know their frailty and aspire to no more than the acquisition of the essentials of life. Their ability to suffer with dignity demonstrates their humanity. Although they are persons of character, they have little respect for the letter of the law and live by a universal sense of justice. Because they are generous and giving, they are also capable of love. The decency of these two outsiders stands in stark contrast to the bourgeois smugness of the woman who informs on them to the conductor. And above all, the story manifests a touch of sentiment in the motif of love at first sight. This meeting is no liaison but a permanent union that lasts through "hard times." This romantic concept of love that Böll embraced appears in many works : *Das Brot der frühen Jahre*, 1955 (*The Bread of Those Early Years*), *Ansichten eines Clowns*, 1963 (*The Clown*), *Entfernung von der Truppe*, 1964 (*Absent without Leave*), *Gruppenbild mit Dame*, 1971 (*Group Portrait with Lady*), and in other stories as well. At times his critics claim this tendency to sentiment passes into sentimentality.

In *Das Vermächtnis*, written 1948, published 1982 (*A Soldier's Legacy*), Böll demonstrated for the first time the intimate political and psychological connection of the postwar era with the war years. Böll saw clearly that the ruthless, egotistical personality capable of committing and repressing war crimes was the type to rise to the top after the war. The story is a report written in 1948 to the brother of a Lieutenant Schelling about the circumstances of the lieutenant's murder by Captain Schnecker on the eastern front in the summer of 1943.

Critics reviewed this novella[4] as they had reviewed much of Böll's fiction: praised it for its power, its serious themes, its manifestation of talent, but, nonetheless, regretted its failure to achieve its full potential. An example of this kind of critical response was Joel Agee's review for the *New York Times*. He called *A Soldier's Legacy* "a simple and affecting tale that reads like a draft for a first rate novel. It addresses important themes but doesn't explore them for all their implications. It assembles the ingredients of a gripping conflict, but fails to bring them to dramatic maturity. One reads the book with the active sympathy and participation that are the effects of real narrative power, and finishes it with the wish that one could send it back to the author for a more complete development" (9).

What such reviews fail to mention is that Böll's stories always contain something that makes them triumph over their shortcomings. That something can vary from use of language, the brilliant reproduction of ordinary speech, to a consistent and convincing presentation of the essential dignity of people, but ultimately it comes down to the manifestation of an unobtrusive moral power achieved with deceptive ease. This novella shows this talent was Böll's early in his career. With few words, Böll was able to point out the fundamental distinguishing traits of his characters.

The murderer's name, Schnecker, from the word *Schnecke* (snail, slug), suggests an ambitious person who leaves behind an unpleasant trail as he moves relentlessly toward his goal. In this case Schnecker steps cold-bloodedly over bodies on his way to success. On the opening page, the narrator, Corporal Wenk,[5] Lieutenant Schelling's former orderly, sees Schnecker by chance in a café with a young woman as the two celebrate

Schnecker's newly acquired Doctor of Law degree. She says to him: "My, how you did it! Fast and certain, the only one with 'honors' " (*V* 9). Wenk immediately comments that Schnecker has not changed: "He was a little fuller, younger rather than older, with the beginning of a steer-like neck, the kind some Germans from a better class develop when they are about thirty-two, the right age to join the party of their fathers and start a politically active life" (*V* 8).

The novella is primarily a political work. Its purpose is to inform the German public that criminal opportunists, against whom no crime will ever be charged, will soon be the lawyers and judges, politicians and leaders of business, the people in power who will run the country. As a new "democrat," Schnecker is the model for the ruthless, ambitious Nettlingers (*Billard um halbzehn/Billiards at Half-past Nine*) and Gäselers (*Haus ohne Hüter/The Unguarded House*), the villains without memory who appear so frequently in Böll's later novels. With ironic understatement Böll makes this political intention of Wenk's report clear. Wenk says he is writing his report not only to tell Lieutenant Schelling's brother the truth about the lieutenant's death but also to do his "duty for the fatherland," to justify the receipt of his veteran's pension of thirty marks a month (*V* 12). Elsewhere he reinforces this message: "I can't be quiet. Fear and anxiety have seized me after looking behind the rosy façade of all the 'rebuilding' and 'restoring' going on and looking into Schnecker's face" (*V* 22).

Wenk's bitterness is typical of Böll's heroes in this period. They believe that too many of Germany's best citizens were killed in the Hitler period, often because they, like Schelling, possessed the one quality irreconcilable with fascism, decency. The Nazi Schnecker, in fact, hates Schelling for this reason. The lieutenant is courageous, humane, democratic, religious, concerned for the welfare of his men, and worst of all, dangerously moral.

Wenk is assigned to Lieutenant Schelling while they are stationed in France. Later their division is sent to the East. The war appears, as in all of Böll's war stories, as the source of boredom, hunger, loneliness, despair, and above all as the cause of senseless destruction of people and things. Lieutenant Schelling realizes their fate as soldiers in full contradiction of the propagandistic concept of German destiny (*Schicksal*). "We are not born to be happy," he theologizes to Wenk. "We are born to suffer, and to know why we suffer. Our pain is the only thing we have to show" (*V* 65). Schelling's speech is about redemption, both in this world and in the next. Social and spiritual redemption for Schelling is based on knowing why one suffered; redemption is related to critical memory of the Hitler years and knowing the real causes of suffering. When Wenk seems not to understand this message of responsible Christian existentialism, Schelling states it for him again more directly: "Then you will understand that we are not born to forget. . . . We are born to remember. To remember rather than to forget is our job" (V 66). Thus, in Schelling's theology, the human condition requires suffering, and human dignity requires remembering it, both the suffering one experiences and the suffering that one causes.

This theme of memory dominates Böll's work. He fought unceasingly in his writing against the tendency in Germany to forget the crimes of the Hitler period. In his last years, this message was even more important to him than in the forties and fifties.[6] In 1985, at the celebrations commemorating the fortieth anniversary of the end of World War II, the Germans became determined to draw a line under the balance sheet of the war years. In this regard, Böll's early work can still be read as a profitable corrective to the Bitburg sentiment currently popular in West Germany and actively propagated by conservative German politicians and revisionist historians. These thinkers argue that most of the war generation is dead, most living Germans were born after the war; therefore, it is legitimate now to set a new course, to stop dwelling on past wrongs, and to be proud of current achievements. Böll's writing argues that a nation, like an individual, cannot live a healthy, productive life without a full memory intact. A selective memory is the disease of national amnesia.

The structure of the A Soldier's Legacy varies the form of the detective story. Here the crime and the murderer are announced on the first page, and the rest of the tale is explanation. This structure serves well the theme of remembering. With this variation of the detective form, Böll is able to concentrate his story entirely on why—not on what or who. This structure might properly be called a "why-done-it." Böll employs this structure in several works, notably in Der Zug war pünktlich, 1949 (The Train Was on Time)—where how a person dies is important—and Ende einer Dienstfahrt, 1966 (End of a Mission)—where again why a crime is committed is the point of the novel.

In A Soldier's Legacy, the novella's key sentence occurs in an argument between Schnecker and Schelling. Lieutenant Schelling says to Captain Schnecker: "I can imagine nothing worse than cheating a soldier of his food and his sleep. In the final analysis we, in our officer's uniforms, represent the power that forces these people to let themselves be shot to pieces or to bore themselves to death. This responsibility is enough for me. I do not want to be responsible for their hunger any more than is required"

(*V*102). Schelling is here a Michael Kohlhaas in his struggle for justice, seeing that his subordinates get all the food and sleep to which they are entitled. And like Kleist's Kohlhaas, Schelling's thirst for justice results in his death.

In this novella, as in other war stories by Böll, the "good" Germans hate fascism and desire liberation from it. Still, on the eastern front, they fight tenaciously to stay alive and to avoid Russian imprisonment. Lieutenant Schelling confides in Wenk: "The worst thing is, we don't know whom we want to win" (*V*, 143). The representatives of decency in *A Soldier's Legacy* are the narrator Wenk and Lieutenant Schelling. Captain Schnecker, on the other hand, is a committed Nazi, a fascist by nature. He delights in his medals and his authority. He uses power to create privileges for himself. Since power exists only in relationship to others, the army is the place par excellence for his ambition, where resistance to his will is dangerous. Only Schelling dares to stand in his way, and for his defiance Schnecker shoots him just at the moment the Russians attack. Only Schnecker and Wenk escape.

The Train Was on Time also takes place on the eastern front, but in contrast to *A Soldier's Legacy,* most critics have praised it for its perfection in execution. Gert Kalow claims it has a "design of genius" (428), and Ziolkowski writes, "Never again has Böll written a story of such closed perfection and inevitability. . . . It is an artistic *tour de force*" ("Conscience and Craft" 217).

On the first page, the ominous certainty of death becomes tangible as fear seizes the soldier Andreas as he is about to board a train for the front. Passive in the extreme, he resigns himself to his fate. He says to his friend Paul, a priest accompanying him to the station: "I don't want to die . . . I don't want to die, but the most terrible thing is that I will die . . . soon!" (*WRE* 1: 66). The sonorous voice over the loudspeaker invites the passenger to board the train that departs "on time," as the title of the work has already announced. From this moment on, death is as certain in this novella as it is in any tragedy. The exposition of the story is complete. There is nothing more for the tale to relate except how the prophecy of death is fulfilled. Inevitability and fate now hang heavy over all that happens.

The smooth, soft, comforting voices over the stations' loudspeakers accompany Andreas on his way. They embody the anonymous forces of the world that control the events of history. Andreas concludes, "All misfortune comes from these sonorous voices; these sonorous voices have started the war, and these sonorous voices control the most terrible aspect of the war, the coming and going of the train stations'' (*WRE* 1: 72). These voices function like a chorus in a Greek tragedy; their pronouncements about time and place are as invariably correct as they are precise. The only questions open after the first page are where and how Andreas will die.

On the train, Andreas takes out his map and sets his finger on the place where he will die. From then on, only the manner of his death is unresolved. Here the distinction between story and plot is helpful in understanding the novella. The story line of *The Train Was on Time* is simply: a man believes he will board a train and ride to the place where he is to die. This kind of a story is no different in structure than many classical tragedies. In the Oedipus story, a man is told he will kill his father and marry his mother. The plot is how the prophecy or premonition comes about and what happens to the hero as a result. In *The Train Was on Time* the plot is what occurs between departure and arrival at the destination of death. The plot develops when Andreas meets Willi and the blond soldier on the train and when they visit a bordello and meet the Polish prostitute, Olina.

The episode with Olina threatens to destroy the story's prophecy of death. Olina works for the Polish underground, passing information to the partisans. Olina realizes after meeting the lamblike Andreas that she also is part of the impersonal machinery of death that kills the innocent with the guilty. Andreas realizes through Olina that life can still have meaning and gives up his passive acceptance of death. Together they, along with Willi and the blond soldier, decide to flee the world of war by escaping to the mountains. At this point the tragic dimensions of the story seem about to fall asunder. At this turning point in the drama, the two lovers, Andreas and Olina, with Willi and the blond soldier, steal a German officer's car that is parked before the bordello and flee to the refuge of the mountains. When they reach the mountains, partisans see the car filled with German soldiers and destroy the vehicle. Death arrives on time, as the title had predicted, and at the place where Andreas had laid his finger.

In my analysis of the novella elsewhere, I emphasize not only the similarity of the story and structure to Greek tragedy but also the Christian theology that supports the structure of the tale. Olina identifies Andreas as an innocent lamb, and their chaste relationship is more reminiscent of the one between Jesus and the prostitute Mary Magdalene than it is between two typical lovers. Accordingly, Andreas is a Christ figure and the structure of the story derives from the structure of the Catholic mass, which in turn re-creates the sacrifice of the death of Christ on Calvary. Several parallels in the text reinforce this interpretation. Andreas's priest friend Paul promises to pray for him as Andreas boards the train, and Paul is actually saying mass for Andreas at the moment of his death.[7]

Critics who approach *The Train* from the standpoint of its structure, development, and execution react positively to the work; critics who approach the work from the standpoint of its political message react more negatively. Hans Joachim Bernhard, the East German critic, is most typical of the latter group. He praises the story for its strong antifascist sentiment, its pervasive humanism, and its critique of capitalist profiteering from the war—the last point derived from revelations by the blond soldier that his father's flag and banner company made enormous profits after Hitler came to power and the war started. Regarding these aspects of the novella he concludes, "Böll's critique of the war is principled and without concessions" (26). Nevertheless, Bernhard finds that Böll's lumping of all the participants in the war into just two simplistic categories, victims and executioners, blurs the distinction between Allies and Axis. For Bernhard, Olina's conclusion that each death in the war is a murder removes the novella too far from historical reality (30). Bernhard regrets that Böll did not incorporate into the story his deeply held conviction expressed in the essay "Brief an einen jungen Katholiken," 1958 (Letter to a Young Catholic), where the author expresses the true historical reality, "Bolshevik Russia found herself in 1941 in a position of justified self-defense when the German army attacked the Soviet Union" (Bernhard 30–31).

The novel, *Wo warst du, Adam?*, 1950 (*Adam, Where Art Thou?*) has many similarities with *The Train Was on Time*. Foremost among them are the love between the soldier, Feinhals, and the Jewish school teacher, Ilona, the antifascistic, pacifistic spirit of the work, and its tendency to ahistorical treatment of the war.

The novel is composed of nine chapters, related to each other by theme and the reappearance of characters. While structurally the episodes in these chapters form a connected whole, they are sufficiently independent to stand alone. In 1952 Böll transformed the bridge-building episode in chapter eight into radio play (see *WHTDG* 1: 45–58). Similarly, the stories of Lieutenant Greck, Sergeants Schneider and Finck, and the murder of the Jewish school teacher Ilona can be excerpted and read as self-contained narratives.

The novel opens toward the end of 1944 with the description of a "tragic-faced" general (*WRE* 1: 308), standing before a thousand men. He is about to send this division of reserve troops into battle against the advancing Russians. The perspective of the narrator gradually focuses on smaller and smaller units within the division under the command of a colonel, major, captain, lieutenant, and so on, until the narrator's attention is on the single soldier Feinhals, the main character of the novel. The chapter ends with Feinhals receiving the password of the day, "victory," just as he is reading "defeat" in the general's weary face (*WRE* 1: 318).

This simple device of framing and varying perspective aids Böll in binding together the independent episodes of the novel. In the final chapter, Feinhals sees the general again as he is being interrogated by American officers. He now proudly wears an Iron Cross that was conspicuously lacking from his neck in the first chapter as he addressed his troops; his jaundiced color has become a rosy complexion, and he appears "handsome, relaxed, educated, humane" (*WRE* 1: 435).

Jochen Vogt perceives in this scene a theme from *A Soldier's Legacy:* officers who lost the war were destined to be victorious in peace. Vogt suggests, "Here the victory of the defeated military is anticipated; a theme which becomes central in Böll's social criticism in the novels of the postwar period" (43–44).

Although the general frames the story, Feinhals is the person through whom Böll links most of the various episodes. He is either the main character or on the periphery of all the stories. When his own story is not central, other characters come to the fore. These individual episodes are then united by a similarity of theme, in Vogt's words, the "absurdity and senselessness of war" (38) or, as Bernhard prefers to express it, "the psychic and moral deformation of men under fascism and their despair of being forced to serve an unjust cause in war" (45). The separate accounts of Sergeant Schneider and Dr. Schmitz in chapter three, of Lieutenant Greck in chapter four, of the procurement officer Finck in chapter six, all end in death deprived of all glory and heroism. Chance and irony characterize the deaths of Schneider and Schmitz, who volunteer to stay behind with the wounded in a field hospital. As the Russians approach the evacuated building, Schneider, waving a white flag, stumbles on an unexploded shell that was ordered removed from the premises days ago. The ensuing explosion causes the Russians to open fire on the hospital. Only after all firing has stopped do the Russians realize that "not a single shot came from the other side" (*WRE* 1: 348). The fastidious Lieutenant Greck dies covered with excrement as a grenade lands by him in the latrine. And Finck becomes the victim of his egotistical colonel, who sends him to Hungary to bring back genuine Tokay wine. Finck dies when a shell hits his suitcase filled with sweet, blood-red wine.

The central story is, however, the love story of Feinhals and Ilona. As in *The Train,* love temporarily loosens the bonds of tragedy only to have them draw tighter in sudden death. In this novel Böll intensifies his motif of love at first sight by having the sensitive Feinhals (his name, fine throat, suggests a perfect model for a Botticelli or a Modigliani) fall in love with Ilona before even meeting her, merely by looking at her class picture in the hall of the school where she teaches. When they meet, he feels he already knows her. Here, also as in *The Train,* the affair remains chaste. They have only brief meetings, but between the two the bond is permanent.

They agree to meet again after Ilona returns from a visit to her family in the village ghetto. But while there she is rounded up and taken to a death camp. Upon her arrival she is shot. Feinhals, sensing the tragedy, deserts and returns home to the Rhineland.[8] As Feinhals reaches the door of his mother's house, in no-man's-land, where white flags are flying, one of several mortar rounds fired by a fanatic German soldier lands next to Feinhals. The white sheet from his mother's house falls over him like a shroud. Again Böll's message is apparent. The good and the sensitive are the primary victims in war, the morally ambivalent like the general, Finck's colonel, and the absolute villains like Commandant Filskeit are the survivors who go on to thrive in peace. Since the symbolic qualities of the novel are unmistakable, Hans Schwab-Felisch criticizes Böll's tendency to "overladen symbolism" (221).

This criticism is, however, more justified in the novel *Billard um halbzehn,* 1959 (*Billiards at Half-past Nine*), which will be discussed later. Still, Schwab-Felisch praises Böll for finding the right artistic form for his work. He lauds Böll's natural talent for economy of literary means and for his unusual mastery of language, all of which, he concludes, make *Adam, Where Art Thou?* "one of Böll's most beautifully successful books" (221). Böll himself, although for personal rather than artistic reasons, also granted this novel preferred status. He called it his "favorite book" (Bienek 151).

Böll placed the action of his first novel in the few months from the end of 1944 to the last days of the war in May 1945. Böll's desire for tight forms, controlled by well-defined temporal structures, led him in future novels to concentrate even more on the action of his plots. Future novels often transpired over a single weekend or in a few hours.

In *Adam, Where Art Thou?,* as in *The Train,* Böll placed the burden of humanity primarily on his female characters. This role is characteristic for Böll's positive women. Negative women certainly exist in his work, such as the informer in "Kumpel mit dem langen Haar" and especially Frau Franke in *Und sagte kein einziges Wort,* 1953 (*And Never Said a Word*), but a major function of Böll's heroines is to bear the essence of decency. In *Adam* as in *The Train,* Feinhals's and Andreas's contact with Ilona and Olina represents proximity to incarnate virtue. But these female characters are not the only characters who bear the burden of preserving moral values. In the episode of Sergeant Schneider, the Hungarian peasant woman who delivers vegetables to the field hospital represents the epitome of simplicity and decency. Sight of her is enough to raise Schneider out of his despair. In the bridge episode, which typifies the senseless waste of social wealth in war, the widow Frau Susan, as she goes about her daily routine of cleaning and working, radiates humaneness and a desire for peace.

This role played in the novel by Ilona, the Jewish Catholic school teacher, climaxes in the scene of her death. As she begins to sing before Filskeit, the commandant of the camp, Filskeit is forced to recognize what he has been seeking in life: "Here it was: beauty, greatness, and racial perfection, combined with something that totally lamed him, faith. . . . And in her face, although he saw that she was shaking—in her face was something that was almost like love" (*WRE* 1: 407–8). His only response in confrontation with humanity and moral perfection is to destroy it. He shoots her on the spot and gives the command to murder all the other prisoners. Not every reader responded favorably to this idealized treatment of the Holocaust. Marcel Reich-Ranicki in *Deutsche Literatur in West und Ost* complains of positive stereotyping, "As soon as Jews appear as victims of national socialist persecution, a well-intended primitive philosemitism is noticeable even by the best authors" (222). For Reich-Ranicki characters like Ilona are in the final analysis too "noble, touching, and completely ungenuine" (222). And Susan E. Cernyak-Spatz complains of a lack of authenticity in that there were actually no extermination camps in Hungary, and she finds in Filskeit a mere stereotype of evil (56).

Commandant Filskeit, however, embodies more than the evil of Nazism; he also stands for the perversion of art, exemplified in his sterile love of music. His inclination to correctness, exactness, intolerance of error finds expression in his career as a choir director. The camp provides him the opportunity for inhuman perfection. Here people are forced to sing for their lives and pay for mistakes with death. In Filskeit's love of music, Böll expresses the final perversion of Nazism, for the first purpose of art is to make people more humane. Manfred Durzak maintains in *Der deutsche Roman der Gegenwart* that in the figure of Filskeit, Böll "demonstrated with a convincing model the irrationality of national socialist logic, that even with the distance of time . . . has lost nothing of its effect'' (35).

Böll's treatment of the Holocaust in this novel is one of the first in German literature. It is the forerunner of works such as Rolf Hochhuth's *Der Stellvertreter,* 1963 (*The Deputy*), and Peter Weiss's *Die Ermittlung,* 1965 (*The Investigation*).[9]

The circumstances surrounding Ilona's death can also be read as a commentary on what Hannah Arendt was later to call "the banality of evil," the way in which ordinary people with no particular proclivity to criminality go about their ordinary daily business, which at this time happened to be participation in mass murder.[10] In the same year that Arendt published her book on Eichmann and the banality of evil, Carl Amery published a book, *Die Kapitulation oder deutscher Katholizismus heute,* 1963 (*Capitulation: The Lesson of German Catholicism*), with an afterword by Heinrich Böll, which espoused a similar theory of the Holocaust. Amery distinguishes between primary and secondary values—primary values are the traditional Christian virtues of faith, hope, and charity; secondary are the values of the milieu, such as honesty, cleanliness, reliability, obedience, punctuality, chastity, industriousness. Amery maintains that during the Hitler period the Catholic church (implied is the Protestant church as well) emphasized the secondary and neglected the primary virtues.[11] Amery argues that in such a moral atmosphere, "I can be punctual serving the parish or working in the Gestapo-cellar; I can be fastidious in the 'final solution' or in social work; I can wash my hands after a day's work in the field or in the crematorium of a concentration camp"(23).

Böll's novel illustrates this Arendt-Amery theory of milieu morality in his presentation of the chaste and proper Commandant Filskeit and in the two drivers of the van carrying Ilona and others to the concentration camp. The drivers Schröder and Plorin are normal, law-abiding family men doing their job as citizen soldiers, seeing that the extermination of people proceeds like any other legitimate project. They are not Nazis, not ideologues, not in the party. They are politically indifferent. On their way to the camp with their truck filled with screaming people, they talk of their families and sing popular songs. In many ways this novel sets a pattern for treating the Holocaust that many writers and sociologists have since followed.

Böll's early war stories, besides containing this implied theory of the Holocaust, also reflect his most recent experience in the war. They manifest an earthly fatalism that death is larger than life and proclaim a religious optimism that heavenly consolation is greater than suffering. The novel *Adam* is typical of these early stories in that the book's motto reveals an ahistorical attitude toward the war. Böll took the motto from Antoine de Saint-Exupéry's *Flight to Arras:* "When I was younger, I took part in real adventures: establishing postal air routes across the Sahara and South America. But war is no true adventure; it is only a substitute for adventure. War is a disease just like typhus." Paul Konrad Kurz points out the imprecision of this analogy. He argues that war is not like a sickness derived from the realm of nature (22). Rainer Nägele furthers Kurz's critique by adding that war comes from the realm of politics and economics and has historical causes (126).

This ahistorical perspective in the novel and in the other early war stories is also easily perceivable in *The Train,* when Andreas attributes the causes of the war and all its misfortunes to the "sonorous voices." Certainly the sonorous voices come from people, but, nonetheless, they represent mysterious powers, unknown and unaccountable. Alan Bance claims that this apolitical attitude toward the war was typical of German literature in the forties and fifties. He even sees a kind of realism in this vagueness because, as he says, "war is not conducive to clear thinking" (120). In Böll's case this unanalytical response to the war (seeing international conflict as a natural illness) was compounded by his feeling of being a lucky survivor. Few young men of Böll's generation came home from the war. In the essay "Jahrgang 1917," 1966 (Those Born in 1917), Böll put it this way: "Someone born in 1880 had far more chance to become sixty-six years old than someone born in 1917 had to become twenty-eight. In fact, the chances of survival were only one in three" (*WESR* 2: 234). Böll believed his generation had played Russian roulette with four bullets in the six chambers of the gun of history. Böll's sense of destiny forced him to deal subjectively rather than objectively with the suffering of the Hitler years. This narrow perspective manifests itself in Olina's (*The Train*) simplistic division of people caught up in the war into two groups, victims and executioners, with the victims often being the Germans themselves. Böll's dichotomous view of World War II is understandable and even accurate for someone who was himself an antifascist and a sufferer of twelve prolonged years of oppression. Still, the simplistic dichotomy prevalent in the war stories cannot reveal what the war was about because the limited categories of suffering—innocents and brutal henchmen—are too unrefined. Such dualism, as Walter Sokel calls it, characteristic of Böll's work in this period, disappears from later stories as they become more sophisticated in their characterizations.

But Böll's novel *Adam* borrows a second motto, this one from the wartime diaries of the Catholic writer Theodor Haecker, *Tag- und Nachtbücher*. Böll quotes from Haecker's entry of 31 March 1940: "A world catastrophe can serve many ends, one of which is to find an alibi before God. Where were you, Adam? 'I was in the world war.' " Of these two mottos the one from Haecker is clearly the more important, for Böll takes the title of his novel from it. Clear also is Haecker's irony, which informs Böll's novel: war is no excuse before God. Ultimately people like Schröder, Plorin, and Filskeit are responsible for what they do. This message goes far to undercut the metaphor that war is like typhus or some mysterious disease that runs its course, especially since the main narrative sections of the novel tell the story of the deaths of Feinhals and Ilona. Within the economy of the novel, such excuses as "We did not intend what happened," "We did not know," or "We only did our duty" find no support.

Though Böll under the influence of Christian existentialism may have viewed the world unhistorically in the forties and early fifties, he learned quickly that without recognizing the forces of history he could not understand what was going on in the world around him. The development from ahistoricity to historicity—from presenting one-dimensional characters to presenting morally complicated characters, to writing stories without historical background to novels rich in historical explanation—is a fundamental change in Böll's writing.

NOTES

1. See Conrad, *Heinrich Böll*, 28–31.
2. Of the twenty-five stories in *Wanderer*, twenty-two are in the first person.
3. Böll himself acquired the habit of smoking during the war and could never give it up. It was ultimately the cause of his death due to circulatory problems.
4. Although Böll uses the expression *Erzählung*, meaning simply "story," for most of his fiction, many of the *Erzählungen* are, in fact, models of the classical novella genre characteristic of German literature of the nineteenth and early twentieth centuries. When Böll's stories are, indeed, novellas, I will call them that throughout this book. Furthermore, I will also indicate when an *Erzählung* is a novel.
5. Corporal was also Böll's rank after six years of military service. Wenk expresses Böll's sentiments and ideas in this novella.
6. See Böll's essay, "Brief an meine Söhne oder vier Fahrräder," 1985 (in *Fähigkeit* 79–112), and his last novel, *Frauen vor Flußlandschaft* (1985).
7. See Conard, *Heinrich Böll*, 96–103.
8. These elements of desertion and returning to the Rhineland are strongly autobiographical.
9. For treatment of the Holocaust in German literature see the appropriate sections in Lawrence Langer, *The Holocaust and the Literary Imagination* and *Versions of Survival: The*

Holocaust and the Human Spirit; Hamida Basmajian, *Metaphors of Evil: Contemporary German Literature and the Shadow of Nazism;* Sidra Dekoven Ezarahi, *By Words Alone: The Holocaust in Literature;* and Susan E. Cernyak-Spatz, *German Holocaust Literature.*

10. Hannah Arendt, *Eichmann in Jerusalem: A Report on the Banality of Evil.*

11. Böll's essay, "Brief an einen jungen Katholiken," 1958 (*WESR* 1: 261–76), is an example of his use of this thesis of milieu Catholicism. The letter is based on his experiences in 1939 of participating in a retreat for young Catholics about to enter service in the *Wehrmacht.* Böll recalled exhortations by the chaplain to chastity, sobriety, obedience, doing one's duty, and maintaining a happy disposition but could remember no recommendation to follow one's conscience or to love one's neighbor. This essay was, in fact, influential in Amery's developing his theory of milieu Catholicism.

CHAPTER THREE

The Satires

In his conversations with Eckermann, Goethe claimed, "In general the personal character of the writer influences the public more than his artistic talent" (*Conversations with Eckermann* 30 March 1824). Goethe illustrated his point with Corneille, whom, Goethe said, Napoleon did not read, but nonetheless wished to raise to a prince, and with Racine, whom, Goethe said, Napoleon did read, but of whom he made no such statement. Goethe's observation would actually have found more support in the case of Böll. His integrity as a man of conscience was never in doubt, not even by his opponents. His importance as a man of principle and as a critic of society was well recognized. But nowhere did his character and talent blend so well to form a unity than in his satires. Böll's work in the satiric mode has no equal in postwar German literature. As a satirist Böll has won his highest critical acclaim.

The satire "Nicht nur zur Weihnachtszeit," 1951 ("Christmas Not Just Once a Year"), written at the time of Böll's growing displeasure with political, psychological, and social developments in the Federal Republic, was his breakthrough in this genre.

"Christmas Not Just Once a Year"
("Nicht nur zur Weihnachtszeit")

In writing "Christmas Not Just Once a Year," Böll began to distance himself from the general approval of Germany that he felt immediately after the war in the nation's return to what he thought were fundamental values. This change in attitude found praise among critics. James Henderson Reid in his 1973 book on Böll claimed, " 'Nicht nur zur Weihnachtszeit' [is] possibly Böll's most telling satire . . . and must be ranked among

34

Böll's most unreservedly successful works'' (16, 62). And Erhard Friedrichsmeyer wrote in his study of Böll's satires: "This text ['Christmas Not Just Once a Year'] is a satiric gem. The work's comic richness as well as its virtuosity . . . are indisputable'' (83).

The work soon became widely anthologized both in Germany and abroad and in 1970 was made into a film for television.[1] Its acceptance abroad paralleled its success in Germany, where it was frequently used as a school text. Although the work's reputation continues to grow, there is still no consensus about the meaning of the story, even when most critics agree the satire deals with the relationship of Germany's present to its past.[2] Despite disagreement about the target of the satire, the critics are unanimous in their praise of its quality.

In January 1979, West German television broadcast the American television serial "Holocaust." Millions of Germans saw all or part of this dramatized treatment of the Final Solution of the "Jewish problem." The response of the nation to the series again made clear that thirty-four years after the war, many Germans who had lived through those years had not yet dealt honestly with the past. Some still claimed not to have known of the crimes of the Hitler period, and a few even denied that they took place. The phenomenon of German repression of the events of the war years was once again a subject for the world press.[3] The German claim of limited knowledge of the extent of Nazi war crimes was justified at the end of the war, but during the postwar years of the "economic miracle" many Germans slipped into willful ignorance and denial. While many German writers have treated this theme,[4] Böll's bizarre and humorous tale "Nicht nur zur Weihnachtszeit" was one of the earliest works in German literature to deal with this refusal to face reality, and that theme is arguably the real meaning of the story. But the story in its carefully chosen symbolic form transcends the limits of a national satire and contains a message for other nations as well.

The satire is easily summarized. It relates the tale of tyrannical Aunt Milla, who desires to celebrate Christmas every day, and of her tantrums, which force the members of her family to yield to her strange and destructive demand. To recount the tale, Böll chose a first-person narrator, but one not immediately involved in the events. As nephew to Aunt Milla, he is close enough to events to be informed but not close enough to lose his objectivity. He witnesses some of the action and hears about the rest from members of the family. Despite his effort to be detached, he is more sympathetic to his aunt's attempt to have Christmas every day (to hide reality) than he admits. Because of his sympathy with the older generation, because of his desire to put his relatives in a good light, he becomes a German Everyman, who shares the responsibility of that generation for the repression of history. Most exemplary of his cooperation in the repression of the past is his failure, in an entire story about the Hitler period, to hint at, much less refer to, concentration camps or the Final Solution; he mentions only Germany's own suffering in the war years. What results is a narrative fraught with understatement of bizarre antics. The discrepancy between the understatement and the extraordinary events of the story contributes to the irony of the tale.

In "Christmas Not Just Once a Year" the object of Böll's satire is not primarily false Christian piety or hypocrisy, the commercialization of Christmas, the sentimentality of Germans, or the state of religion in West Germany—all suggested interpretations. Certainly the satire can be read as a critique of these social realities. But the work attacks, first and foremost, West Germany's desire after the war to avoid coming to terms with the Hitler years and that nation's reluctance to learn from recent historical experience. Since this aspect of West Germany's national character is characteristic of all nations' psychological behavior, the satire acquires intercultural importance.

Remarkable about "Christmas" is the way it presents its message with objectivity and cool detachment in a genre not noted for either of these virtues. Böll's satire is in this regard in the manner of the satirist Jonathan Swift, who creates tension in "A Modest Proposal" by confronting outrageous events with calmness. (In fact, Böll uses Swift as a model in another story, "The Thrower-away," discussed later in this chapter.) While the very idea of Christmas every day is a form of hyperbole, the work retains a matter-of-factness and directness that results in a thorough analysis of Germany's postwar social sickness.

The opening sentences of the story suggest Böll's intention:

> Among our relatives, symptoms of disintegration are beginning to show up that for a while we tried silently to ignore but the threat of which we are now determined to face squarely. I do not yet dare use the word "collapse," but the alarming facts are accumulating to the point where they represent a threat and compel me to speak of things that may sound strange to the ears of my contemporaries but whose reality no one can dispute. The mildew of decay has obtained a foothold under the thick, hard veneer of respectability, colonies of deadly parasites heralding the end of the integrity of an entire clan. (*WRE* 2: 11, Vennewitz translation from *The Stories of Heinrich Böll* 419)

The narrator's story is to be understood as a tale of his countrymen. He achieves this breadth of context with the words, "among our relatives," which indicate the story is one of more than the immediate family and refers to all relations and kin, with the phrase "entire clan," which indicates a tribe, a family group in the largest sense, and with the expression "contemporaries," which informs the reader that the unusual story he is about to hear is a parable ("whose reality no one can dispute") for and about the entire German nation. Lothar Huber in his essay on Böll's satiric method also identifies the family with the German nation, for he sees in "distinguished old" Aunt Milla the figure of "Germania" (52).

Early in the story the narrator humbly apologizes for having to mention the war, admitting he preferred not to run the risk of making himself "unpopular" (WRE 2: 13) but was forced to raise the unpleasant topic simply because it had an "influence on the story" (WRE 2: 13); however, after once having put the "boring" (WRE 2: 13) detail aside, he promises not to bring it up again. With this use of understatement, Böll both sets the tone and provides the background necessary to understand the message of his tale.

The choice of Christmas as a symbol of Germany's forgetfulness (a people's desire not to conquer the past) is actually quite natural. Christmas, in fact, abrogates the concerns of the day. For a brief period people forget their troubles or at least disguise them behind a festive spirit. Traditions by their nature stress the past and in that manner distort the present and neglect the future, but Christmas more than other celebrations emphasizes an idealized and romanticized past. Hence, the Christmas season functions as institutionalized escapism as it is employed in the work, a permanent flight from reality extending from December to December, a point reinforced in the satire by the twelve narrative divisions Böll gives the story.

The past that Aunt Milla wishes to forget is implicit in the tale, "The war was registered by my Aunt Milla only as a power which began in 1939 to endanger her Christmas tree" (WRE 2: 13). Two conclusions are necessary from the narrator's observation. First, some Germans only reacted to the war to the extent that it touched adversely upon their personal lives, and second, Germans could hate the inconvenience of war without relating it to the Hitler dictatorship. Both conclusions reveal that the war might be condemned as something not directly resulting from National Socialism and fascism. The leitmotifs of the story—"the good old days" and "Everything should be as before"—refer specifically to the period prior to1939, not to 1933. "The good old days" refer then to the prewar period when Hitler was in power, Nazism was triumphant, and all was going well for the nation. Böll is saying in this satire of 1951 that the German failure to conquer the past is more than merely a desire to forget the war and a refusal to assume responsibility for it, but it is also a failure to condemn fascism.

The time references in the story are specific. It was "the middle of March" 1947 (*WRE* 2: 16) when the narrator discovered the first signs of permanent Christmas among his relatives. But the family gave in to Aunt Milla's hysterical demand for Christmas every day by treating it as a "harmless weakness" (*WRE* 2: 13), and thus, with the "participation of all" (*WRE* 2: 14), they took up the "costly" (*WRE* 2: 14) burden of continuing the celebration.

The costs are, indeed, more than financial. Aunt Milla's husband, Uncle Franz, described prior to the permanent Christmas as a "goodhearted man" and a "model of a Christian businessman" (*WRE* 2: 12) soon manifests signs of moral decay hinted at in the opening paragraph. He becomes estranged from his wife, takes a mistress, and becomes a greedy, manipulating merchant—the last change a necessary development to maintain the costly permanent Christmas. As the narrator sums it up, "In his case the decay was complete" (*WRE* 2: 29).

Aunt Milla's children, Cousin Johannes, Cousin Lucie, and Cousin Franz, are equally ill affected by the tacit decision not to conquer the past. Johannes, a successful lawyer, becomes a Communist; Lucie has a nervous breakdown. Her husband Karl plans to emigrate to a country "not far from the equator" (*WRE* 2: 31) in order to save his wife and to restore their children's deteriorating health. Thus, the children of Aunt Milla turn to political activism, emigration, or succumb to poor health because of conditions in the German family. These desertions from normal German life are positive alternatives in the story if one considers that their other choice is to accept permanent social deceit.

In order to make his criticism more analytical and historically accurate, Böll departs momentarily from the tradition of satire that conventionally makes no claim to fairness. In fact, satire is normally the least objective of all literary genres because its intention is to present a revealing insight into the condition of society; therefore, it makes no pretense of equity nor claim of realism, relying instead on disproportion either as overstatement or understatement. Such methods are justified in satire because its purpose is not to offer solutions to social problems, but only to point out what the problems of society are.

In "Christmas Not Just Once a Year," Böll departs from the normal exaggeration of satire to tender a fuller view of reality. Although he never accepted the idea of collective guilt in relation to the Hitler period, he did accept the term in relationship to Germany in the postwar period after the currency reform of 1948, when most Germans rushed into the economic miracle at the expense of the past. In the essay "Hierzulande," 1960 (In This Country), he claimed, "If there is anything like collective guilt in this land, then it starts with the moment of currency reform when the sellout of suffering, sadness, and memory began" (*WESR* 1: 374). And in the same essay he declared with outrage, "Whoever has a memory that goes back ten years is considered sick and deserves to be put in a deep sleep so that he can wake up strengthened for the present" (*WESR* 1: 333). Nonetheless, Böll still knew that not all Germans were guilty of even the postwar cover-up. Thus, he provides Aunt Milla's family with a symbolic redeeming member in Cousin Franz, whose function in the satire is to act as a foil to his tyrannical aunt. He is a typical Böllian black sheep, a boxer with an inclination to piety. He warns the family from the beginning of the "terrible consequences" (*WRE* 2: 11) of permanent Christmas and is fully aware that what appears to be " 'in itself' a harmless event" (*WRE* 2: 11) is in reality a dangerous undertaking.

At no time does Cousin Franz personally take part in the celebrations. He even enhances his unpopularity in the family by suggesting that his screaming mother be subjected to an exorcism or committed to an institution. In this detail Böll points out his view that the refusal to confront the past is, indeed, a devilish obsession or, as a case of willful amnesia, a form of mental illness. Because Cousin Franz as a young man was a mediocre student, became a boxer, and associated with questionable companions, he "possessed . . . too little reputation for the relatives to listen to him" (*WRE* 2: 12). The family considers him of unreliable character and treats him as an outsider. Cousin Franz exemplifies a type common in Böll's stories, the ethical asocial individual. His life is a model of humanity. During the war he treated Polish and Russian POW's with kindness, and after the war he reluctantly assumes the role of a prophet, of one crying out in the wilderness, warning his relatives of the dangers of catering to escapism; later he even intervenes to save Lucie's and Karl's children. However, at the conclusion of the story, he retreats to a monastery to continue his battle to save his German family by other means. He dons a monk's habit and turns to prayer, accepting the fateful conclusion, "We are punished by life" (*WRE* 2: 34).

It is typical of Böll in these early years that he puts religion and the church in a favorable light. Besides Cousin Franz, two clerics, a pastor, and a chaplain refuse to take part in the daily Christmas celebrations. But in the prelate who cooperates with the family, one sees the earliest example of Böll's criticism of the church. Also, the manner in which the wealth of the family determines the institutional church's treatment of the pastor and chaplain reveals Böll's belief that the wealthy bourgeois class influences the church as it does the state. Also implied is Böll's belief that it is the wealthy who benefit most from a society with a façade that conceals the relationship of the present to the fascist past. Erhard Friedrichsmeyer's analysis of the satire also supports this interpretation. He concludes, "Reactionary tendencies establish themselves so that parallels begin to develop between the fascism of the past and growth-obsessed capitalism (*Leistungskapitalismus*)" of the present (60).

Uncle Franz, because of his wealth, has connections in the hierarchy of the church; he sees that charges are brought against the pastor and the chaplain for their "neglect of pastoral duties" (*WRE* 2: 23). Although the two clerics are exonerated in the canonical court, the incident reveals a working relationship between the financially powerful and the church hierarchy. Through this relationship, Böll's story shows that the church shares in the guilt of the postwar repression of the past by its failure to provide moral leadership, or, in the words of the story, begins to share in the responsibility for the "mildew of decay" (*WRE* 2: 11) developing in the heart of West German society.

By being balanced in his presentation, Böll departs from the tradition of satire, but he also deviates from satirical practice in yet another way. He uses satire not only to criticize but also to analyze social reality. Each character has a parabolic role in relationship to the permanent Christmas, and the players fall into more than two camps: those for and those against the celebrations, those who cooperate and those who do not. Within the family only Aunt Milla is totally dedicated to the restoration of "the good old days." She feels no remorse nor does she demonstrate any recognition of the consequences of her actions. Therefore, her physical health is not endangered by the repression of the recent past, "Only my Aunt Milla enjoyed the best of health, smiled, is well and happy as she almost always was" (*WRE* 2: 12). Aunt Milla, therefore, represents the people who see nothing wrong with the years 1933–1945, except that the war years after 1939 began to endanger their Christmases.

For other persons not in this category of the willfully deceived, the repression of the past produces psychological disturbances, family divisions, and generational animosity with undesirable social effects. If such are the negative results of the permanent Christmas, the reader must ask why one would begin—much less continue—such a practice. The answer is indicated in the story. At first the extension of Christmas seemed " 'in itself' harmless" (*WRE* 2: 16). "The terrible consequences" (*WRE* 2: 11) were not foreseeable (except by Cousin Franz, to whom no one listened). It was easier to cooperate with the celebrations than to oppose them because the "costs" were not immediately obvious. It was also an easy way to achieve normality, for, as the narrator states, "Everything seemed to be in order" (*WRE* 2: 20).

The story speaks to the German social situation in the 1990s as effectively as it did in 1951. The current desire of Germans for normality in relationship to the Hitler period and, since unification, in relationship to the crimes of the Stalinists in the former German Democratic Republic is again a major issue of contention with philosophers, historians, politicians, journalists, and intellectuals. Their debate centers on the uniqueness or commonplaceness of Germany's aberrations. In this climate, Böll's formulation of the problem in "Christmas Not Just Once a Year" gives the story a continuing actuality.

Furthermore, the satire suggests a close connection between the repression of the past and the headlong rush into the economic boom. It implies that the more one wants to do away with the unpleasantnesses of recent history, the more one must lose oneself in frantic economic activity. Uncle Franz, representative of the entrepreneur class, is forced to earn more, increase his profits, participate in the *Leistungsgesellschaft* (performance society) in direct proportion to his cooperation with the needs of permanent Christmas.

Böll's satire is effective for at least two reasons. The first derives from the technique of exaggeration used to execute the author's idea and the second from the choice of permanent Christmas as a symbol to represent the theme. While the election of the dual perspective of Aunt Milla's nephew with its advantage of intimacy and objectivity, involvement and detachment, has already been mentioned, this point of view also performs another aesthetic service. The teller of the story is not consciously committed to any of the factions within the family. He tries to be neutral in his presentation, friendly with all, sympathetic to everyone. He sees with the aunt's, uncle's, and the cousins' eyes. He even ends his story with a visit to Cousin Franz in the monastery. This middle position of the narrator (although in reality he is somewhat more sympathetic to Aunt Milla's generation than to her children's) reduces the unpleasant didacticism and overbearing seriousness satire can often have. The narrator's stance aestheticizes and socializes the aggression inherent in the satire by the principle of indirection.

The technique of exaggeration deserves further mention in relation to Böll's development as a satirist because it was his first use of a method that later proved so successful and simple for him to apply that he gave it up as no longer challenging. That is the principle of *executio ad absurdum*, the carrying out of the details of a story to their ultimate self-parodying conclusion. Böll explained this method in a conversation with Karin Struck: "In essence writing a satire is nothing but the development of a very simple mathematical formula, let's say, a plus b in parentheses, squared. A basic idea consistently exaggerated until it can't be exaggerated any more, then you have a satire. To to do that you need imagination, not information" (*WI* 1: 297).

In "Christmas Not Just Once a Year," this technique is seen in the details of the daily celebration, in the effort to prolong the life of the tree, the itemization of the daily cost of providing the feast, the replacing of the children with wax figures and the hiring of the actors to replace the adults, the sending of the children to cut trees in the state park, the bribing of officials to get out-of-season items, the melting of the candies on the tree in the summer heat, and the angels' constant whispering of "peace, peace." Klaus Jeziorkowski refers to this process in Böll's satires as "a mass of details, nonsense, scurrility, and fantasy" stabilized by a "precise calculated static framework of inner form" (13). The success of Böll's method as employed in "Christmas Not Just Once a Year" and in most of the other satires of the fifties—first-person narrator with a tendency to confessional revelation and the accumulation of details leading to an absurd conclusion—is no doubt the formula that Böll had in mind when he explained in an interview with Marcel Reich-Ranicki in 1967 why he wrote so few short stores in the sixties: "Probably it is a weariness with my own ability. I would like to make the short story the middle point of my work again. But when I try it, I fall again and again into the same pattern. I'm making every effort to change this. Perhaps I will be successful. The short story is still the most beautiful of all prose forms" (*WI* 1: 67).

In fact Böll published few short stories after the fifties, together no more than about twenty-one are spread throughout various books; about half of these could be called satires, the best of which are "Anekdote zur Senkung der Arbeitsmoral," 1963 ("Anecdote Concerning the Lowering of Productivity"), "Veränderungen in Staech," 1969 ("The Staech Affair"), "Epilog zu Stifters 'Nachsommer,' " 1970 (Epilogue to Stifter's *Indian Summer*), "Berichte zur Gesinnunglsage der Nation," 1975 (Report on the Attitudinal State of the Nation), and "Erwünschte Reportage," 1975 (A Desired Report).[5]

The second reason for the effectiveness of "Christmas" is that the symbol of Christmas is timeless. Most satire has a short life because of its usual relationship to rapidly changing current affairs. Böll's story, on the contrary, remains alive because in it he chose to criticize conditions which, though specifically German, still retain a general validity. In the choice of Christmas and the critique of "the good old days," Böll created a certain universality, which transcends the single interpretation of Germany's desire to forget its Nazi past. The story can, in fact, be read with equal application in any country where for political, economic, or psychological reasons a shameful national past has not been adequately dealt with. In such a country where national policy is changed out of opportunism or expediency, where the perpetrators of injustice assume the role of victims, "Christmas Not Just Once a Year" will be rewarding reading. Erwin Theodor Rosenthal makes this point about Böll's popularity in Brazil, "Böll's works are received in Brazil as contemporary critical observations which do not apply exclusively to Germany, but to the entire Western world (and perhaps not only there!)" (150). In "Nicht nur zur Weihnachtszeit" Böll created not only a national classic but a satire for all ages.

"The Thrower-away" ("Der Wegwerfer")

Böll's best satires follow not only the pattern that he referred to in his conversation with Karin Struck, where he defined satire as an idea carried to absurdity, but also another pattern easily discerned from the structure he repeats in "Der Lacher" ("The Laugher"), "Bekenntnis eines Hundefängers" (Confession of a Dogcatcher), "Im Lande der Rujuks" (In the Land of the Rujuks), "Hier ist Tibten" ("This is Tibten"), "Es wird etwas geschehen" ("Action Will Be Taken"), and "Der Wegwerfer" ("The Thrower-away"). All are first-person narratives of a confessional nature where the narrator has an unusual occupation or pursues an exceptional way of life. These eccentric characters give Böll an opportunity to expose society's shortcomings. The laugher is a successful professional audience stimulator with an infectious laugh who never lets a natural laugh escape his lips. The dogcatcher is a man who never registers his own dog because he is the person who enforces the registration law. The scholar in "Rujuks" spends a lifetime mastering a language no one speaks and for which there is no literature. The protagonist in "Tibten" has two doctorates but opts for a stressless job announcing "this is Tibten" in the train station in the town where he lives. In "Action" an eager businessman learns to handle thirteen telephones at one time while another masters the art of working with a phone in each hand as he takes notes with a pen in his mouth and operates a knitting machine with his toes.

This pattern of first-person narration, unusual occupation, and exaggeration of plausibility is best illustrated by "The Thrower-away," 1957. Klaus Jeziorkowski, taking a phrase from Theodor Adorno's analysis of Aldous Huxley's *Brave New World,* calls Böll's technique "lengthening the line" (29–30). It is, in fact, another way of explaining Böll's own description of his method as explained to Karin Struck. In Adorno's own words, "Huxley projects observations of the present state of civilization along the lines of its own teleology to the point where its monstrous nature becomes immediately evident" (99). Certainly Adorno's observation about Huxley's satire can readily be applied to Böll's. Still, it is most likely that Böll, if he had a conscious model at all, had Jonathan Swift in mind.

When Böll visited Ireland in 1955, one of his first excursions was to the tomb of Swift, Böll's "godfather in satire," as Theodore Ziolkowski calls him ("Conscience and Craft" 220). Böll records this event in his *Irisches Tagebuch,* 1957 (*Irish Journal*):

> At Swift's tomb my heart grew cold. St. Patrick's Cathedral was so clean, so empty, so full of patriotic marble figures, and the desperate dean appeared to lie so deep under the cold stone—by his side Stella: two rectangular brass plates, highly polished as if by a German *Hausfrau*: the large one for Swift, the smaller one for Stella; I ought to have brought thistles, hard and large, with long stems, and a few shamrocks, also a few thornless mild blossoms, jasmine perhaps or honeysuckle: that would have been the right greeting for the two. (*WRE* 3: 19)

This account documents Böll's familiarity with Swift's life and work: the prickly thistles for his bitter satire, the shamrocks for his Irish patriotism, the thornless blossoms and sweet flowers for his tender relationship with Esther Johnson, his Stella.

But even more convincing of Böll's knowledge of Swift's work is the similarity of his method of satire to that of the Irish moralist. A comparison of the two writers indicates the probable source of Böll's technique of amalgamating humor, wit, irony, burlesque, and the grotesque, and thus, explains why Böll's satires are free of the characteristics of classical Latin satire: sarcasm, invective, and innuendo.

In "A Modest Proposal" (1729) and in "The Thrower-away," the similar styles of these men can most easily be recognized. Characteristic of their technique is an extremely realistic method of description, combined with fanciful exaggeration, minute observation, and precise calculation in a pseudo-scientific manner, designed to intensify estrangement from what is natural and to produce comic, grotesque, ironic, and satiric situations with moral implications. In this case of Böll's "The Thrower-away" and Swift's "A Modest Proposal," the nucleus of the works is a plausible idea worked out in great detail, calculated with simulated expertise, expressed in detached language with appropriate jargon, and carried out unemotionally to a horrific conclusion.

Swift's "A Modest Proposal" is a *coup de main* against Ireland's poverty and the people and policies responsible for England's foreign trade practices. Böll's "The Thrower-away" assails the belief that people and nature exist to produce profit through exploitation. Böll's work satirizes the waste of human and natural resources—that senseless destruction of things—that often results from the profit motive of capitalism. Furthermore, both authors also attack an impersonal world by creating nameless characters. In Böll's case, his anonymous narrator even works for an anonymous insurance company identified only by the unexplained acronym "Ubia." And in Swift's case, his anonymous persona places total confidence in the detached indifference of numbers to solve the human equation of labor, poverty, and population. Böll likewise assaults the statistical method of manipulating society, the computer, and he volleys away at sacred time-study methods that promise increased productivity by reducing a person's natural movements to an unvarying mechanical routine. It is an important detail in Böll's story that the thrower-away learns to hate the practical application of his theories when he is required to live by them, although he still claims to love the stimulating mental activity that leads to their development. Here Böll reveals a further critique of advanced technology by reproaching the scientist who joyfully pursues detached research without concern for the ultimate application of his discoveries. The thrower-away's assertion concerning the ethical—"I would like on principle to keep away from morality. My area of speculation is pure economics" (*WRE* 3: 281)—is representative of an attitude of many researchers to the application of knowledge they produce.

Böll's "The Thrower-away" also attacks society for its false hierarchy of values and criticizes a world in which a false pluralism prevails. This critique is latent in the encyclopedic ordering of the thrower-away's junk collection in which "Art History" (*Kunstgeschichte*) is placed next to "Artificial Honey" (*Kunsthonig*), suggesting the only remaining valid principle of order is the alphabet. Thus, Böll is saying, if there is no priority that acknowledges people as the highest good, then it is perfectly natural to handle people as objects. In both "A Modest Proposal" and "The Thrower-away" a critique obtains against the tendency in society to the total administration of things. Such satire is not comparable to Horatian or Juvenalian satire or to the classical tradition in general because in a classical satire the prevailing norms of society are accepted, and merely the deviations from accepted standards are condemned or criticized. In contrast, Swift's disdain is precisely for the accepted principles of his day, for the economic planners who commit the error of trying to solve human problems by indices. Swift's economic "projector" is addicted to numbers as other men are to alcohol. His counterpart is Böll's thrower-away, who admits to being "intoxicated" by his figures. In their use of statistics both Swift and Böll reveal their disregard for the classical theory of satire as summarized by Schiller in his essay, "On Simple and Sentimental Poetry." Here Schiller explains that the satirist "takes as [his] subject the distance at which things are from nature, and the contrast between reality and the ideal," explaining further that "in satire, the real as imperfection is opposed to the ideal considered as the highest reality." (7: 296–97)[6]

Instead, Swift and Böll favor a technique of setting a fantastic intensified projection of the real world against existing reality to permit the reader, by means of contrasting exaggeration, to see what the real world is becoming, thus reflecting the moral hope that the reader will acknowledge and reject the direction the world is taking. This analysis is also perfectly in keeping with Adorno's analysis of Huxley's *Brave New World*.

Recently Umberto Eco has in the form of the novel, *The Name of the Rose*, reconstructed Aristotle's theory of comedy derived from general knowledge of the lost second book of the *Poetics*, and Leon Golden, independently of Eco and by different means, has arrived at similar reconstructions of Aristotle's theory.[7] These reconstructions also provide unifying theories to cover modern forms of satire. For both Eco and

Golden, and here they follow Aristotle, comedy is an instrument of truth that preserves humility and makes doubt possible. Both see Aristotelian laughter as an instrument of reason which in the service of truth refutes false propositions. Laughter makes possible a humane and just response to the depravities that human beings are capable of committing. According to Eco and Golden, comedy creates catharsis (understood by Eco as "purification" and by Golden as "intellectual clarification"), and this catharsis originates in indignation toward presented ignoble actions. In the "Modest Proposal," that would be cannibalism and by inference British economic policy, and in "The Thrower-away" the planned and calculated destruction of things. Hence, laughter in Böll's and Swift's work is a subversive force against arrogance and unquestioned concepts of social truths. They use satire to chastise and modify social behavior. Golden, in his essay, "Aristotle on Comedy," restates Henri Bergson's view of comedy in *Le rire* for its close correspondence with what he concludes is Aristotle's position. Bergson's attitude is also descriptive of Swift's and Böll's satires:

> The subject matter of comedy [is] whatever is rigid, automatic, and mechanical in human mental, spiritual, and physical behavior. These rigidities, these automatic responses, these mechanizations of the human spirit, all subvert the optimum level of human social behavior . . . Comedy is to bring the powerful admonishing force of laughter to bear on this kind of socially disruptive human behavior and thus to alter it for the better. . . . The basic goal of comedy is the correction of such negative behavior by the punishing humiliation of laughter." (Bergson 284, trans. Brereton/Rothwell)

Swift's persona, the modest proposer, and Böll's narrator, the thrower-away, are remarkably similar types, eccentrics who try to conceal their perversity and megalomania behind the guise of solid burghers. The modest proposer hides behind such measured phrases of restraint as, "I think it is agreed by all parties" and "I do therefore humbly offer it to public consideration" (439), while the thrower-away conceals himself behind a business suit, his mundane streetcar conversations, and the politeness of offering his seat to an elderly lady, all of which leads to his observation, "Thus I complete the picture of a careful citizen" (*WRE* 3: 273). Despite the meticulously constructed public images of these characters, they both secretly entertain doubts about the morality of their endeavors: the destruction of work of others and the proposing of cannibalism.[8] But in anticipation of reproach, they have well-formulated defenses.

The thrower-away expresses his fear of discovery in the first sentence of his narrative, "For the last few weeks I've been trying to avoid contact with people who might ask me what I do for a living.'' That fear is the reason he hides himself behind the protective guise of a perfect business manner. The modest proposer, besides concealing himself behind dissembling turns of phrase, defends himself against the accusation of infanticide by asserting his concern for humanity: ''It is improbable that some scrupulous people might be apt to censure such a practice [of eating children] (although indeed very unjustly) as a little bordering on cruelty, which I confess, hath always been with me the strongest objection against any project, howsoever, well intended'' (442). But the fear of being considered employed with morally dubious ideas does not prevent either character from overcoming his moral hesitancy and expressing pride in his precisely calculated theory. The thrower-away calls himself ''inventor,'' ''private scholar,'' ''student,'' and ''unacknowledged genius'' (*WRE* 3: 272). The modest proposer esteems himself as one who ''would deserve so well of the public as to have his statue set up for a preserver of the nation'' (439).

Both men do, in fact, intend to better their worlds.[9] They think of themselves as humanitarians striving for goals that everyone can applaud. The modest proposer seeks ''a fair, cheap, and easy method of making . . . children sound and useful members of the commonwealth'' (439) and desires to create an ''innocent, cheap, easy, and effectual'' (445) means to ''aid the public good, advance trade, provide for infants, relieve the poor, [and] give pleasure to the rich'' (446). The thrower-away hopes to develop the national use of goods and resources in a system of maximum utility that will ''spare humanity that useless effort under which it groans'' (*WRE* 3: 278). ''Daily,'' he claims, ''billions of discarding movements are made, energy wasted, which, if it could be harnessed, would suffice to change the face of the earth'' (*WRE* 3: 278). But in their language and phraseology as much as in the proposals themselves, these men betray the horror of their good intentions. To the modest proposer, people are ''commodities,'' children ''yearlings,'' and babies merely ''carcasses,'' the ''fattest'' of which are to be brought ''to market'' and ''dress[ed] . . . hot from the knife.'' A mother is a ''breeder'' who like a ''dam'' does not give birth, but ''drops'' her young. The thrower-away is less coarse in his vocabulary because he is more aware of the moral implications of his theories, but he, nonetheless, also gives himself away in his choice of words. Jeziorkowski points out that the nominal and abstract quality of the thrower-away's vocabulary—the tendency to nouns ending in *-heit, -keit, -tät,* and *-nis*—represents the vocabulary of science, industry, and administration, the language of institutional functionaries (59). It is an attempt to order reality into concepts in order better to control and to dominate the milieu. It is a parallel to the modest proposer's borrowing the diction of merchants, economists, stock breeders, and butchers. At this point Swift and Böll have the same object of satire: man's pride in his rationality. Each writer shows where insensitive scientific theorizing can lead—to the slaughterhouse or to the refuse heap.

Although Swift's "A Modest Proposal" is in the form of an essay and Böll's "The Thrower-away" takes the shape of a short story, there is, in fact, little difference between the two.[10] Both works, despite their varying forms as tract and confession, manifest one of the most prominent characteristics of satire: the absence of plot, i.e., both works conclude where they begin. The social conditions and the personality of the modest proposer remain constant throughout the essay. And the thrower-away ends his narrative as he began, still reveling in his theories and enjoying the "icy intoxication produced by formulas" (*WRE* 3: 274). Although in a final nightmare he is visited by a prophetic vision of exploding calculations and demonic laughter, true to the form of satire, he fails to recognize the warning. In satire, plotlessness is necessary to prevent the reader from concluding that the criticized situation has changed. Plotlessness is actually part of the meaning of satire. From the satirist's point of view, society still needs improvement.

In both "A Modest Proposal" and "The Thrower-away" the plotlessness is also accompanied by contrived reasoning. The modest proposer calmly adds and subtracts people by the thousands, estimates the number of miscarriages, calculates the quantity of adults needed for breeding, allows for a ratio of males to females more generous than that allowed sheep, cattle, or swine, reckons the average price each body will bring, suggests alternative ways of preparing the human product for consumption, and suggests the avoidance of waste by indicating that an infant's skin can be made into fine hand and footwear. No better example exists in literature of the confusion of kind (people for animals) and, hence, the confusion of means (slaughter for population control). The result is that Swift's "A Modest Proposal" is not only great literature as satire but also as prophecy, for it is the first and best analysis of the Auschwitz phenomenon and the personality that produced it. The modest proposer is a model of the dedicated servant, the banal Eichmann, who calmly plans and carries out the systematic mechanized liquidation, starvation, and exploitation of millions for the "good" of his country. The societal tendency toward total administration of things, the concern of Swift's essay in the eighteenth century, became reality in the twentieth. And it is precisely this aspect of the "Modest Proposal" that "The Thrower-away" most closely parallels.

The thrower-away calculates no less accurately and distorts equally his logic. He reports on his work routine by the minute and describes his activity in a manner characteristic of a do-it-yourself manual, "I enter the workroom, change my coat for a gray smock . . . I open the sacks . . . empty them into wooden trays . . . ," etc. (*WRE* 3: 274). At another point he informs the reader of the obvious materials needed for his research: graph paper, colored pencils, and even gives their prices; he further relates how with the help of a stopwatch he determines the minimum and maximum time necessary for opening packages, for instance, 5–25 seconds for printed matter. Thus, Böll appears to create the image of a precise, reasonable person sensitive to facts and dictates of sequential thinking. However, the opposite is true. Böll comments on this paradoxical method of narration as follows: "When work procedures are described exactly, they are raised to the level of the abstract. The more correctly that which is experienced is [related], the more abstract it becomes" (*WESR* 3: 192). Hence, the more conscientiously and precisely these fictional "geniuses" relate their procedures, the more absurd—and especially here—the more inhuman their procedures become and their proposed cures are revealed to be worse than the maladies they intend to remedy.

These reasonable men go astray because they start by rejecting realistic, practical solutions and submit to no humane principle above themselves or their theories. The modest proposer discards out of hand such ideas as taxing absentee landlords, buying domestic manufactures (445) as methods impossible to implement. Therefore, he opens the way for his extreme remedy. The thrower-away, likewise, never considers the real cause of the problem of material waste (production for profit instead of for human needs); hence, he treats only the symptom of waste. Böll reveals the true mental capacity of the thrower-away in the passage where he suggests, "It would be important to acquire access to experimentation in department stores to see . . . if an experienced thrower-away should be stationed by the packing table to unpack what has just been packaged to get the wrapping paper ready for the scrap dealer" (*WRE* 3: 278), and where he concludes that superfluous packaging is leading the nation into mental hospitals, "In the psychiatric clinics the number of patients who have had a breakdown while trying to unwrap a bottle of perfume, a box of candy, or open a pack of cigarettes has greatly increased" (*WRE* 3: 279). These magnificent fallacies reveal Martin Price's statement about Swift—his technique is characterized by a "meeting [of] false rhetoric [meaning logic] with even falser rhetoric" (72)—to be equally valid for Böll.

By looking at these two works in detail and tracing the multiple parallels of style, point of view, and satiric object, it is fair to conclude that Swift is one of the writers that has most influenced Böll and that this influence extends far beyond this single satire to the many that follow the same pattern. Swift is, indeed, as Ziolkowski says, Böll's "godfather in satire" ("Conscience and Craft" 220).

NOTES

1. By 1975 "Christmas Not Just Once a Year" had appeared in twenty-three German and foreign anthologies. See Werner Martin, *Heinrich Böll: Eine Bibliographie seiner Werke.*

2. For a summary of the broad range of interpretations, see Conard, "Heinrich Böll's 'Nicht nur zur Weihnachtszeit.' " The interpretation given here is based on this article.

3. For a sample of the reporting of the German reaction to the "Holocaust" series, see, for example, *Der Spiegel* 29 January 1979, cover article; *Die Zeit*, North American Edition, 26 January 1979: 15–16; *Time* 5 February 1979: 115; *Newsweek* 5 February 1979: 62. The "Holocaust" series was rebroadcast in November 1984 and attracted ten million viewers, one-sixth of the West German population.

4. See Judith Ryan, *The Uncompleted Past: Post-war German Novels and the Third Reich.*

5. See *Werke: Romane und Erzählungen,* vols. 4 and 5, *Du fährst zu oft nach Heidelberg, Gesammelte Erzählungen,* 2 vols., and *Das Heinrich Böll Lesebuch.*

6. See Conard, "The Relationship of Heinrich Böll's Satire 'The Thrower-away' to Jonathan Swift's 'A Modest Proposal,' " for treatment of Böll's relationship to black humor and the theater of the absurd.

7. See Leon Golden, "Aristotle on Comedy" and "Eco's Reconstruction of Aristotle's Theory of Comedy in *The Name of the Rose.*"

8. From the earliest stories to the latest novels, the theme of destruction and waste remains one of the most consistent in Böll's work.

9. Klaus Jeziorkowski in *Rhythmus und Figur* divides all of Böll's satires into three groups: 1) utopian satires, 2) narratives with satiric character, and 3) non-utopian satires. He places "Der Wegwerfer" in the first group because of the narrator's desire to better the world. For Jeziorkowski's three lists see notes 36, 37, and 38 on p. 84.

10. See Conard, "The Relationship of Heinrich Böll's Satire 'The Thrower-away' to Jonathan Swift's 'A Modest Proposal,' " for an analysis of the similarity of the structure in the two works.

CHAPTER FOUR

The Major Novels

The Mythological-Theological Problematic

Böll's interview of 1976 with René Wintzen entitled "Eine deutsche Erinnerung"/A German Memory (*WI*: 504–665) is not only one of Böll's longest interviews but also one of his most important. In one passage Wintzen pursues the relationship of history to Böll's work. Wintzen believes, as do most of Böll's critics and readers, that there is an intimate connection between the two, that his writing is bound up with his experience during the Hitler dictatorship, the war, the restoration, the economic miracle. Böll disputes this point. He argues that the concrete events of history after 1933 affected him very little, that without this history, he would have written essentially the same works.

Böll's position has in its favor that it leads to revealing insights into his work that a strict historical approach is unlikely to produce. The methodology is simply to ask what is a novel about when its concretization is stripped away, when its time, place and specificity of details are removed. What is its theme? What is the story in essence about? This approach makes some basic structures immediately apparent and helps explain why Böll's work is popular in the West, in the East, in the Third World, in societies that seem to have little in common. One answer is that readers recognize the universal quality of Böll's themes, which communicate to readers in all circumstances.

Böll explains: "Let's assume there had been no war and no Nazis. . . . I am quite sure that I would have written *Und sagte kein einziges Wort* [*And Never Said a Word*] . . . almost exactly the same." It is a novel about the "decay, decadence and fragility of structures people believe last forever: marriage and the church" (*WI* 1: 515). He calls the novel "an existential statement about the institution of marriage" (*WI* 1: 519). These remarks are actually very similar to a statement he made in the 1967 interview with Marcel Reich-Ranicki where he says, "As author only two themes interest me: love and religion" (*WI* 1: 68). Obviously missing again is a reference to politics. Böll explains this omission in the interview with Wintzen. He continues: "I do not believe that this novel, except for a few contemporary details, would have come out very differently without the war. One has to go back to what is important for the writer, to what molds him existentially, temperamentally, geographically and topographically, to his milieu, religion, and his background and education" (*WI* 1: 516).

Böll then illustrates his thesis further with *The Train Was on Time*. "It was basically a love story. Let's take away the war and its decor. The question is, if we did, would this novel be any different? . . . I am convinced that what comes to one from the outside does not change one very much. When one applies that idea to literature, it means all that history throws under one's feet: war, peace, Nazis, communists, the bourgeois, all that is secondary. What counts is a thorough-going mythological-theological problematic that is always present" (*WI* 1: 516).

This ever-present "mythological-theological problematic" in Böll's novels can be sketched quickly, for it pervades his work, and relates, as he has indicated, to his concept of love and religion. From Böll's earliest short stories up to the end of his career, his central theme has had to do with lovers coming together, trying to stay together, and being driven apart. His problematic is the struggle between forces of union and forces of separation. This concept of love, however, is not limited to lovers in the narrow romantic sense. It applies also to people coming together in community, friendship, brother- and sisterhood, and in the family.[1] In *The Train Was on Time*, 1949, and *Adam, Where Art Thou?*, 1951, independent of the convergence and separation of Andreas and Olina and Feinhals and Ilona, there is the fellowship of Andreas, Willi, and the blond soldier and the striving of Feinhals at the end of *Adam* to return to his mother. Characteristic of this pattern in Böll's early work is that achieving the ideal is impossible because of fascism, war, and related forces. Thus, what condemns the forces of separation is that they destroy love and prevent the goodness that can come from a grace-filled union.

Therefore, Böll's mythological-theological problematic, reduced to its simplest form, shows that Böll's work struggles for love and battles against hate. Ultimately this simplicity is the basis of Böll's universal appeal, what people acknowledge when they, with praise or derision, call Böll the "good man from Cologne" or "the conscience of the nation." This simplicity is the essence of Böll's humanity. Fundamental to this vision is the belief that people are social beings. What furthers community is good; what hinders it bad. Böll's work shows that German fascism with its emphasis on *Volksgemeinschaft* is in reality the antithesis of it. Still, the evil forces in the stories that take place in the postwar years are not essentially different from those of the Hitler period. Fascists and Nazis are social types that are always present. From this perspective, fascism is a matter of the exercise of power. Fascism resides not only in officers in the *Wehrmacht* and commandants in concentration camps but also in members of a family, bosses in a company, teachers in a school, commissars of the police force, journalists for newspapers, politicians elected to office, and bishops of the church.

A concomitant part of this mythological-theological structure in Böll's work is the need for a place of refuge where love can thrive. In *The Train* it is the bordello where Andreas, Olina, and Andreas's friends find peace, tranquillity, happiness, and freedom from the dangers in the world waiting to drive them apart. In *Adam,* the schoolhouse provides this protection for Feinhals and Ilona, as well as the room in his dream where they perfect their love, and also Feinhal's home in the Rhineland where his mother's house stands for the same kind of desired security. That these refuges are often in the mind or short-lived only emphasizes more their importance in Böll's vision. In their temporariness and illusoriness, they emphasize that in spite of its material resources existing society cannot create conditions for the thriving of this essential human necessity. Böll's vision forcefully condemns society that separates people more than it unites them. When Böll says in his "Brief an einen jungen Katholiken," 1958 (Letter to a Young Catholic), "We are forced to live from politics and that is questionable fare," and adds, "We do not live from bread alone," his statements reinforce his religious humanist message that a healthy society provides its members with all the prerequisites for a humane existence (*WESR* 1: 275–76). In both *The Train* and *Adam,* Böll's Catholic theological orientation finds further expression in the implied eternal union of the lovers that takes place after death.

This pattern continues throughout Böll's oeuvre. In *And Never Said a Word,* 1953, one finds this pattern in the love and marriage of Fred and Käte Bogner. The forces that bring them together are religion and prayer. The forces that separate them are physical poverty and ecclesiastical indifference. Their place of refuge is not their one-room apartment but a snackbar that is owned by a gentle old invalid who welcomes everyone and that is run by a beautiful young girl who cares for her retarded brother as she serves the customers. Here in this secular church the brotherhood of man becomes a reality. In *Haus ohne Hüter*, 1954 (*The Unguarded House*), the pattern undergoes another variation as widows and half-orphans permanently separated from their husbands and fathers represent the legacy of war. They long for a family unity that has been destroyed forever. Only "Uncle" Albert represents the force trying to restore the balance of good to an imperfect world. In this novel, the place of refuge where peace reigns, social differences are abrogated, and widows and orphans experience hope is the country inn of Albert's mother. In *Billard um halbzehn*, 1959 (*Billiards at Half-past Nine*), three generations of the Fähmel family are torn apart by events in the Hitler period. But the novel concludes with a restoration of the family in Heinrich Fähmel's studio, where the generations unite to celebrate a birthday. In *Ansichten eines Clowns*, 1963 (*The Clown*), Hans Schnier's short-lived union with Marie is destroyed by the power that separates, in this case the church with its juridical concept of marriage. In *Ende einer Dienstfahrt*, 1966 (*End of a Mission*), the Gruhls find friendship, understanding, and support for their anti-military protest in their village. Communal solidarity maintains them against the forces of separation represented by the army, the law, and the big city.

After the reader once identifies this pattern, it is easy enough to recognize its variations in succeeding novels. It is this pattern that comes to mind when Böll claims he would have written essentially the same works without war, bombs, ruins, and the events of the postwar period (*WI* 1: 519). But there is still one more important aspect of this paradigm: the Böllian ideal of anarchy. Böll's refuge tends to be a little utopia, a modest paradise where people relate to one another as equals. It is a community without a leader, a group of people, a petite polity without an imposed authority. A passage from Böll's essay "Straßen wie diese," 1958 (Streets Like These), suggests his almost idyllic conception of anarchy. Böll claims society is good when "life transpires anarchistically, that is, according to strict rules that are all unwritten" (*WESR* 1: 255).[2] The origin of this anarchism lies in Böll's prewar experience, his recognition at that time that the forces of separation always represented in some way the malevolent exercise of power. Böll explains the roots of this knowledge in his fear of the Nazis as they destroyed the tranquillity and security of the streets of

Cologne. He says to Wintzen: "This fear will be with me till the end of my life. But I feared them long before they came to power" (*WI* 1: 517). This fear of fascism taught Böll an unforgettable hatred of all disregard of human rights, and it manifests itself in his abhorrence of the exercise of power over others. In his novels, Böll's good people seek instinctively to avoid authority and long to find a refuge from its abuse. They know that it is always the forces of "order," represented by seekers of advantage—people who follow authority, idolize ideology, pursue wealth, desire power, and write rules—who endanger their refuge. In the novels these purveyors of power are people like the madame in *The Train* who starts the process that destroys the idyll in the bordello. In *Adam*, they are the drivers of the van who transport Ilona to the concentration camp and Commandant Filskeit who murders in the name of ideology. In *And Never Said a Word*, they are the bishop who lives and rules his diocese like a sovereign prince and Frau Franke who controls the living conditions of the Bogners. One recognizes easily these servants of order. Their presence creates in simple hearts the anarchistic longing for freedom from all merchants of power and panderers to authority who engineer tyranny and process death. The very existence of these purveyors of suffering establishes the need for a humane refuge where decent people in voluntary association can peacefully harvest the modest fruits of unpretentious humanity.

And Never Said a Word
(Und sagte kein einziges Wort)

The novel is told by Fred and Käte Bogner in thirteen chapters of alternating first-person narratives. To tell the story Böll uses a simple structure and the technique of simultaneity. The events take place over a single weekend from noon on Saturday until noon on Monday, during which time the main characters reveal the fifteen years of their life together and their own and each other's characters. All the uneven-numbered chapters are narrated by Fred and the even-numbered ones by Käte. Chapters one and two cover Saturday afternoon, and chapters three through nine cover from Sunday morning to five o'clock Sunday evening, when Käte and Fred meet in a hotel room. The main chapters are ten to twelve, which recount the time Fred and Käte are together from five o'clock Sunday to seven-thirty Monday morning. The final chapter, thirteen, treats the unusual event that causes Fred to return to his family. This tightly structured novel has aspects of a short story and a novella. It treats as essential internal—not external—developments, concentrates on a single event (Fred and Käte's meeting in a hotel), is based on character, not action, has only two central figures, is framed with Fred's narration in chapters one and thirteen, begins and ends with Fred's relationship to money, starts and finishes with the important technique of a "mirror reflection" that permits Fred to see the truth about himself in chapter one and allows him to recognize his love for Käte in chapter thirteen.

Fred Bogner is a telephone operator in the ecclesiastical chancery of an unnamed city—recognizable, however, as the Catholic city of Cologne. The time is 1951 or 1952. The economic miracle is just beginning. Store windows are full, and advertisements are ubiquitous. The exhortations to "Trust in Your Druggist," to buy "Doulorin" for hangovers, and to find security from undesired pregnancy in "quality" prophylactics by "Gummi Griss" function throughout the novel as leitmotifs suggesting the commercial and secular orientation of postwar West German society. In contrast to this picture of dynamic buying, selling, and consuming is the portrait of Fred and Käte Bogner struggling for the essentials of dignity in the midst of humiliating poverty. As the novel opens, Fred has recently left his family because he can no longer tolerate the stress created by the crowded conditions of their one-room apartment where frustration causes him to beat his children. Although he now lives away from home, he maintains his marriage by arranging meetings with Käte in cheap hotels and by sending her his entire wages to support the family. He manages on his own by sleeping where he can, earning extra money tutoring the children of friends, and by borrowing from whoever will help him.

During one hotel rendezvous with Käte (the central episode of the novel when the two perspectives of the story come together), Käte tells Fred that she is again pregnant and is no longer willing to meet him like a prostitute. She delivers the ultimatum for him to return home or to end the marriage. The next day Fred sees a "gentle tragic profile" of a woman in a "green" skirt reflected in a store window. He is inexplicably drawn to her, eventually recognizes the "tragic" figure as his wife, and decides to return to his family. The last word of the novel is "home."

While the surface meaning of the ending seems sentimental in offering love as the solution to the problems of life, the deeper meaning of the story is quite different. The hopefulness symbolized by Käte's "green" skirt and her turning at the decisive moment into "Green Street" suggests

57

something more is in play than merely love. What causes Fred to return home can be explained best by the illogic of grace, of which love is only the most obvious aspect. In various passages of the novel Käte speaks of the power of prayer. She tells Fred, "Prayer is the only thing that is not boring" (*WRE* 2: 183), and "the only thing that can help us" (*WRE* 2: 181).[3] When Käte meets Fred at the hotel, her first words of greeting are, "We have to go to mass" (*WRE* 2: 151). She also consoles Fred, who is given to self-pity, with the wisdom that "God is not far away" (*WRE* 2: 182). Later Fred makes the connection himself between his decision to return home and prayer. He says when he recognizes the "tragic figure" as Käte: "What unites people more than sleeping together is praying together. And there was a time when we prayed together" (*WRE* 2: 203).

Fred is a typical protagonist in a Catholic novel of the fifties. In many ways he is similar to the whiskey priest of Graham Greene's *The Power and the Glory* and Georges Bernanos's curé in *The Diary of a Country Priest*. These heroes suffer from self-doubt and wavering faith, but they, like Fred and other believers in the novels of the *renouveau catholique,* ultimately are redeemed by faith. At one point Fred tells Käte he is "interested only in God and the quiet of churchyards" (*WRE* 2: 162). Despite Fred's bouts with bitterness and self-pity, there is an important spiritual dimension to his life that makes the essential difference in his decision to return home.

Here a similarity to Böll's own life is striking. In 1942, while serving in France, Böll wrote a letter to his wife that contains these lines: "I am happy because I went to mass today and received communion. I never would have thought that a mass could be so precious." The same letter tells of his waiting for the arrival of the priest in the churchyard to go to confession (*Rom* 32–33). These intimate lines about religion reflect sentiments similar to Fred's and Käte's in the novel.

The religious aspect of the novel has caused Ralph Ley to call the story "one of Böll's best, a work which may some day be regarded as the finest Christian novel of post-war Germany" (xiv). Understandably, however, it is precisely this aspect of the novel that has caused some readers to criticize it. James H. Reid in *Heinrich Böll: Withdrawal and Re-emergence,* writing twenty years after the novel appeared, called it "considerably dated" (41), and Manfred Durzak in *Der deutsche Roman der Gegenwart* doubts the "effectiveness of the Catholic aura" (44).

Certainly, none of these statements represents any form of literary criticism. These opinions are simply reactions to the religious content of the novel. But the religious content of the work cannot be ignored; it is all-pervasive. The novel's themes of poverty and money, its methods of characterization, and its social criticism all appear in the framework of religion.

Through religion the novel receives its social dimension. It condemns the Bogners' misery by showing that their poverty does not derive from Fred's lack of intelligence, education, or unwillingness to work, but from the inadequacy of the social system itself. It is true that Fred lacks ambition, drinks, and squanders time and money playing pinball machines, but he does not do these things to excess. He is employed full-time and even takes odd jobs to provide for himself and his family. The Bogners' miserable conditions derive more from the decisions of the housing commission that refuses them a larger apartment and from the low wages the church pays Fred at the chancery than from any shortcoming in Fred or Käte. A lack of living space and little money create most of the Bogners' problems. While Käte recognizes that part of their difficulties lies in Fred's attitude (they do not all come from the smallness of their apartment [*WRE* 2: 180]), she still does not hesitate to put the blame on society, "You beat the children because we are poor," she says to Fred. And Fred acknowledges this truth, "Yes, poverty has made me sick" (*WRE* 2: 158). The weight of evidence in the novel suggests that the organization of society is more at fault than the Bogners themselves.

But despite Böll's understanding of the suffering caused by distressed circumstances, the novel betrays a Franciscan tendency to the glorification of poverty. Suffering is, indeed, misery, but, nonetheless, ennobling. Another war letter from France written by Böll in 1942 explains this attitude, "Surrounded by the greatness of poverty and its suffering, the beggar is made the equal of a lord" (*Rom* 34).

Böll depicts the characters of the novel as either sympathetic or despicable by the manner in which they practice their religion. The bishop's "goose-stepping" through the St. Jerome's Day procession, his wearing of the cross like a military decoration, his forcing workers to rent tuxedos to carry the baldachin in the procession, his affecting a tinge of dialect in his sermons, his friendship with the "gangster" or "general" who owns the empty thirteen-room villa, and the use of this "English gangster's" private library for his Dante research characterize the bishop as autocratic, hypocritical, and indifferent.

The lay counterpart of the bishop is the Bogners' landlady, Frau Franke. She receives communion every day and kisses the bishop's ring every month. She knows best the Bogners' problems and their unbearable circumstances, but as head of the housing commission she prevents the Bogners from receiving a larger apartment. Her reasons are not even selfish, for if the Bogners move to a better place, she becomes the beneficiary of their vacated room. Her motive for denying the Bogners better housing is simply that they do not deserve it.

But religion has its humane aspects in the novel as well. The peasant priest at the Church of the Seven Sorrows who hears Käte's confession and whose questioning worked like "skilled hands pressing pus from a wound" (*WRE* 2: 135) comforts Käte with his concern for her marital situation. He even confesses to Käte that he shares her hatred for the well-kept priests who live in big houses and have skin like in ads for face cream. Even in the chancery itself, where Fred works, a friendly secretary tells him that he has more friends there than enemies. And Prelate Serge, the diocesan authority on marriage, one of Fred's superiors, is the most reliable source of funds when Fred needs money. Prelate Serge's humanity expresses itself also in his secret blessing of Fred when he is unable to help Fred with his advice.

As there are good and bad people within the institution of the church, so too is the case with the laity. Most important in contrast to Frau Franke is the "beautiful young girl" in the snackbar. Her unselfish loving care of her retarded brother and invalid father and her friendliness to Fred and Käte create a spiritual aura in the snackbar that makes it a secular temple. Here, through simple goodness, the social mission of the church and the spiritual needs of people are met in the normal course of serving coffee and breakfast. In fact, it is actually in the snackbar, not in church, that Käte receives absolution from the peasant priest.

The religious dimension of the work is found also in its criticism of the growing commercialization of society. Consumption is becoming the new religion of salvation. Every ill can be cured with a purchase. The pharmaceutical industry exemplifies this new postwar secular society. It can cure hangovers, prevent tooth decay, and avert unwanted pregnancy. The advertisement that subsumes all the others in the novel is the flashing neon sign in "all the colors of the spectrum," dominating the city and advising Christians to "Trust in Your Druggist" (*WRE* 2: 178). The novel, through the lives of Käte and Fred, makes clear that the alternative to trusting in consumption is to trust in God. The very title of the novel reinforces its religious message, for the words are a translation of a Negro spiritual that Käte hears on the radio, "They nailed him to the cross, and he never said a mumbling word" (*WRE* 2: 107).

The Unguarded House
(*Haus ohne Hüter*)

A year after the appearance of *And Never Said a Word*, Böll's new novel, *Haus ohne Hüter*, 1954 (*The Unguarded House*) was published. The work makes up the second of the family novels. In *House* Böll tells the story of two young boys who have lost their fathers in the war. The title and the subject matter illustrate how Böll used immediate postwar problems as sources for his narratives, a continuing effort that earned him the reputation of "chronicler of the republic."

Martin Bach and Heinrich Brielach are two eleven-year-olds in the same school class. Martin knows no material needs. He lives with his mother and several family friends in the house of his wealthy grandmother Hostege. His widowed mother gives him no supervision and little care as she retreats into a dream world where she lives out her life with her dead husband, the now famous antifascist soldier-poet, Raimund Bach. She abandons this dream world only to seek diversion with opportunists interested in associating with the widow of an important literary figure.

In contrast to Martin, Heinrich has been burdened with responsibility. His poverty has taught him early economic maturity and forces him to learn arithmetic on the black market before going to school. His mother, in contrast to Martin's mother, is compelled to deal with problems of existence in the form of "uncle" marriages and egoistic lovers rather than with problems of psychological adjustment to widowhood. The friendship of the two boys, their different social positions, and their similar emotional needs form the main story of the novel. The plight of the widowed young mothers provides additional depth and breadth to the novel. Within the thematic of the problems of orphans and widows, Böll pursues the question of social justice and personal responsibility.

The choice of children as Böll's focus of narration is not surprising. He used this perspective in several earlier short stories, most notably in "Lohengrins Tod," 1950 ("Lohengrin's Death"), about an orphan fatally injured stealing coal from a train, in "Mein Onkel Fred," 1951 ("My Uncle Fred"), about a boy's relationship to his eccentric uncle just returned from the war, and in "Erinnerungen eines jungen Königs," 1953 ("Recollections of a Young King"), a humorous tale about a carefree child monarch. The advantage of the adolescent narrative is that it permits Böll a naive approach to the novel's subject matter. It allows him to assume an attitude unaffected by adult experience. The children see the problems they face directly and without illusions tempered by conventional wisdom. Their path to knowledge has the immediacy of first-time experience. Their emotions are undisguised, their questions uninfluenced by mature thought or clouded by developed intellectuality. Martin and Heinrich, in trying to understand their own personal situations and their different circumstances, learn from one another.

Martin learns from Heinrich that a few pennies mean an extra egg for breakfast, and Heinrich discovers through Martin that wealth does not guarantee a mother's nurturing. Together they pose questions about justice. They learn to distinguish between the stated norms of society and real social practice. Martin recognizes that what he learns in school about the Nazis (they were "not so bad," *WRE* 2: 469) conflicts with what he learns from the artist friend of his father, Albert Muchow. Heinrich recognizes that the sexual morality taught in religion class does not take into account the circumstances of his mother's life. He sees that morality is determined by class in an atmosphere removed from material reality. The children learn that society makes claims and judgments that are at variance with their experience. Experience teaches them that fair treatment is dependent on social position. Martin discovers that his tardiness at school, his poor work, and his petty transgressions are treated with deference because he is the son of a respected poet and the grandson of a wealthy manufacturer, and he sees that the same misdemeanors committed by Heinrich, the son of a poor and "immoral" woman, bring punishment and chastisement.

Along with the two children, their mothers and the artist Albert Muchow are the central characters in the novel. The two worlds of the Bachs and the Brielachs come together not only through the friendship of Martin and Heinrich but also through Albert who is an "uncle" to Martin and a friend to Heinrich. He not only cares for Martin but also tries to save his mother from her addiction to dreams and shallow diversions. At the same time he supports Heinrich's attempt to take responsibility for his baby sister while Frau Brielach is away at work. In his efforts for the two families, Albert becomes a model of social responsibility.

The two levels of the story, that of the children and that of the mothers, run parallel but in opposite directions. The children are concerned with the present and the future because they have no past. But their mothers, although still young, are caught up in memories of the war and the prewar period. Each blames the war for destroying her life. For Frau Brielach, her husband's death has robbed her of a loving provider and a handsome companion and forced her to rear children in a world for which she is ill prepared. Without training or education she is suited for only the most un-skilled jobs. Wealth has spared Nella Bach this ordeal but has condemned her to dreams and idleness. Both women see themselves as victims, but because Nella Bach perceives her situation with more intellectual sophis-tication, she sees history as male-dominated and for this reason refuses re-marriage and the responsibilities of motherhood. While Frau Brielach lives with one ''uncle'' after another, seeking in the real world what the war took from her—security and companionship—Nella Bach lives alone, seeking in dreams an idyll that never existed. She moves in a half-conscious state motivated by the circumstance of her late husband's fame.

Albert's role in the novel is to provide a stable element for the two women as he does for the two boys. His strength derives from his remem-brance of the past, but in contrast to the women, he is secure in the present because his undistorted knowledge of the past is the basis of his sure vision of the future. Albert is the embodiment of Böll's concept of a moral man. He recalls the Hitler period and speaks openly of its criminality. In caring for the victims of fascism, he takes up his responsibility for the tragedy of the war. He sees that the children are taught the truth, that adults do not pervert history, and tries to see that no one forgets the past. He is not im-paired by grief or self-pity. His moral position is that social responsibility manifests itself in confronting injustice and helping people.

In the figure of Albert Muchow, a change from personal to social re-sponsibility takes place. In the previous novels, *The Train Was on Time*, *Adam, Where Art Thou?*, and *And Never Said a Word*, the heroes, whether those of the war or those of the immediate postwar period, are unable to care for themselves, much less for those around them. In the *Train* and *Adam*, Andreas and Feinhals and those closest to them cannot preserve their own lives; in *And Never Said a Word* Fred is forced to abandon his family. In *House*, Albert's primary concern is not for himself, but for oth-ers. He sees himself as a social being, a member of society, not as an isolated individual. Since he has no pressing material needs and is psychologically healthy, he is able to take an interest in others. With this novel the individual concerns of the war and the postwar hunger years are past; problems now become societal more than personal. In this sense *House* is a turning point in Böll's work. The social point of view now be-gins to dominate.

The theme of a ''new life'' is a motif that runs through the novel. When Albert returns from the war, he wants to marry Nella and start again. Nella, however, rejects marriage for the very reason that it is a new start,

"I hate all of you [men] because you permit life to go on" (*WRE* II: 325). Nella's objection to marriage is the fear of becoming a widow again, of seeing a new husband sent to war, and of being left again with children who will in their turn die in battle. She rejects marriage and the call to a "new life" because she sees people and society unchanged from before the war. She sees the postwar world being formed in the mold of the prewar period. Too many old fascists have become new democrats without essential change. It is this knowledge that warrants Nella's rejection of active participation in the present and justifies her passivity.

Paradoxically, a new life begins for Nella when she plans to kill Gäseler, the "murderer" of her husband. In her confrontation with this former Nazi officer who indifferently ordered Raimund Bach into a situation of certain death, she herself changes. She recognizes that this legal murderer embodies the epitome of political opportunism. She despises the ease with which he has adjusted to the new Germany without changing, simply by excising all unwanted memory from his mind. Nella challenges him with his past, but to no avail. He responds, "All is forgotten . . . systematically cut out of my memory" (*WER* II: 436). He has forgotten, Nella realizes, "the widows and orphans and everything that was dirty" (*WER* II: 436). He has built a "beautiful, clean future" (*WER* II: 436) over a void.[4] It is this kind of a new life that Nella rejects. She realizes in this encounter the moral emptiness in men like Gäseler. In his presence she is surprised that "hate did not come, only a yawn" (*WER* II: 435). She discovers that he is not worth shooting and that she must give up further association with the Gäselers of the world, people whom she has until now befriended as cultured and charming. In her circle besides Gäseler, who is the culture editor of a Catholic newspaper and the erstwhile editor of an anthology of Raimund Bach's poems, are the critic Schurbigel, who wrote his dissertation on the "The Führer in Modern Lyric Poetry," and Father Willibrord, who in his private war letters, blessed Hitler. These men, Nella realizes, are now what they were then: opportunists supporting a new order that could just as well be fascist as democratic. When she arrives at the monastery where she and Gäseler are to attend a conference on poetry, she undergoes a symbolic cleansing in the garden fountain and returns home, presumably to a more responsible life.

Another variation of the theme of a "new life" is Frau Brielach's relationship with "Uncle" Karl. Karl speaks so often of starting again that Heinrich calls him "New Life Karl." He is not a vicious man as was "Uncle" Leo, who mistreated Frau Brielach, Heinrich, and his baby sister, but when Frau Brielach refuses to marry him, Karl heartlessly rejects the Brielach children in the name of religious morality.

In contrast to the negative motif of a "new life," there is the positive motif of "things will be different." These words are the substance of Albert's promise to Martin. He takes Martin to the casemates to show him where the Nazis tortured his father and killed his father's friend Absalom Billig. The difference between a "new life" as desired by Gäseler and a "different" life as desired by Albert is that the former separates the past from the present by willful, opportunistic forgetting and the latter joins the present to the past by intentional, responsible remembering. Albert fulfills his promise that "things will be different" when he takes Martin to live in the country with Frau Muchow, Albert's mother, and when he rescues Frau Brielach from another unfortunate uncle "marriage" at the end of the novel.

In Böll's novels, content and form always work together to reinforce one another. Form here is understood as structure and content as Böll's emphasis on the relationship of Germany's fascist past to its democratic present—themes that deal with the problems of orphans, widows, marriage, family, opportunism, or social responsibility. Here the idea of content applies to the whole of Böll's oeuvre. In many ways the tension of this historical dichotomy (past-present) is the mainspring of Böll's writing. All his themes of love, religion, and politics can be understood as conditioned by this historical problematic. The past-present, forgetting-remembering antitheses frame Böll's religious, political, personal, and moral concerns.

Two broad general principles can be discerned operating in his work. For Böll, whoever does not remember the past is socially irresponsible; whoever remembers the past is a responsible person. Throughout Böll's work the sympathetic characters are set apart from the unsympathetic ones by their acknowledged relationship to the German past. In the simplest terms Böll's past means Hitler, fascism, National Socialism, and war. In specific situations it means also proto-fascistic tendencies in the pre-Hitler period. But Böll is not, as an historian would be, interested in the past for its own sake, but as a contemporary, trying to explain how the past conditions the present. This preoccupation makes Böll the preeminent chronicler of West German life, and at the same time it explains the structure of his novels. From this observation, one can see how his novels live from the structural tension between what is called "narrated" and "narrative" time.

Böll developed this method of handling his thematic early in his career and thereafter merely varied it from one novel to the next. From *A Soldier's Legacy* (1948) to *Frauen vor Flußlandschaft* (1985) (*Women in a River Landscape*), the technique manifests itself in the temporal structure of one work after another. Böll concentrates the present, his narrative time (*Erzählzeit*), into a few days and expands the past, his narrated time (*erzählte Zeit*), into several years. This structure permits Böll to show how the present moment, the present historical situation, is no anomaly but the result of historical events. There is no zero hour (*Stunde null*) for Böll in his view of West German history. There did not suddenly develop a new and different German people and German community in May 1945. The end of the war did not end one society and start another. Böll's novels try to show the economic, political, psychological, and moral continuity between Germany before and after 1945. For example, if one looks at economics or politics in his novels, one sees that what *is* resulted from what *was*. Capitalism returns to dominate economic life, and old Nazis maintain their political influence as democrats.

In Böll's novels, those who choose not to recognize what has happened in West Germany are the villains no matter how prominent, successful, or popular they become; furthermore, Böll shows that their prominence, success, and popularity often derive from their choice to repress the past. These characters possess a wonderfully clear conscience that still now in the postwar period offers no resistance to any expediential, self-serving, opportunistic decisions, just as it offered no resistance to their accommodation in the Hitler period.

These people are, according to the psychoanalysts Alexander and Margarete Mitscherlich, willfully psychologically impaired. Their impairment consists of an intentional obliteration of their connection to the past; the result if an "inability to mourn."[5] In Böll's work these deformed people become the dominant type in postwar West Germany.

In contrast to these villains, Böll makes his heroes the people with memory and conscience. They are the ones capable of suffering because they remember and have the virtue of compassion. These are Böll's decent people no matter what their failings, their inconsistencies, their harsh words, their unfair judgments, their weaknesses, and their desire for revenge. They are still the humane population of his oeuvre. They illustrate the overriding ethical maxim of his work: "Wer nicht leidet ist kein Mensch" ("Who does not suffer is not human"). Naturally, Böll's maxim also translates as he who has no compassion fails as a human being. Compassion then becomes the essence of Böll's ideal of humanity. These people who have acknowledged human suffering and have learned to mourn have by that ability demonstrated their humanity. To these characters Böll accords respect. These persons are often unsuccessful, and often their lack of success is caused by their burden of grief. They have become incapacitated by what they perceive to be past and present injustice. They tend to passivity rather than to action. They mourn while their dynamic counterparts succeed. In this sad fact alone resides much of Böll's criticism of West German society. No doubt, there is also implied here a rejection of the competitive, aggressive personality required for success in capitalist society.

The reader can find these two types of people even in the earliest war stories, but they dominate in his work treating the postwar period. In *And Never Said a Word* Käte and Fred Bogner contrast with Frau Franke, and the peasant priest from the Church of the Seven Sorrows contrasts with the princely bishop. In *House* Albert, Nella, Grandmother Holstege, and Frau Brielach stand opposed to Gäseler, Schurbigel, Father Willibrord, and Frau Brielach's rapacious lovers.

Böll enhances this historical, moral thematic by incorporating it into the temporal structure of his novels. By concentrating the narrative present and expanding the narrated past. The two levels of time confront one another just as do the two types of characters. This literary device is reminiscent of Proust. In *And Never Said a Word* the mirror is the physical object that precipitates Käte's and Fred's excursions into recollection. In *House* Nella's memories become a movie running in her mind as she looks out the window at the street where she played as a child. For Albert, his visit to the torture chamber in the casemates and his review of his prewar drawings force him to recall the past. Such objects as a mirror, a street, a drawing function like Marcel Proust's *madeleine,* invoking what Proust in his novel *A la recherche du temps perdu* called *mémoire involontaire.* This influence of Proust is not sheer chance. When Böll was about twenty, that is, after he had decided to become a writer, his reading of Proust in a German translation left a permanent impression (*WI* 1: 591). Proust's mark on Böll's technique of using objects, smells, and taste to evoke past time is noticeable throughout his entire oeuvre.

In *House* Böll organizes the temporal structure of the work by concentrating the present time of the novel into a single week in the late summer of 1953, with most of the slight action occurring on Friday of that week. As in a drama, he assigns each chapter a special function. For example, chapter 1 introduces the characters and the problematic of the novel. An omniscient narrator relates the random thoughts of Martin as he contemplates his relationship to his friend Heinrich and the various people living with him in his grandmother's villa. Thus, Böll quickly presents the two worlds of the novel and the main characters in them.

Chapter 2 centers on the Brielach family, chapter 3 on the life of Nella Bach, and chapter 4 again on Frau Brielach. In chapter 5 the focus turns again to Martin's world and chapter 6 to Heinrich's. It is clear Böll is varying the same structure he used in *And Never Said a Word*, where the chapters switch between the worlds of Fred's and Käte's thoughts. In *House* the first six chapters alternate between the spheres of the rich Holstege-Bachs and the poor Brielachs, revealing the differences money and wealth make, not only in how one lives but also in how one thinks and acts. This alternating pattern, contrasting the two worlds, changes in chapter 7. Chapters 7 through 10 present the Holstege household by concentrating on the several unusual residents of the old mansion. Böll shows how their pasts have made them what they are.

Chapter 8 is important in this sequence. Coming near the middle of the novel, it develops the house as a symbol for Germany's major postwar problem, that of conquering the past. The old house needs repair. The roof leaks, windows are broken, water and rats are in the basement. Nella and Grandmother Holstege are so burdened by the past that they cannot function in the present. They have not balanced their suffering in the past with their needs in the present. They are burdened by memory and have lost their capacity for prudent behavior. Nella cannot come to grips with the house, and Grandmother Holstege is indifferent to it. Grandmother Holstege is too old to care about life, and Nella is too burdened to think of changing hers. Nella avoids the basement; she refuses to deal constructively with the past in order to give purpose to her life. And for the attic she merely buys pails to catch the rain. The burden of repairing the German house falls on Albert. He realizes that if the house is to be made livable, he must put it in order. Albert eventually calls the repairmen and the exterminators and goes in the basement to retrieve the valuable things stored there. His descent into the past saves his, Raimund Bach's, and Nella's correspondence of the Hitler years. It is a necessary excursion into the nether region and a return to the present. It is a journey the novel insists every German must take. While in the dark basement, Albert discovers the

"Sunlight Carton" containing his prewar drawings. They symbolize, as the name on the carton suggests, the light that the past can shed on the present. Important also for its symbolic quality is the monetary value of the drawings. Albert is able to live well from their sale. The descent into the past brings its natural rewards and provides the means for a healthy life.

Careful analysis will reveal that each incident in the novel relates the past to the present. For example, "New Life Karl" falls into the moral trap of failing to see how his desire for a new life ignores consideration for Frau Brielach's past experiences. In chapter 10 Martin's visit with his grandmother to the Vohwinkel Restaurant provides the impulse for his recollection of his first visit to the restaurant in 1947, when he was five, during Germany's postwar hunger period. Now, in 1953, at the age of eleven, Martin realizes that the restaurant is a refuge for the rich who pay more for a meal than the Brielachs live on for a week. Furthermore, when Grandmother Holstege explains to Martin how the Holstege jam factory earned its greatest profits during World Wars I and II, he recognizes that their wealth is related to Germany's wars. Every episode reinforces Böll's message that there was no *Stunde null* (a time from which one begins anew without a past).

Beginning with chapter 11, the remaining action of the novel, except for the last few pages, occurs on the Friday on which Nella meets Gäseler. The next eleven chapters present this day concurrently in alternating chapters from the perspective of several characters. As the first six chapters varied the method of *And Never Said a Word,* chapters 11 through 21 anticipate the method of Böll's next novel, *Billiards at Half-past Nine,* where the entire action transpires in a few hours on the eightieth birthday of one of the characters.

To keep the complicated structure of his novels under control, Böll invented a system of charting his longer works to minimize inconsistencies in the stories. In fact, some such errors of conflicting ages of characters and the days on which events transpire still occur in the published German editions, although they are often corrected in the English translations. To keep such mistakes to a minimum and to provide himself with an instantaneous overview, Böll developed a system of detail management by representing characters, motifs, and present and past time with various colors applied to paper with felt pens. In this way he could glance at his chart and see in which chapters characters appeared in association with which motifs and at which level of time an event had occurred. The graphs for *House* and *End of a Mission* have been published (Schöter 64–65, 74–75), and

Böll sent a colored reproduction of the chart for *Group Portrait with Lady* to friends as an acknowledgment of his Nobel Prize. Also, the original outlines for *House, The Clown,* and other novels are framed and hang as abstract paintings in the Böll house in Merten. Böll's descriptions of his work as possessing qualities like pictures and watercolors and sketches (*WI* 1: 642) have their counterparts in reality.

The appearance of Gäseler is the central event of the novel. The arrival of the "murderer" of Nella's husband forces each of the main characters in the Holstege household to bring the past up to the present, forces each to see the historical continuity between the dictatorship of the thirties and forties and the democracy of the fifties. This day forces Albert to assess his situation in the Holstege constellation. On this day, too, Martin comes to realize that the conditions in the Brielach family are not as immoral as he has heard at school. Martin's new awareness and Albert's intention "to make things different" are summed up in his advice to Martin, "Don't forget." This counsel stands in direct contradiction to Gäseler's formula for postwar success of systematically expunging his memory.

For Heinrich and his mother this Friday is also a day of change and hope. Frau Brielach decides to move out of the small room she shares with "Uncle" Leo. She meets Albert and there is an immediate attraction between them that changes her life: "A gleam of hope was in his mother's and Albert's eyes. 'Promise' stood for a moment in both of their eyes and it seemed that an agreement existed between them" (*WRE* 2: 483–484).

Their meeting concludes the novel with optimism. The last sentence comes from Heinrich's consciousness, "He thought of the hope which for just a minute was in his mother's face, for just a minute, but he knew a minute can mean a lot" (*WRE* 2: 498).

Billiards at Half-past Nine
(Billard um halbzehn)

Billiards at Half-past Nine (1959) was published in the same year as Günter Grass's *The Tin Drum.* Both works have as their central concern the relationship of the Nazi past to the social-political problems of the present. This topic occupied the minds of many German intellectuals during the fifties, but for Böll it took a central place in his work from his early short stories, especially his satires "Nicht nur zur Weihnachtszeit," 1951 ("Christmas Not Just Once a Year"), and "Doktor Murkes gesammeltes

Schweigen,'' 1955 (''Merke's Collected Silences''), through his middle works, especially *Ansichten eines Clowns*, 1963 (*The Clown*), and *Gruppenbild mit Dame*, 1971 (*Group Portrait with Lady*), to his final novel *Frauen vor Flußlandschaft* 1985 (*Women in a River Landscape*).

In *Billiards* the theme is embedded primarily in the novel's structure. The members of the Fähmel family reflect on the past as they prepare to celebrate the eightieth birthday (6 September 1958) of the family patriarch, Heinrich Fähmel. On this single day, three generations of Fähmels recall the years of their primary socialization in three different eras, the Wilhelminian period, the Third Reich, and the postwar period. Dominating the novel are the architect Heinrich Fähmel, who established the Fähmel dynasty, his wife Johanna, still living in a sanatorium because of her ''insane'' opposition to Hitler, their son Robert, who in the last days of World War II, ostensibly to create a field of fire, destroyed the famous Abbey of Saint Anthony built by his father, and Robert's daughter, Ruth, and his son, Joseph, the latter presently restoring the abbey identified with the Fähmel family. The important characters besides the Fähmels are the ex-Nazi Nettlinger, a schoolmate of Robert, Robert's friend Schrella, a victim of Nettlinger's persecution, and Joseph Fähmel's fiancée, Marianne.

As in *House*, the key to comprehending the novel lies in understanding its complex structure. The places of the action are not always clear without close reading, and the interweaving of narration, interior monologue, and stream of consciousness at times obscures the point of view and the chronology of events. Furthermore, this complicated structure also presents Böll's main paradigm for dealing with the past, that is, the concentration of the narrative present and the expansion of the narrated past. As a result, in *Billiards,* fifty years of history are treated in eight hours of a single day. Böll summarized his desired structure in an interview with Horst Bienek with this exaggeration: ''Ideally . . . a novel ought to be able to take place in a single minute'' (*WI* 1: 19).

Although *Billiards* is generally recognized as one of Böll's most important works, it is especially relevant now that the question of the German past is again being revived.[6] From this point of view, the novel is as important today as it was for the fifties. Critics of Böll's oeuvre have often doubted its lasting importance because of its close relationship to the history of the times in which it was written. A number of factors contribute to its continued timeliness, however. Among them are the renewed debate by historians;[7] Helmut Kohl's idea of the ''grace of late birth'' (of being born too late to be guilty or responsible for Nazi crimes);[8] and German unification, which has brought 16 million East Germans into the Federal Republic who have known the Holocaust primarily as a crime against antifascists, not as a crime against Jews, Roma, Sinti, Slavs, and homosexuals. The East German perspective also creates the need for another kind of *Vergangenheitsbewältigung* (conquering the past) in the form of the hundreds of thousands of East Germans who worked officially or privately for the hated *Stasi* (secret police). The importance of the past in assessing the present is again a pressing issue and makes *Billiards* relevant reading for another generation.

Despite a favorable reception, the novel has not escaped negative criticism. Because of Johanna's attempt on the life of the minister at the end of the novel and Robert's complicity in the attempted assassination of the sadistic Nazi Wakiera, some critics have seen in the book an endorsement of violence. These critics fail to recognize that Böll is not condoning violence through these positive characters but showing the inevitable consequences that arise in a situation when citizens believe that no societal solution to injustice exists. Böll's point is that a nation as a whole must deal responsibly with its crimes at both the personal and societal levels if the social cycle of violence is ever to be broken. Böll's definitive literary answer to the problem of social violence, however, is his novella, *Die verlorene Ehre der Katharina Blum,* 1974 (*The Lost Honor of Katharina Blum*), which will be discussed later.

Besides the problem of violence, critics have pointed to other less-than-satisfying aspects of the novel, among them its reliance on obscure motifs, its weighty symbolism, and its very complex structure.[9] In addition to these difficulties, Johanna's assassination attempt seems too casually accepted by the Fähmels. Johanna fires her shot at seven o'clock, but at seven-thirty her friends and relatives are gathered in Heinrich's studio celebrating his birthday. What has happened to Johanna in regard to her arrest, booking, contacting of a lawyer, seems almost of no concern to the gathered clan. Böll seems to abandon realism in favor of the symbolic significance of the birthday celebration. When Heinrich remarks that "this day is great, it has returned my wife to me" (*WRE* 3: 533), he seems to ignore the fact that she is about to be permanently incarcerated. No one notices that Johanna, the seeker of justice for others, is also herself a victim of the German past in her passion for righteousness.

From a different perspective, the work has often been criticized in a way that fundamentally confuses the world of the novel with the real world and too closely identifies the ideas of the characters with those of the author. These critics conclude that the behavior of the positive characters offers an inadequate solution to the problem the novel raises, namely, how to bring about a better society. In general this argument asserts that the positive characters act privately, not publicly, and that private acts cannot effect social change, only public acts can. An example of such criticism is Judith Ryan's comment on Schrella's insult to Nettlinger at their meeting in the Prince Heinrich Hotel. Ryan concludes:

> Because of the personal level on which it [Schrella's insult] takes place and the discreet milieu which conceals it from public view, it remains ineffective as a protest against the continued existence of Nettlinger and his kind of postwar Germany. All it does is assuage Schrella's personal sense of justice. The polite formal tone in which the two enemies converse throughout the scene indicates Schrella's retreat from further political engagement. (83)

Peter Demetz also exemplifies this kind of criticism:

> Johanna's shooting of the minister is an act of a trigger-happy grandmother who fires a misdirected shot at a parading Bonn functionary (a piece of anti-fascist *Kitsch* much admired by Georg Lukács): it is fascinating to see how quickly the absolute purity of the "lambs" is likely to change into absolute terrorism. The trouble is that Böll's good people are good German petits bourgeois who do not want to get involved with the daily business of politics; traditionally unable to think except in the most extreme terms, they continue to dream of an absolute idyll and are unwilling to soil their hands with something disturbingly relative. (198)[10]

Donna Baker, referring to the symbolic gestures of the Fähmels, concludes that they "will probably effect . . . little desired change in society" (99) and adds that Böll "suggests in actuality a commitment that is far less political than he would have us believe" (99). The latter point also agrees with Manfred Durzak's that an apparent contradiction exists between Böll's public image and his literary work, "On the one hand, the combative critic, who fearlessly takes a stand, and on the other, the literary apologist for the virtuous *Kleinbürger*" (*Der deutsche Roman der Gegenwart* 26).

Implied in Ryan's criticism and in others of its kind is that Schrella and the Fähmels, or any character that withdraws from society or offers social criticism privately, betrays an obligation to change society because his or her act is not public. Schrella's action, Ryan complains, is only "personal" instead of societal, takes place in a "discrete milieu" instead of in a public forum, remains "ineffective" protest instead of effective protest that changes society, and satisfies only personal justice rather than public justice. Ryan calls Schrella's behavior a "retreat from further political engagement," and she accuses him of wishing to "clear his own name" rather than desiring to "expose crimes committed during the Nazi era." This type of criticism makes a fundamental philosophical error of confusing the fictional world with the real world. If one recognizes that the goal of the author and the novel is to change existing society, as Ryan's and similar criticism does, it does not follow that a passive character or a character acting privately cannot effect this goal as much as a politically active one. The desired change is for this world and not for the fictional world. The point is that the reader, not a fictional character in a fictional world, must act for change. If in the novel Schrella came back to Germany as a political activist with a social agenda, a social commitment, and an appropriate ideology, what difference would it make in the real world? The novel is as politically active, or socially effective, as it can be, when it raises the necessary social questions in an enlightened manner with philosophical and artistic consistency. These social questions are raised powerfully and rationally just as well by passive, melancholy figures as by active, optimistic ones. The important point, assuming social enlightenment and political change are the desired goals, is the effect the work has on the reader. It is not important whether Schrella's or Johanna's fictional contemporaries in the novel understand their motivation, but it is important that the reader understands their motivation. The novel is a public argument. The thoughts, ideas, and social points of view of the characters reach the reading public through the novel and have their (albeit unknown) effect in the real world. From a political and sociological point of view, criticism of this kind misses the mark because it confuses the world of fiction with the reception of the novel.

The whole structure of the novel as it moves from the past to the present demonstrates how the Fähmels break out of their shells of memory and become subjects of history. This single day is the day on which they transcend the barrier of recollective inactivity and begin to apply their morality, derived from contemplation, to a more responsible, active life. With small, concrete acts the Fähmels alter their circumstances and confront the reader with truths about the relationship between the first half of this century to the second half, or more specifically, the Hitler past to the postwar present. The private steps of Fähmel's adopting the bellboy Hugo, rejecting the old fascist Gretz, changing a routine of fifty years are not ends but beginnings and are the psychological prerequisites for future actions. Even if one believes such acts are unlikely to change society because society can only effectively be changed through institutions, political organizations, and consistent and persistent pressure, one should not conclude that these acts of the Fähmels are without social consequences. They make a powerful statement, and their effect on readers, both personally and politically, is incalculable.[11]

The open ending of the novel raises another question: Does Böll's work perpetuate the bourgeois attitude that the individual is essentially alone in society, at best a member of a family or of a small circle, an insignificant element acted upon rather than a dynamic force capable of determining history? Since many of Böll's works end with people finding comfort in small groups, securing themselves from the outside world, one must ask if Böll's essential social model in this regard is historically regressive instead of progressive. The answer is not clear. *Billiards* illustrates the dilemma that occurs in any attempt to deduce Böll's position entirely from his novels. But even Böll's life provides no definitive answer. He was both a very private person who cherished the private sphere of the family and a public person aware of his social responsibility. Judging from Böll's life, one would conclude that he believed the individual has an obligation to serve and protect his own circle and that in return the individual has the right to expect support from friends and relatives, because without this interconnection between the person and the group the individual is alone and lost. In addition, Böll's life shows that he recognized not only a narrow social responsibility, but also believed that what he did as an individual could influence the whole of society.

In *Billiards* this social conviction is paradigmatically present. During World War I Heinrich Fähmel refers to the war that kills innocent people as an "act of God" ("höhere Gewalt"), but during the Nazi period he comes to realize that people are responsible for war. In the Hitler period Robert recognizes that individually he can act for justice, and in the postwar era Johanna believes she can prevent the minister from becoming the murderer of her grandchildren. It is not a matter here of condoning the means employed but a matter of recognizing the importance of individual action.

Böll's novel shows that "people make history" as well as that people are victims of social events. Böll's works are not one-sided in their handling of this problem. They do not end as do Bertolt Brecht's with the clear appeal to ordinary people to become active in the process of social change, but they certainly give political morality priority. This point of view distinguishes the novel *Billiards* from the purely socialist, Marxist perspective which holds that a changed society will change people. *Billiards* suggests the opposite: changed people will change society.

This problem of the individual as subject or object of history is inherent in the symbolism Böll chose for the novel. Ryan goes to the heart of the symbolic problem, "The lamb-beast scheme implies that there always are and always will be beast and lambs, thus removing the issue from its specific historic anchoring" (91). Horst Haase, the East German critic, concludes from a socialist perspective that the symbolism is not able to explain the complicated economic roots of the conflicts of the twentieth century; by reducing history to the symbols of lambs and buffalo, Böll implies something not human is behind historical conflict (225). These objections to Böll's dualism are well taken, even if one recognizes that Böll has created a third category of "shepherds" and assigns them the role of protecting the innocent.

In his early work Böll tends to see war as a natural catastrophe. In the motto of his first novel *Adam,* he calls war a disease, like typhus. But *Billiards* is actually the beginning of a move away from this naive position. Still, the symbolism endangers the social effectiveness of the novel if it leaves the impression that lambs and buffalo are permanent aspects of human society. The reader must ask himself if this, indeed, is his own response. How the text is read depends on the reader.

In interpreting the novel, one must also keep in mind the nature of symbol and metaphor. They are only attempts to provide a perspective for looking at phenomena via artistic means. They are always limited and inadequate as analysis. They merely give a focus that can aid understanding, but they distort reality by narrowing the view. Symbol and metaphor can never do more than provide a unique angle of vision, at best an insight. They always fail as explanation.

Böll's novel, therefore, is not an attempt to explain fascism. It tries only to show some of fascism's characteristics and to present the relationship of fascism to the post-fascist era. At the novel's center of values is a moral imperative to reflect on the present in light of the past. If this coming to terms with the past occurs, then, the novel suggests, society will become more humane. If this is not done, then, the novel argues, recent history will repeat itself.

Böll became very much aware of the shortcomings of the novel's symbolism. In 1975 in an interview with René Wintzen, he criticized the lamb–buffalo dichotomy for its simplified condemnation of people who aspire to power and its glorification of those who do not:

> I would not do it that way again today. The concept of power in the novel is not sufficiently differentiated. There are some people who desire power in order to do good. I would not try this dualistic symbolism again. . . . This dualism is based mainly on my concept of Hindenburg and the German nationalist criminals . . . together with the industrialists and the bankers, [those who] brought [the Nazi party] to power. This powerful constellation, this dark, rather mysterious power group, this connection of Junkers and bankers and German nationalists, they made up for me the buffaloes . . . because together they simply trampled over everything like a herd of beasts. (*Q* 113–14)

Böll's view of history is in large part justified by what the Hamburg historian Fritz Fischer calls "the alliance of the German elites." His study of the alliance is now available in English under the title *From Kaiserreich to Third Reich: Elements of Continuity in German History, 1871–1945*. Fischer, famous for the "Fischer controversy" of the sixties concerning Germany's responsibility for World War I, argues in this latest work that the close ties of Germany's two major elite groups, the agrarians and the industrialists, allowed them to provide German leadership from the Kaiserreich to the surrender in 1945. Fischer sees continuity in Germany's leadership through World War I and World War II. This continuity of power is what is symbolized in the buffalo in Böll's novel.

The novel also reveals another consistent element in Böll's work: the connection between fascism and religion. In *Billiards* this critique manifests itself not only in the monks' lack of moral opposition to Nazism but more forcefully in the church's continued postwar adherence to fascism's ideological anti-communism. This latter critique comes in Schrella's conversation with Robert. Schrella asks whatever happened to Enders, one of their school friends whom Schrella characterizes as a "man of nonviolence" (*WRE* 3: 526). Robert says: "He became a priest; after the war he gave a few sermons that were unforgettable. . . . So they transferred him to a village so small that it doesn't even have a train station. . . . There he tells the peasants all men are brothers, and they think he's a communist. . . . He's suspect because he preaches too often about the Sermon on the Mount; maybe one day they'll declare it an addition to the Gospel, and they'll expurgate it" (*WRE* 3: 527). Postwar Germany, Robert informs Schrella, has reduced the number of pejorative epithets to the single word, "communist" (*WRE* 3: 527). Here, the criticism of the institutional church is even more stinging than in the passages about the monks' behavior during the war because the church has failed to learn from its mistakes under Hitler. It has again accepted the political truth of the milieu. The church is shown again to choose, as it did under Hitler, the moral standard of the dominant ideology.

Böll sees still another danger in the prevailing religious situation, the danger that the existing spiritual void will be exploited by unscrupulous religious leaders. He satirizes this kind of religious exploitation in the figure of the sheep-priestess. She recognizes the existing hunger for guidance and moral leadership but feeds her followers falsehoods and easy solutions for her own enrichment. She lives in luxury in the Prince Heinrich Hotel as she preaches asceticism to her flock and promises salvation to those who wear sheepskin and drink sheep's milk. The sheep-priestess recognizes that the "good society" has produced a vacuum that religion can fill, and she succeeds in meeting this spiritual need with a marketable product.

Billiards is by all standards a modern novel not only because of its complex temporal structure but also because the structure relies on a series of motifs. Like a piece of music, the characters and the themes are announced with set phrases. The most obvious ones derive from the realm of religion, literature, and the military: "Must have a gun" ("Muß haben ein Gewehr" appears eight times), "Intrigue and Love" ("Kabale and Liebe," the title of Schiller's famous play, nine times), "The rotting bones tremble" ("Es zittern die morschen Knochen," a line from a song, nine times), Whywhywhywhy" ("Wozuwozuwozuwozu," nine times), "The eternal heart remains firm in compassion" ("Mitleidend bleibt das ewige Herz doch fest," a quotation from the poet Hölderlin, six times), "Their right hand is full of gifts" ("Voll ist ihre Rechte von Geschenken," six times), and "Feed my lambs" ("Weide meine Lämmer," seven times). These poetic and biblical references suggest the content of the novel by connecting the thoughts of the characters and revealing their attitudes toward the moral values manifested in the work. Because the purpose of the combination of the structure and the motifs becomes clear only after the novel as a whole has been understood, Böll's interweaving of these formal elements confers on the novel its modernity. The novel demonstrates thereby one of the principal aspects of experimental literature of the 1950s, the concept that the whole explains the parts rather than the parts the whole.

The Clown
(*Ansichten eines Clowns*)

In 1985, shortly before his death, Böll wrote an epilogue to *The Clown*. It was an attempt to explain why this work published in 1963, which dealt with the problem of German Catholicism in the fifties and sixties, still held the attention of the public. It is, indeed, interesting that this most parochial of Böll's works remains one of his most popular books worldwide and especially in the United States.

In the epilogue it is clear that Böll sees the problem addressed in the novel as one of religious organizations speaking for individual Christians, that is, of a few church functionaries speaking for millions of Catholics. The problem is, then, a political one of national and international dimensions. It is essentially the problem of democracy: who speaks for whom, who represents whom? In other words, *The Clown* treats in a broad sense the question of freedom. In the case of the main characters Hans Schnier and Marie Derkum, the matter is localized within the context of love and centers on the issues of what constitutes marriage, of who legitimizes a couple's living together, and who controls the social aspects of marriage.

Since 1963 some of these personal, social, and moral problems raised by the novel have been resolved in favor of more freedom for the individual, but in 1963, the question of the appropriateness of living together without marriage was far from decided. Böll's novel in 1963 was a love story on the cutting edge of controversy. No other German novel of the sixties produced such an active response. The religious press chastised the book as immoral, the conservative press condemned it for political irresponsibility, and the mainstream press argued over its artistic merits. In *Die Zeit* alone, eight reviews appeared between 10 May and 21 June 1963. Germany's most prominent critic, Marcel Reich-Ranicki, felt obliged to review the novel twice in that period.

In 1963 the Roman Catholic Church was the focus of attention for its role in Europe during the Hitler period. Rolf Hochhuth's play *The Deputy* appeared, presenting the Pope as a responsible actor in the tragedy of the Holocaust. In the same year Böll's colleague, Carl Amery, published *Die Kapitulation oder deutschen Katholizismus heute* (*Capitulation: The Lesson of German Catholicism*), indicting the church for its silent complicity in the crimes of the Hitler years, but judging the church more harshly for its behavior since the war because of its continued complicity with the government in power, its failure to learn from the past, its continued acceptance of bourgeois values, and its lack of moral leadership. Thus, the capitulation referred to in the title of Amery's book was not as much to the church's surrender to National Socialism as it was to its acceptance of the restoration politics of the Adenauer era. Also, in 1963 the Second Vatican Council, which Pope John XXIII opened in 1962 with the intention of renewing the church and bringing it into the modern world, was in full swing. These important religious-political issues find expression in the novel within the framework of a love affair between an agnostic clown and a believing Catholic. Further woven into the story is harsh criticism of capitalist society. Hans's condemnation of the values of his bourgeois industrialist family and his praise of the proletarian values of the Derkum family suggest wealth is exploitively ignoble and poverty humanely virtuous. Thus, the novel is typical of Böll's oeuvre, for like his other works, especially the preceding novella *Das Brot der frühen Jahre*, 1955 (*The Bread of Those Early Years*), it treats love, religion, and political economy from a moral perspective.

When Böll wrote his epilogue in 1985, *The Clown* was just twenty-two years old, but it had already become an "historical" novel through its accurate depiction of the moral and political milieu of an age about to be challenged by the spirit of the sixties, the student revolution, the New Left, and progressive Catholicism. This undercurrent of turmoil surfaced in the novel in the context of a love story that raised theological and political questions. Regarding the nature of marriage, the novel gave an answer that satisfied neither the liberal nor the conservative. While the official church condemned the book, Carl Amery considered it "too pious" (See Böll, *Fähigkeit* 289). By taking the sacrament of matrimony out of the hands of the church and marriage out of the hands of the state and placing the union of lovers in the hands of the lovers themselves, Böll took a radical, anti-institutional, anarchistic position, but by arguing that the union of lovers was equivalent to an indissoluble marriage, he became an ultra-conservative. Böll agreed with Amery that the work was "pious" for, he said, it opposed "promiscuity" and pleaded for a kind of "chastity" (*Fähigkeit* 290).

The key passages showing that Hans and Marie considered their union a permanent commitment with the force of a sacrament occur in the consummation scene of chapter 7. In their conversation and by their actions, the two lovers show the mutual acceptance of their new status. Hans says, "I was proud that Marie was my wife [Frau]" (*WRE* 4: 103). And Marie tells

Hans to inform his brother Leo about their new relationship before he hears of it from someone else. She also purposely kisses Hans at the street door so the neighbors can see them, and she refuses after this day to return to school because she is starting a new life (*WRE* 4: 104–5). When Hans comes home, he says to his brother, "I was with a girl, with a woman [Frau]—my wife [Frau]" (*WRE* 4: 108).[12] In chapter 13 Hans defends his "marriage" theologically in a telephone conversation with Father Sommerwild. Sommerwild takes the official position that marriage is a status in canon law requiring formalization by a priest and witnesses. Hans, arguing from an anthropological standpoint, maintains that marriage is a condition of commitment between two people. He calls Marie's present marriage to Züpfner "adultery" (*WRE* 4: 164) because, he believes, only a formality binds them together.

One way to approach the novel is to see the essential theme as a conflict between the abstract and the concrete, between rules and behavior, principles and practice, between the force of order and the desire for freedom. Seen from this point of view, the novel reveals the durable qualities that give it universal meaning in its tension between the desire to control and the wish not to be controlled.

Another aspect of the novel warns of milieu morality. It illustrates that people who become too accepting of institutions and who identify too much with the values of society forfeit their critical responsibility. This forfeiture is a path of destruction that, the novel suggests, leads to capitulation of conscience. The freedom of conscience of the thinking, moral person is at stake in Marie's acceptance of the morality of the Catholic circle. (See the comments by Evelyn T. Beck [19–24] for a feminist reading of the novel.) On the other hand, the clown, with all his weaknesses and failings, becomes a prototype of freedom.

Böll criticized the critics of the novel for making what he called the "most stupid of all mistakes," that of identifying the clown with the author (*Fähigkeit* 288). While it is clear that Hans is not Böll—nothing in their biographies is even similar: age, background, class, religion—the critics that suggest an identification are not entirely wrong. One need only read Böll's essays of the late fifties and early sixties to discover some of the ideas of the clown. Böll's "Brief an einen jungen Katholiken," 1958 (Letter to a Young Catholic), which treats the failure of the church to provide moral leadership under Hitler and its continued failure to do so after 1945, reflects some of the ideas of the novel. Many of the sentences relating to marriage, sex, and the church in this open letter echo the sentiments of Hans Schnier. Also the essay, "Das Brot von dem wir leben," 1958 (The Bread from Which We Live), which clarifies some of the ideas in "Brief an einen jungen Katholiken," contains sentences reminiscent of the clown:

> The sacrament of marriage without [sexual] union is not conceivable, not complete. It alone does not make up marriage, but without it there is . . . no marriage. . . . [Just as] without bread and wine there is no mass or communion, without sexual union marriage is impossible. . . . I am certain that every act of love contains a mystical dimension of paradisiacal origin. . . . For me everyone is a theologian who carries out a priestly function. (*WESR* 1: 278–79)

Regarding the church and politics, Böll continued in this essay, again in the spirit of *The Clown*, to chastise the political orientation of the church, "The only word that reaches the people is the political message, the election advice [to vote Christian democratic]; is that not too little, when that is all there is?" (*WESR* 1:280). And Böll's ire is close to Hans's in the words, "I admit my letter [to a young Catholic] was written in anger, but not in anger alone, [it was intended] for the good of the cause [to reform the West German Catholic Church]" (*WESR* 1: 281). Böll's views on anti-Semitism in the essays "Antwort auf eine Umfrage zu antisemitischen Ausschreitungen," 1960 (Answer to the Questionnaire about Anti-Semitic Excesses), and in "Zeichen an der Wand," 1960 (Writing on the Wall), also show marked similarities to Hans Schnier's views in the novel. Böll wrote in the former, "I believe that the number of anti-Semites now is not greater, but also not less than in 1933," And like the clown he did not fear the anti-Semites as much as "the mass of completely indifferent democrats." And Böll's anarchism in the latter essay, expressed in the thought, "To write on walls 'Down with the government!' will never hurt anybody" (*WESR* 1: 344), corresponds perfectly with Hans's anti-establishment stance. Hans's anti-capitalist sentiments can be recognized in Böll's essay "Hast du was, dann bist du was," 1961 (If You Possess Something, You Are Somebody), where Böll attacks not just the capitalist tendency to value a person for his possessions but finds fault especially with the church for its uncritical endorsement of the capitalist system. In the novel the nonbeliever Schnier, who is the acting Christian of the story, after rejecting his father's fortune and family position, concludes—much as did Böll in this essay—that the philosophy of acquisition produces the theology of "If you own nothing you are no Christian" (*WESR* 1: 457).

The parallels between Böll's public position at the time of *The Clown* and Hans's attitudes in the novel are even more pronounced by comparing the theological-philosophical-political expression of the periodical *Labyrinth* to those of the novel. The periodical was founded in 1960 by Böll, the artist HAP Grieshaber, the Catholic pacifist Werner von Trott zu Solz, and the philosopher Walter Warnach. The periodical attempted to develop a Christian way out of the existing religious-political labyrinth into which the Catholic church had been led by accepting the prevailing social morality. According to the editors, the tragedy of German Catholicism was that there was no Ariadne (hence the title *Labyrinth*) to lead the church out of its danger. The periodical found little reader support and ended circulation in 1962 after just six issues. The novel, *The Clown*, is by Böll's admission in the program notes to the stage version of *The Clown* (1970) a private response to the lack of public response to the journal (*WESR* 2: 450). Hans's hatred of what he perceives as the unalterability of institutional Catholicism (represented by Father Sommerwild, Leo's seminary training, and the Catholic circle), the unreformability of Bonn morality (represented by Schnitzler, Kalick, and Kinkel), and the unchangeability of bourgeois ethics (represented by his father and mother) is, along with his disintegrating relationship with Marie, what creates in him the despair that drives him to the Bonn train station to become a beggar at the end of the novel. In the same program notes Böll also formulates the theme of the novel as the "ostracizing of a person who . . . is infected with religion like leprosy" (*WESR* 2: 449). For that reason he says Hans could just as well end the novel begging, with a rattle in his hand to warn people of his infection, instead of, as he does, playing his guitar and singing protest songs, for the final image is that of an outcast person with a contagion that could dissolve the existing order of society (*WESR* 2: 449).

The novel is easily summarized. After a declining career as a clown due to a severe case of melancholy brought on by Marie's desertion after five years of cohabitation, the twenty-six-year-old clown, Hans Schnier, finally falls on stage and injures his knee. At about six-thirty in the evening with a single mark in his pocket, he returns to Bonn to recover his mental and physical health. In his apartment he begins to telephone friends to borrow money, to discover the whereabouts of Marie, and to berate the Catholic circle for frightening Marie into worrying about her own soul instead of his. As a result of which Marie has left Hans and married the Catholic Züpfner. Between these conversations, he recalls scenes with his family and friends that span the years from near the end of the war to recent times. These recollections in the form of interior monologues and his quarrelsome phone calls are interrupted only by an unpleasant visit from his father. At about ten-thirty, realizing he must provide the necessary money himself, he returns to the train station to beg. Thus, the novel follows Böll's preferred structural paradigm of the fifties and early sixties in which the narrative time is abbreviated, to a period of four hours in this case, and the narrated time expanded, here to eighteen years.

The novel also deals with conquering the past. In the early sixties this topic was of national concern because numerous former Nazis were in all levels of government. The estimate was that eighty percent of government positions were held by old party members. The argument for their reinstatement had been that the government could not run without these experienced people.

In several scenes Böll tries to show how complicated this problem of rehabilitation was. Part of the difficulty in judging fairly the conversion of fascists is worked into the story by the reader's uncertainty in evaluating the biased narrative of the idiosyncratic clown. Hans is so thoroughly egocentric in his point of view that the reader is forced to question his judgment and interpretation of events. It is his lack of balance that makes him a truly fictional character and not a simple mouthpiece for the author.

Before making his first call to his mother, he remembers the final days of the war as she sent Hans's seventeen-year-old sister, Henriette, to the air defense to protect "the holy German soil from the Jewish Yankee" (*WRE* 4: 79). Shortly thereafter, a notice arrives that she was killed near Leverkusen. Now his formerly anti-Semitic and nationalistic mother is the president of the central committee of the Society for the Reconciliation of Racial Differences. She speaks at the Anne Frank House and travels to America to talk about repentant German youth. When Frau Schnier answers Hans's phone call with her official voice, the shocked Hans asks to speak to Henriette. His mother says, "You can't forget, can you?" and Hans responds, "Forget, is that what I'm supposed to do?" (*WRE* 4: 86). This exchange sets up the theme of conquering the past. Implied is that the new democrats like Frau Schnier have made their accommodations to the postwar era by repressing recent history.

Hans then asks about her friend Schnitzler because it was this parasitical author who lived with the Schniers at the end of the war who "forced" (*WRE* 4: 87) Frau Schnier to send her children Hans, Henriette, and Leo to the Hitler youth organizations. Schnitzler wrote at the time an innocuous love story about a German girl and a French POW, entitled *A French Affair*, which brought him a ten-month ban on writing. After the war he was able to use this proscription to sell himself to the Allies as an antifascist writer. On the day before the Americans occupied Bonn, Hans remembers Schnitzler saying, "The Führer has our salvation in his hands" (*WRE* 4: 87). His mother now reports how well things are going for Schnitzler, "He's in the Foreign Office, and they can't get on without him" (*WRE* 4: 87).

Other memories of the war haunt Hans. He remembers his teacher Brühl telling the class that all deserters should be shot for not defending the sacred German soil. Now Brühl is a professor at the Pedagogical Academy, enjoying a good reputation as a man with a "brave political past" because he was never in the party (*WRE* 4: 79).

Hans also recalls his and Leo's military training in the family garden under the guidance of the fourteen-year-old youth leader Herbert Kalick. When Hans called Kalick a "Nazi swine," Kalick and the teacher Brühl demanded extreme punishment, but the local party leader Lövenich saved Hans by acting "reasonably," insisting that everyone "keep in mind that the boy is not yet eleven years old" (*WRE* 4: 81). Hans's father also responded positively at this moment by putting his hand on Hans's shoulder saying, "The boy doesn't know what he said" (*WRE* 4: 82). Later, Georg, one of Hans's friends, blew himself up mishandling a grenade in the garden. Hans's mother reacted with a warning to Leo, "You better do it better than that stupid boy" (*WRE* 4: 84), and Herbert Kalick responded simply, "Thank God, Georg was an orphan" (*WRE* 4: 82). Kalick, only a few years older than Hans, has now received the Federal Service Cross for his work of instilling democratic values in German youth.

Obviously, these examples of the past illustrate the difficult task of judging rehabilitation after the war. The party member acted humanely and saved Hans, but he has disappeared from postwar history.[13] The writer Schnitzler, Hans's mother, the youth leader Kalick, and the teacher Brühl, whether in or out of the party, were Nazi fanatics who have succeeded as democrats after the war. The reader has no way of judging the sincerity of these conversions because Hans's narrative includes no parallel scenes from the postwar period. From his perspective the war generation is essentially hypocritical. At one point Hans says, "it is easy to repent big things: political mistakes, adultery, murder, anti-Semitism, but who forgives the details" (*WRE* 4: 215). Hans believes it is too easy now to denounce fascism and to proclaim democracy. Conquering the past must be done, he believes, with honest sorrow for small things. Repentance and retribution must be made at a personal as well as at the social level. People like Frau Schnier must mourn their lost children and acknowledge their own responsibility in their deaths. Honest sorrow requires that Kalick and Brühl remember beating the table demanding "hardness, unyielding hardness" (*WRE* 4: 215) in their desire to see Hans punished.

Hans recounts only one postwar episode that relates to his wartime experience. He and Marie visit Kalick for a reconciliation. During the visit, Hans remembers Kalick demanding in school that their classmate Götz Buchel bring in proof of his Aryan ancestry. Hans sees Kalick grabbing Götz by the shirt in front of class yelling, "Look at him, if that's not a Jew, I never saw one" (*WRE* 4: 215). Vivid still for Hans is the fear in Gotz's face that lasted till the end of the war. Hans knows truth lies in details, and in Kalick's eyes he sees no change.

The direct, uncompromising honesty of *The Clown* is what gives the novel its strength. While the theme of the past in this work repeats the treatment in *House* and *Billiards*, it is more artistically refined in *The Clown* by being more exact in its particulars and less certain in its condemnation. Although Hans is viciously sure of his judgments of others, the reader is suspicious of the one-sidedness of his narration. Böll originally entitled the novel *Augenblicke* (Moments). In many ways this original title is more revealing of its intent and content, for the story is, in essence, a series of recalled moments—exact, precise details that illuminate the past and reveal the present.

The problem of the unreliable narrator must also be kept in mind in judging Hans's relationship to Marie. The single perspective of the narration makes it difficult to understand Marie's desertion of Hans except in Hans's own terms. Evelyn T. Beck, analyzing the novel from the perspective of Marie, concludes that Hans treats Marie as an unintelligent person, uses her to comfort him, cook for him, look after him, and satisfy him sexually. In Beck's words, Hans "sees her as a valuable piece of property . . . as someone who could be counted upon to fill his every need" (19).

Although Hans is aware of Marie's sacrifice of friends and education to be with him, he never shows appreciation of her selflessness. He demeans Marie's intelligence; he does not treat her as a thinking person capable of good judgment. That is why he attributes her decision to leave him to the influence of the Catholic circle. Hans believes their relationship was perfect until her friends began to meddle in her life, but Beck perceives this explanation as Hans's rationalization of Marie's departure, that Hans was incapable of conjecturing "that she grew tired of being nursemaid, cook, mother, and comforter to someone who did not understand her and who, on occasion, even bullied her" (21). According to Beck, it was perhaps "easier to leave him than to confront him" (21). This feminist critique contributes to a better understanding of the novel by reading the work against the grain, from seeing the narrator as a negative rather than a positive character.

Hans challenges the idea that rational order is better than natural order, that law serves the individual, that principle produces right. The novel reveals Böll's own tendency to creative humanistic anarchy by confronting the abstract with the concrete. Laws and rules represent for Hans the desire of those with power to impose their will in the powerless. The main example in the novel is the church and state's conceptual view of marriage, which in the specific case of Hans and Marie destroys their relationship and undermines their love. Because of her Catholic education, Marie's life with Hans creates in her "metaphysical fears" (*WRE* 4: 120), that is, not "real" fears, fear based on a physical danger, but only spiritual anxiety produced by an abstract concept of order. Even when Hans agrees to convert to Catholicism and to sign a contract to rear their children as Catholics, when he is willing "to do anything . . . to have her with me the rest of my life" (*WRE* 4: 121), Marie complains, "You're doing it out of laziness, not because you are convinced of the correctness of the abstract principles of order" (*WRE* 4: 121). For Hans, the expression "abstract principles of order" is the prelude of "torture chambers" (*WRE* 4: 121). Hans is thinking not only of the Inquisition but of Nazism as well, of imposed values being the basis of social discipline. Hans abhors also in the economic realm all coercion that derives from abstractions. His father's visit reveals that the principles of capitalism force Herr Schnier's generosity to be justified as an investment. Hans summarizes his dread of abstraction most succinctly with the sentence, "One never knows what a person will do under the compulsion of a world vision" (*WRE* 4: 114). For Hans, abstractions tend to lack mercy and violate human nature.

For the clown, the opposite of abstraction is detail. This is clear in the way he deals with fascism. He sees fascism as a concept of order, an abstraction producing the misery he associates with Henriette's death, Kalick's hard eyes, his teacher's gestures, his mother's words. Only these concrete realities give meaning to the abstraction of fascism. Hans's aversion to the abstract is nearly total. For him Marie's adultery lies in the detail of brushing her teeth in Züpfner's bathroom as she did in his hotel room. In the realm of economics Hans complains of his father's "abstract money," numbers on paper or figures in a bank account, something that exists not to be spent but to be invested. Herr Schnier feels morally obligated to see his money increase and multiply. It is not a means of exchange, but a means of wealth, power, influence, respect. It exists to produce profit. For Hans it is the equivalent of food and rent; it is a means of providing pleasure by satisfying human needs. The Catholic intellectual Kinkel entitles his pamphlet, which impresses the Catholic circle, "Ways to a New Order" (*WRE* 4: 129), and it is Kinkel who, in his phone conversation with Hans, complains that the clown "obviously lacks a mind for the metaphysical" (*WRE* 4: 137). Also, in this conversation Hans reveals what he thinks is the true crime of the Catholics: putting Marie's natural goodness in conflict with the supernatural. In Hans's conversation with Father Sommerwild the abstract-concrete dichotomy finds expression in Hans's statement that the church only tolerates sex in marriage as a defense against human nature. While sex is accepted by Hans as something natural, for Sommerwild it is a complicated social matter that should be regulated.

What makes *The Clown* one of Böll's important novels is that it requires the reader to deal with its unresolved contradictions. It is a metaphysical novel that argues against metaphysics. It leaves questions unanswered. Is Hans a positive or a negative figure? Although he expresses many of the humanistic concerns of the author, he is also biased, unfair, and intemperate in his judgments. While he argues for the concrete against the abstract, he is, nonetheless, aware that a life without order produces more pain than pleasure. And as an artist Hans is forced to contradict his own philosophy. He defines a clown as one who abstracts the essence from the details of life and presents studied exaggerations of reality as life itself with the purpose of showing the absurdities of daily existence. Thus, in creating his routines of coming and going in the train station and of meetings of boards of directors, the clown becomes himself what he most despises, someone who lives in the lifeless world of abstraction. Still the clown has his integrity. On his visit to Erfurt he is asked by East German functionaries to perform some of his anticapitalist numbers. He refuses on the grounds that a clown must criticize the society he lives in, not one that exists elsewhere.[14] It is precisely in fulfilling this function of social criticism that the novel succeeds best. The clown as daring court jester gives the work its lasting vitality.

Absent without Leave
(*Entfernung von der Truppe*)

In the late 1940s and through the 1950s Böll was a prolific writer of short fiction as well as a master novelist, but in the 1960s he produced few short stories. He explained this change in interest by claiming he had grown tired of his own ability (*WI* 1: 67). He believed that he was merely repeating formulaic writing. Thus, in the years after *The Clown* he began to try new ways of telling a story. His work of the fifties was essentially modern, characterized by experiments with time, interior monologue, stream of consciousness, shifting points of view, and extensive reliance on leitmotifs, but his work after the middle sixties became post-modern. While the latter term lacks any cohesive definition and is an umbrella for works with little similarity, it is descriptive of some consistent characteristics in a broad range of Böll's stories and novels after 1963. *Entfernung von der Truppe*, 1964 (*Absent without Leave*), "Die Kirche im Dorf," 1965 (The Church in the Village), "Warum ich kurze Prosa wie Jacob Maria Hermes und Heinrich Knecht schreibe," 1966 (translated as "The Seventh Trunk"), "Er kam als Bierfahrer," 1969 ("He Came as a Beer-truck Driver"), "Epilog zu Stifters 'Nachsommer,' " 1970 (Epilogue to Stifter's *Indian Summer*), *Gruppenbild mit Dame*, 1971 (*Group Portrait with Lady*), and *Die verlorene Ehre der Katharina Blum*, 1974 (*The Lost Honor of Katharina Blum*) all possess characteristics of post-modernism. The distinguishing marks of post-modernism in these works are the use of the mystery format; recourse to frequent literary references and allusions; interjection of hidden quotations from legal documents, reference works, newspaper reports, and trivial literature; structuring the work on the process of an activity such as painting or an engineering project; implying that the writing is the result of mundane research rather than an artistic creation; and imposing on the reader the burden to act as coauthor by forcing on him the responsibility to produce meaning out of the confusion of the work. The egocentricity of German post-modernism represented by Peter Handke, Bodo Strauß, or Patrick Süskind, which focuses the work of art on the author himself or emphasizes fantasy and betrays a profound disinterestedness in the political world and a lack of social engagement, is absent in Böll's writing. No matter how much he experimented with structure, style, and form, Böll always showed in his writing the commitment of a chronicler and the concern of an active participant in German affairs.

Typical of Böll's post-modernism is *Absent without Leave*. Here the process of narration is likened to a child working with a coloring book, where the reader is asked to connect the dots to make the outlines and to complete the pictures by choosing the colors to fill in the spaces. The narrator in his first-person story compares his work to that of various writers, composers, and philosophers, uses motifs from fairy tales and history, employs symbolic names (explained in the text and then denied), quotes from prewar and wartime documents, makes direct appeals to the reader, and concludes with the teasing remark: "The narrator is hiding something. What?" (*WRE* 4: 322). The result is that the reader is forced to look at the whole again to discover what he or she has missed. The point that no reader is likely to miss, however, is that the title *Absent without Leave* refers not only to the narrator's wartime desertion but also to his rejection of the values of postwar West Germany. Through his act of withdrawing, the narrator discovers his own humanity and implies strongly that his readers will discover their humanity if they desert the established positions of their society. *Absent without Leave* is an uncompromisingly radical book and proclaims the author's manifesto of humane anarchism.

The story embodies the attitude that was to develop into the revolutionary spirit of the 1960s. But the indirectness of this novella let it pass by the public as an uncontroversial work. The same idea of the novella, however, expressed more directly in the speech "Die Freiheit der Kunst," 1966 (The Freedom of Art), contained lines that brought Böll the enmity of the conservative establishment. Here he wrote what might be called the radical summary of the novella, "There where the state could have been or should be, I see only the rotting remains of power, and these obviously costly rudiments of decay are defended with ratlike rage" (*WESR* 2: 229). In interviews, such as the one with Marcel Reich-Ranicki in 1967, Böll expressed the sentiments of *Absent without Leave*. In speaking with Reich-Ranicki he rejected all the major West German political parties: "One can no longer hope in the SPD. In a land in which there is no longer a true left, just left wings of three predominantly national liberal parties, it is senseless, a waste of time to get involved in partisan politics" (*WI* 1: 60); in the same interview he asserted, "I still consider communism a hope, a possibility for mankind to 'subdue the earth' and give it order" (*WI* 1: 62). Since Böll's idea of communism was never the Stalinism of eastern Europe, the changes in and revelations about socialism that occurred in 1989–1990 would in no way have led Böll to modify this statement had he lived to witness the "October Revolution." Such sentiments by Böll, as one might expect, created enemies on the right, and these enemies considered Böll one of the fathers of West Germany's nonparliamentarian radical opposition. Böll's works, it is true, tend to illustrate extreme positions. The clown, Hans Schnier, formulated very unsubtle equations—ex-Nazi democrats equal hypocrites—and the narrator of *Absent without Leave*, Wilhelm Schmölder, is even more uncompromisingly extreme with the idea that those who do not desert West German society fail the test of humanity. Böll's critics seldom distinguished between narrator and author. What Böll was doing literarily was not understood by his critics. He was simply appropriating for himself as writer the natural radical freedom of art. He believed the nature of art itself escaped all attempts by the state or any institution to place limits or restrictions on it because freedom constituted the essence of art. Art had limits, Böll asserted, but they could only be discovered when art explored beyond charted boundaries. "Art must go too far, to find out how far it can go" (*WESR* 2: 228), he said succinctly in the speech "Die Freiheit der Kunst."

What radicalized Böll's work in the sixties were developments in west German politics. The CDU and the SPD formed the Grand Coalition in 1966 with Kurt Kiesinger, an ex-Nazi propagandist, as Federal Chancellor. Although Kiesinger was exonerated after the war, many people worried about the propriety of having an ex-Nazi official as head of state at a time when neo-Nazi parties were gaining votes in state elections. Besides the Grand Coalition, Böll saw other political problems. The German government was supporting the U.S. war in Vietnam, the question of the eastern borders of Germany was unsettled, the dispute over the emergency laws was still festering, and the generational problem was growing. Also, in 1969 Böll and his wife took the radical step of not paying their church taxes, believing such taxes violated the spirit of the country's pluralistic, democratic constitution and provided money to the church in a way that tied it to the capitalist state and gave institutional religion power it too easily abused. These were the issues in the background of Böll's writing in the 1960s and provide the basis of the rambling autobiography of the narrator of *Absent without Leave*.

End of a Mission
(Ende einer Dienstfahrt)

In *End of a Mission*, 1966, Böll tried to combine three issues that he had not dealt with before: postwar militarism, the injustice of the federal income tax, and art as a means of changing society. In a broad sense these themes were not new. Showing the military as a senseless and absurd waste of time and material, as a mechanism of boredom that destroys people and perverts values, was a central idea in the early war stories. Now Böll treated this military tragedy as a postwar phenomenon. Although the economic system appeared as systematic exploitation of the "little person" by corporate interests in *And Never Said a Word*, in *The Bread of Those Early Years*, and in *The Clown*, it was never before presented as the function of the tax structure. And the idea of the subversiveness of art only hinted at in Hans Schnier's routines and in Wilhelm Schmölder's peculiar narrative became in *Mission* a metaphor for the whole novel (*Erzählung* as Böll calls it). This new novel was on the surface, however, not an angry book in the way that *The Clown* and *Absent without Leave* were. In fact, its humorous satire tended to idealize the humane potential of provincial life, suggesting that the basis of an alternative society exists in the ordinary people who sympathized with the radical social values of the two protagonists.

End of a Mission was an attempt in the spirit of the *Frankfurter Vorlesungen*, 1966 (Frankfurt Lectures), to create in language the elusive "inhabitable land" (*WESR* 2: 53), the alternative society, discussed in these university lectures on poetics. Böll observed in these lectures that not a single postwar German novel presented a picture of a blooming, happy Federal Republic. For Böll the reason was obvious: West Germany was a miserable country hiding its misery with material success, a discontented "sad land without sadness" (*WESR* 2: 60). Because of a feeling of undeserved prosperity, West Germans unconsciously expected social criticism. "They expect a whipping," Böll said, "and since I came to realize it, I am no longer ready to give them one" (*WESR* 2: 36). The result of this attitude is the narrative *End of a Mission* with its light touch of irony. In this spirit of not satisfying the masochists, Böll wrote a social critical story in the form of a provincial idyll, or as he characterized it in the essay "Einführung in 'Dienstfahrt,' " 1967 (Introduction to *End of a Mission)*, a pleasant story packaged "to blow up the padded cell [of society] with a time bomb and to put the director of the madhouse out of action with a poisoned sweet" (*WESR* 2: 253).

The narrative has one of the most perfect introductions of any of Böll's works. The first paragraph summarizes the entire story and suggests the development of the plot. Three local newspapers report in identical words on the completed trial of Johann and Georg Gruhl and reveal that, although convicted as charged, they received mild sentences and were set free. What the newspapers failed to mention was the crime itself. The anonymous third-person narrator assumes the task with his own report of the events behind the official cover-up. The three newspapers, representing the three major German political parties, are shown in collusion to keep the Gruhls' "inexplicable" crime out of the public realm. By concealing the protest of the Gruhls and their motivation, the press keeps contagious social criticism quarantined.

The trial takes place in the fall of 1965 in the small Rhenish town of Birglar. The accused furniture maker, Johann Gruhl, and his son Georg had in June of the same year near a well-traveled highway in the vicinity of Birglar in full public view and in a festive spirit burned an army jeep. Dr. Stollfuss, the popular local judge, presides over the trial as his last case before retirement. He wishes to offend no one, neither his superiors, who desire a quiet trial, nor the local residents, among whom he wishes to live after retirement. One of the witnesses, Albert Erbel, a traveling salesman, reports that on arriving at the fire, he asked if he could do anything to help. The Gruhls, however, responded that "it was a matter of what they could do for him" (*WRE* 4: 381). This testimony sets up the entire narrative, for the author is saying it is not a matter of what the reader can do for the author but what the novel can do for the reader. Other witnesses are Kirffel, the local chief of police, who is a friend of the Gruhls; Dr. Grähn, an economist, who reveals the devastating effects of the federal tax system on self-employed artisans; Erwin Horn, president of the furniture makers guild, who testifies to the superior craftsmanship of Johann Gruhl and to his impoverished state; Professor Büren, an art historian, who explains the concept of a "Happening" as socially committed performance art and attests to the Gruhls' burning of a jeep as an artistic achievement; Father Kolb, the local pastor, who has baptized most of the local residents and who defends the young Gruhl's antimilitarism as consistent with Christian teachings; and finally three career soldiers in the *Bundeswehr*, who served with Georg Gruhl and who unwittingly provide an exposé of the peacetime military by explaining military procedures. The most pertinent revelation is that privates like Georg Gruhl are ordered to drive military vehicles over the countryside to bring their mileage to the necessary level for inspection.

The prosecutor Kugl-Egger is a Bavarian outsider and the butt of the wily procedures of the defense attorney, appropriately named Hermes. Although the Gruhls fail to win acquittal by presenting their jeep burning as art, they receive vindication by being convicted on only minor charges of destroying federal property and causing a public nuisance. All of the Gruhls' costs are paid by the wealthy Agnes Hall, a relative of Judge Stollfuss and a friend of Johann Gruhl. She also arranges for a yearly commemorative jeep burning, pays Johann Gruhl's back taxes, and makes the bankrupt craftsman her heir. The Gruhls have their pretrial detention, which amounted to a vacation among friends, counted toward their sentence, and end the trial not only as free citizens but as heirs to a rich estate. What goes almost unnoticed in this pleasant story is that the Gruhls fail in their main effort to call public attention to serious social evils and that the system is completely successful in achieving its ends. The conspiracy of the state to contain the Gruhls' criticism of society was replicated in the free press that reviewed the book. Here the critics also chose not to deal with the social intention of the work.

Most obvious at the formal level is the work's indebtedness to Heinrich von Kleist. The Gruhls' trial resembles that of Ruprecht's in *The Broken Jug*, even to the point of having a representative of the state witness the proceedings. Only in Böll's work the legal observer's task is not to see justice done but to see protest covered up. Also, the opening of the novel recalls the newspaper report that opens Kleist's story "The Marquise of O." Even the long, syntactically complex sentences of Böll's narrative and the dominance of indirect discourse and the subjunctive mood carry a Kleistian flavor. The lengthy sentences also retard the action and give the story a relaxed, leisurely pace reminiscent of the nineteenth century. The essential facts of the story come slowly to light. Not until well into the story, when the formal charges are read, does the reader discover that the Gruhls' "inexplicable" crime mentioned in the first paragraph is a burning of a jeep, and the Gruhls' motivation comes to light only much later when they testify, and even still later, four-fifths of the way through the story, does the attorney Hermes present the unusual "happening" defense and portray his clients as artists rather than social critics.

The narrative ends with a complete material victory for the Gruhls, although it is a triumph designed in part by the state itself. The reader has learned about the corruption of the military, the exploitative injustice of the tax system, and the collusion of the free press with the established powers. Nonetheless, it is difficult for the reader to be motivated to enact social change in the midst of all the humanity of the people of Birglar, because things seem to be so decent the way they are. The reader is likely to swallow Böll's poisoned bonbon too easily because of its sugar coating.

Group Portrait with Lady
(Gruppenbild mit Dame)
Background

The publisher's blurb of *Group Portrait* called the novel an epic summation of Böll's work. Indeed, the novel makes up a compendium of the author's humanism and is in that sense a summation. For that reason, in fact, the Swedish Academy awarded Böll in 1972, a year after the novel's appearance, the Nobel Prize for Literature. In *Group Portrait* the reader finds the whole of Böll's value system presented with more directness and clarity than anywhere else in his oeuvre. The reason why this novel of 1971 presents so much of Böll's social thought, his frustrations, and disappointments, as well as his idealism and utopianism is that it is the product of the political revolution of the 1960s, that period in West Germany and elsewhere that focused public concern on the idea of a more humane society.

In 1966 the two major parties of West Germany, the Christian Democrats (CDU) and the Social Democrats (SPD), formed a Grand Coalition that represented 86.9 percent of the electorate. Excluded from representation in this center coalition were three groups: the Free Democrats who shared the centrist politics of the coalition, the right wing fringe, and an influential, but unorganized group on the left made up of students, youth, and intellectuals. The support of the Grand Coalition that brought ex-Nazi Kurt Kiesinger as federal chancellor (1966–1969) to power provided the impetus for this leftist group to form what became known as the Extra Parliamentarian Opposition (APO-Außerparlamentarische Opposition).

With no official party to represent them, the supporters of the APO, Böll among them, began to develop a New Left social orientation. Later in the 1970s and 1980s this orientation was considered the embodiment of the "spirit of the sixties." Its main aspects were anti-authoritarianism, directed against the generation of fathers responsible for Hitler, fascism, and the restoration of capitalism after the war; anti-capitalism, directed against the system for its responsibility in dividing the world into have and have-not nations; anti-imperialism, directed against the capitalist West for exploitation of the Third World; anti-militarism, directed against the

Vietnam War, considered a result of Western imperialism; and anti-Stalinism, directed against the Soviet invasion of Czechoslovakia.

Although ill-organized and disparate in approach, the APO did offer a positive program of its own. It advocated democratic socialism, defining socialism as production for the common good rather than for corporate profit. Accepting this broadly defined socialism were groups ranging from orthodox Marxists, who believed their goal could only be reached by replacing private ownership of the means of production with socialist ownership, to liberal non-Marxists, who believed that capitalist property relations could be reformed into a humane system. To the amorphous APO, democratic socialism also meant expanding democracy in both the political and economic realms. It meant working for practical democracy in the social base (the grass roots of the body politic) and in the workplace, giving workers decision-making power in production and economic planning. The means of accomplishing this democratization of society ranged from revolution to co-determination, a system of cooperation between the owners-managers of industry and the unions.

The alienated, the outsiders, the reformers, the idealists, and the utopians, those hoping for a new and different social relationship between people, found their way into the APO. To the APO the Federal Republic had become fat with its newly accumulated wealth and had grown indifferent to the needs of people at home and abroad. Besides the government's submission to American international interests in Vietnam, the APO criticized its acceptance of America's Cold War relationship to the East bloc.

In 1969 the Social Democratic party made significant gains in the national elections and was able to form a new government with the Free Democrats. In that year this new coalition brought Willy Brandt to power as federal chancellor. As a socialist Brandt was sympathetic to many of the goals of the APO. His social-political platform, democratization of a rigid educational system, and rapprochement with the East met with Christian Democratic opposition but had the support of the moderate element in the APO and of Heinrich Böll. Böll, in fact, campaigned for Brandt in his reelection bid of 1972 because of Brandt's *Ostpolitik*, the name given to his broad range of new attitudes to Eastern Europe. Böll wholeheartedly supported Brandt's treaties with the Soviet Union and Poland in 1970 and with East Germany in 1971 that acknowledged the borders of Germany established by the victors after World War II and that relinquished all German claims to the lost territories east of the German Democratic Republic, as well as Brandt's policy of deemphasizing German reunification.

When Brandt was forced out of office in 1974 because of a spy scandal in the chancery (a close friend of Brandt's had been found working for the East German government), Helmut Schmidt succeeded him in office. The spirit of reform and optimism that prevailed when Brandt was in power soon came to an end. Schmidt's goal became the consolidation of Brandt's reforms, not their expansion.

The movement for change in Germany was already ebbing while Brandt was still in office. The radical left in the APO discerned that there was now no longer a chance of achieving their goals through the system. Two events especially disconcerted the radical left. One was the social pact between German industry and the powerful trade unions that tended to perpetuate the bourgeois status quo. The other was the failure of the APO to organize into a cohesive force for social change. The supporters of the APO filtered back into the established parties or became resigned to things as they were, leaving the left fringe to flirt with violence. There remained no effective, credible party on the left to work within the system for socialist goals. The failure of the APO to grow into an effective organization and the belief of its radical supporters that the recent accomplishments under Brandt were inadequate created the conditions for the rise of the Baader-Meinhof Group and the Red Army Faction (RAF). Their disappointment and frustration with the West German social order became the seeds of West Germany's domestic terrorism of the 1970s.

Böll was aware of the impossibility of effecting a revolutionary alternative by a small group of radicals. He expressed the odds mathematically as sixty million (the population of West Germany) to sixty (his estimate of the number of hard-core terrorists). Böll, nonetheless, maintained the viability of radical change by individual conversion to a new social ethic. It is this utopian view, developed in the 1960s, that finds expression in Böll's *Group Portrait*.

The political scientist Kurt Sontheimer attributes to literature the seismographic function of monitoring minute social disturbances. According to Sontheimer, literature is "the most sensitive organ in the public sphere in reacting to the changes and moods of society."[15] *Group Portrait* illustrates well the role Sontheimer assigns to literature, but Böll's novel is more than a mere seismographic record. It is also economic parable, social chronicle, and religious meditation. As such, the book becomes a manifesto of Böll's humanism, individualism, and socialism embodied in the novel's heroine Leni Pfeiffer, a new twentieth-century Madonna, a contemporary secular saint.

Structure

In an interview with Dieter Wellershoff, Böll explained the intention of the novel, "I tried to describe or write about the fate (*Schicksal*) of a German woman in her late forties who had taken on herself the burden of history between 1922 and 1970" (*WI* 1: 120). To tell this story Böll created a narrator, called the *Verfasser* (*Verf.*), rendered ("Au.,") for "Author," in the English translation, who becomes so fascinated by the person of Leni Gruyten-Pfeiffer, the object of his research, that he devotes all his energy to recording her life in minute detail. At no time does Böll explain what first attracted the "Au." to his subject or why he has expended so much time and money to record her life. That the "Au." is writing in some professional capacity, however, is clear, for he keeps a precise record of his expenses for tax purposes.

In an article entitled "The Author as *Advocatus Dei*," Theodore Ziolkowski explains the motivation behind a fictitious narrator like the "Au." by focusing on the "simple form" of the narration and the similarity of events in Leni's life to those in the life of the Virgin Mary. He concludes that the "Au." is a secular postulator and his work a secular dossier on the life of a "holy" woman.

Although Ralph Ley and Margarete Deschner had previously analyzed the parallelism in the lives of Leni and the Virgin Mary, their purpose was to explain the religious and social content of the novel. Ziolkowski, however, employs the typological similarities and the pattern of narration to explain the structure of the novel. He concerns himself with the method that the "Au." uses to acquire his information and the manner in which he records the life of his subject. Ziolkowski concludes that the "Au.'s" document, consisting of the results of painstaking research and numerous interviews, lacks a coherent narrative and cannot thus be construed as a holy legend or as a traditional life of a saint. Instead, the "Au.'s" document resembles the dossier of facts in a beatification process prepared by an *advocatus dei* to confirm the beatitude of a servant of God. Ziolkowski concludes: "The reader is forced by this sophisticated rhetorical strategy to assume the responsibility of the Congregation of Sacred Rites by rendering an ethical judgment. We become *nolens volens* the authority before whom the postulator [the "Au."] lays his report: we must confirm the beatitude of this *anima naturaliter christiana* [naturally Christian soul], or as *advocatus diaboli*, deny her humanity with indifference and contempt" ("The Author as *Advocatus Dei*" 16).

Iconography

In an interview with Manfred Durzak, Böll stated that in *Group Portrait* it was his intention "to destroy iconographic clichés" (*WI* 1: 332) and in the process to create a new iconography. The new iconography is, according to Böll, a new "possibility [that is] transportable into reality" (*WI* 1: 332). In that sense, Leni is a realizable model of a utopian ideal that transcends the assumed limits of our society. Leni is for Böll the model of an achievable humane socialism.

In an interview with Heinz Ludwig Arnold, Böll accepted Arnold's characterization of Leni and Lev as representatives of an "idealized, humane counterculture" (*WI* 1: 170), but this counterculture, Böll insisted, is "absolutely necessary because it is probably the only possibility for people to protect themselves from fascism, automation, and the computer world" (*WI* 1: 170).[16] As Böll saw it, a mechanized, computerized world could be equated with fascism because both mechanization and fascism "reduce a person in his quality as a human being" (*WI* 1: 171). In *Group Portrait* Böll wanted to criticize the capitalist social priority of economic expediency in all aspects of existence. He felt that such a priority relegated the quality of life to a secondary position. The novel is a reaction, he said, to a society in which "profit is now the controlling factor" (*WI* 1: 171). Böll rejected this economic view of life as a depressing ideology presented to young people by the dominant culture (*WI* 1:171). Böll perceived the rejection of this profit thinking as the cause of the unrest of young people.

> The priority of economic considerations in planning cities, work places, even of one's existence is growing more pronounced. Profit is the controlling element. . . . The assertion that this struggle for success is based on equal opportunity is the greatest swindle that there is. . . . Talk about equal opportunity is terribly depressing. I believe that the problem for young people is: they see no way out of this society based on success and profit. What I tried to do [in *Group Portrait*] was to develop and describe a counterculture. (*WI* 1: 171)

When asked if he thought his social model was a real possibility for the West, Böll replied, "It is realizable when there is solidarity along with analysis of the environment" (*WI* 1: 171). The novel demonstrates in several places the kind of solidarity Böll had in mind: life in the "paradise in the tombs," the division of space in Leni's house according to need, the charging of rent according to ability to pay, Lev's support of the sanitation workers, and above all the action of the "Help Leni Committee'' in saving Leni from eviction. All these examples represent success through solidarity.

Finally Arnold asked Böll, ''Can you say what kind of society the figures Leni and Lev represent?'' Böll replied simply, ''a profitless and classless society'' (*WI* 1:172). Arnold, insisting on more clarity, asked further, ''You mean a socialist society?'' Böll answered, ''Yes, certainly'' (*WI* 1: 172).

The new socialist society presented in *Group Portrait* cannot be separated from the iconography of which Böll spoke in his interview with Durzak. For he presents his social model in religious metaphor, wraps it in biblical allusions, and offers Leni as the patron saint of this social order.

Leni is born on 17 August 1922, two days from the Marian feast of the Assumption (15 August), and is christened Helene Maria (*WRE* 5: 133). At the age of sixteen, while lying on her back on the heath, she experiences a spontaneous orgasm, a *Seinserfüllung*, which leaves her with the feeling of having been ''opened,'' having been ''taken,'' and having ''given.'' From that moment on she confesses she would not have been surprised if she had become pregnant and henceforth considers the virgin birth no longer an incomprehensible mystery (*WRE* 5: 31–32).

Leni's inclination to mysticism and sensualism rather than to rationalism and intellectuality renders her taciturn rather than loquacious. The ''Au.,'' in fact, records only a few of Leni's utterances, reminding the reader further of the Mary in the Gospels to whom the Evangelists attribute very few words. Also, the twenty-five-year gap in Leni's life from the birth of Lev in 1945 to his maturity in 1970 corresponds to the lacuna in Mary's life from the birth of Jesus until his public life. Furthermore, at the time of Lev's birth, Pelzer refers to Leni, Boris, and Lev as the ''Holy Family'' (*WRE* 5: 249). Following orthodox Jewish practice, Boris refrains from sexual intercourse with Leni from the sixth month of her pregnancy until the third month after her delivery. And like Joseph in the New Testament, Boris plays a minor role in the accounts of the life of the Holy Family.

The ''Au.'' also emphasizes the miraculous quality of Lev's birth on 2 March 1945 by reporting that there were no daylight raids and no night shift at the wreath factory nine months prior to Lev's birth. However, he reports two daylight raids took place on 28 May 1944, the day which Leni called her ''wedding day'' (*WRE* 5: 220). And the ''Au.'' records Lev's birth on peat moss in Pelzer's nursery as akin to a birth in a manger.

While these episodic similarities between Leni's and Mary's life are striking, more important for the "theology" of the novel is Leni's identification with Mary through her innocence. Dieter Wellershoff calls it Leni's "naiveté" (*WI* 1: 121). But Böll goes even further and says: "The woman [Leni] is certainly naive, but I believe she is also innocent, not in a legal sense but in a moral one, almost in a metaphysical sense. That is the problem that excited me—the problem of presenting an innocent person" (*WI* 1: 121). The "Au." also attempts to explain Leni's personality with the word *innocence*, but when he tries to learn more about it by looking the word up in an encyclopedia, he finds there is no entry. He concludes the world will never understand Leni because "without this word Leni cannot be understood" (*WRE* 5: 132). But he does find the word *guilt*, which leads him to conclude the world knows more about guilt than innocence.

Since Leni is identified with Mary, Boris must be her Joseph, and Pelzer actually calls him that (*WRE* 5: 265). Even Lotte Hoyser makes the same connection, saying, "They lived together as Mary and Joseph" (*WRE* 5: 249), referring to the six-month period of Boris's abstention from sexual intercourse. Thus, with Leni as Mary and Boris as Joseph, Lev must be Jesus and emerge as a savior. This, in fact, is what happens. Lev associates, as did Jesus, with the lowly in society and becomes the prophet of salvation with his secular gospel of "deliberate underachievement" (*Leistungsverweigerung*).

This economic ethic derives from Böll's socialist philosophy that work is the source of wealth and wealth exists to satisfy human need and not the desire for profit, "I believe we are probably killing ourselves with work [*Leistung*]," is his formulation of the problem in a 1971 interview with Dieter Zimmer about the novel *Group Portrait*.[17] And in an interview with Christian Linder in 1975 Böll expressed the same idea: "People shouldn't work for more than they really need. That may be a lot—but should one spend a life time working for things that are superfluous?" (*WI* 1: 409). Böll acknowledged this concept was a form of *Leistungsverweigerung* and even called it utopian anarchy. However, he insisted that such a characterization should be understood as a desirable and achievable social goal because "many people have already made it a reality by working only for what they need, and live luxuriously because luxury is a relative thing" (*WI* 1: 409).

Though defined most thoroughly in *Group Portrait*, Lev's gospel of social salvation through *Leistungsverweigerung* finds expression in several other of Böll's works—most notably in the satire "Anekdote zur Senkung der Arbeitsmoral" ("Anecdote on the Decline of the Work Ethic") and in the novels *The Clown* and *End of a Mission*. Hence Lev's messianic message forms an essential part of Böll's philosophy over many years.[18]

Humor

Related to this iconography is also Böll's concept of humor, which he defines in his *Frankfurter Vorlesungen* (Frankfurt Lectures) as "the representation in its majesty of that which society regards as refuse" (*WESR* 2: 88). This definition is derived from Jean Paul's *Vorschule der Ästhetik* (The Preschool of Aesthetics), from which Böll quotes the following sentence, "For humor there is no individual foolishness, no such thing as a fool, just foolishness in general and a foolish world" (*WESR* 2: 88).

To illustrate this Jean-Paulian idea of humor, Böll chooses the passage from J. D. Salinger's *Raise High the Roof Beam, Carpenters*, in which the narrator's fictitious brother, Seymour, awakes in the middle of the night with the revelation that he understands why Christ said, "Call no man a fool," the reason being, Seymour says, that no one is a fool (*WESR* 2: 88). Another way of defining Böll's humor is to recognize that its principle is the humbling of that for which society has high regard and the exalting of that for which society has low regard. It is the idea that the great will be brought low and the lowly made great, or in biblical terms "The first will be last and the last first." In another passage of the *Frankfurter Vorlesungen* Böll is even more specific, "It seems to me there is only one humane possibility for humor: to show that which society declares trash (*Abfall*) and treats disparagingly (*abfällig*) in all its grandeur" (*WESR* 2: 89).

In *Group Portrait*, this theory of humane reversal results in what Böll meant when he said one cannot create a new iconography without destroying the old one, in other words, the values of the existing order must be overthrown if new ones are to prevail. Thus, Leni, who is disdained as a whore and regarded as a tramp, and Lev, who is imprisoned and denigrated as a lazy good-for-nothing, are presented as the ideals of a new social order. This principle of reversal works throughout the novel. The "Au.'s" narrative objectivity in reporting Leni's life deteriorates to subjective involvement. The arch-opportunist Pelzer develops into a decent human being. The foreign sanitation workers become knights-errant in garbage trucks saving Leni from the clutches of the dragon Otto Hoyser. Not only character and action but also place are subjected to this principle of reversal. In Pelzer's nursery the toilet is where Leni and Boris exchange their declarations of love. Common objects are granted sacramental status. It is a cup (chalice) of coffee that transforms Boris, the subhuman, into a human being. War has the ironic effect of making lovers of the German Leni and the Russian Boris, and war's end, which should bring Leni and Boris together, separates them forever. The bombing raids that cause misery and death provide Leni and Boris with happiness and life. Thus, the principle of Böll's humor runs through every aspect of the novel. Wilhelm Grothmann even sees this principle at work in various linguistic elements, for example, in the expression "sex-oma" (sex-granny), which combines the fearfulness of sex with the gentleness of a grandmother, in the word "Sowjetmensch" (Soviet human being), which connects the pejorative epithet "Soviet" with the concept of humanity, in the phrase "sich aufs Kreuz legen" (to place oneself on the cross—a pun on the word *Kreuz* meaning both "cross" and "small of the back") which animates a religious expression with sexual implication (158–59).

The reversal of society's concept of high and low as a theory of humane humor even has direct expression in the words of Leni's brother Heinrich as he dies a "traitor" opposing the war. His final words to his family before departing for Denmark are "Garbage, garbage—garbage is all I want to be, nothing but garbage" (*WRE* 5: 59), and his last words before the firing squad are "shit on Germany" (*WRE* 5: 79). Leni, called a "communist whore" (*WRE* 5: 13), reveals herself to be not only a Madonna but also a new Eve when she plunges her hand into a stopped toilet and removes an offending apple core. With this gesture she symbolically restores Eden, showing how the lost paradise in the form of an alternative world can still be realized in opposition to the alienation and repression caused by society.

Sister Klementina says of Leni: "She exists and she doesn't exist. She doesn't exist and she exists" (*WRE* 5: 360). With these words Klementina refers to the dual role Leni plays in the novel as real person and as symbol. This dual function raises the question: why is it a woman and not a man who is the carrier of this new ethic? Although Lev has a similar function, he is a minor figure in the novel. He appears primarily in a psychological report ordered by the court, which focuses on his education and employment. Absent totally is any reference to his sex life. Leni, on the other hand, appears in the full range of her human activity. The reasons why the male is unsuited for the role that Böll assigns Leni and why Böll had to write the history of a woman in her late forties derive from the author's idea of humor—inverting the existing order, turning the world on its head—because what Böll wishes to destroy with his humor is a masculine system characterized by aggressiveness, achievement, competition, and obsession with success. It is the male world represented by the Hoysers, the "elevated personage" (Herr Hochgestellt), and at times by Pelzer that must be humanized by Leni. In such a world of supermasculinity, the countermodel must be female. In fact, the rejection of male values is so strong that the positive male figures, especially Lev, demonstrate characteristics usually attributed to women: gentleness, compassion, sentiment. Even the hardened Pelzer "holds hands" after his humanization. Thus, the entire novel is pervaded by Böll's concept of humor, demonstrated by a radical reversal of values.

Utopia
(Freud and Marcuse)

There is no evidence that Böll was an expert on Freud's metapsychology or that he had studied Herbert Marcuse. To argue for intellectual influence is not the purpose here. I intend only to show how Freud's and especially Marcuse's ideas can explain in large part the novel *Group Portrait*. There are enough casual references to Freud and psychoanalysis in Böll's work to prove a certain familiarity with Freud,[19] but there are no references to Marcuse. Still, it is fair to assume that anyone who played the role that Böll played in the intellectual life of Germany in the 1960s would be familiar with Marcuse's ideas. In fact, Marcuse's perspective is so significant to the cultural milieu in which Böll wrote that a brief discussion of his ideas is warranted here.

Few philosophers of this century have enjoyed as much popular influence as has Herbert Marcuse (1898–1979). He was born in Berlin and studied in Freiburg, where he wrote a dissertation on Hegel's ontology and his philosophy of history. When the Nazis came to power in 1933, he came to the United States and, from 1934 to 1941, taught at Columbia University in the Institute for Social Research, which was moved from Frankfurt by Max Horkheimer (1895–1973). During the war he worked for the Office of Intelligence Research in the State Department. And after the war he taught at Harvard, from 1951 to 1953, and at Brandeis University, from 1954 to 1965, spent periods abroad as director of the Ecole Pratique des Hautes Etudes in Paris, and ended his teaching career at the University of California, San Diego, where he was professor from 1965 until his death. His influence on the youth movements in the United States, France, and West

Germany in the 1960s and 1970s rested in large part on his formulation of the "Great Refusal," the idea that the present social order should be rejected because it was repressive and conformist and that this rejection of or "refusal" to cooperate with such a system could begin immediately, without waiting for a social revolution.

Understanding Marcuse's concept of the Great Refusal, a form of *Leistungsverweigerung,* presented in his book *Eros and Civilization: A Philosophical Inquiry into Freud* can contribute significantly to grasping the essence of Böll's *Group Portrait.* In this book, Marcuse counters the cultural pessimism of Freud with a theory of utopian social change. Marcuse asserts that Freud's argument for the continuing need of sublimation to maintain civilization, society, and culture is no longer valid. Marcuse claimed in the 1950s, before robots and computers were the major forms of rationalized production, that twentieth-century capitalist society had reached such a level of abundance that the basic needs and desired luxuries of all its people could be satisfied, thereby allowing the Western world to shift from a repressive to a nonrepressive culture.

According to Freud, sublimation, civilization's form of the reality principle, is necessary in order to repress the passions of the id—the seat of Eros, the source of love, life, and the creative impulse—the id that always seeks gratification of instincts. Accordingly, libidinal desires have to be controlled by the reality principle so that civilization can develop in a world in which nature fails to provide sufficiency without human labor. Under such circumstances it becomes necessary to repress pleasure for the sake of future security and later gratification. Freud's insistence on the necessity of human labor for survival is the basis of his cultural pessimism because he believed that that scarcity would always prevail. Scarcity then reinforces the reality principle; it makes repression necessary in the name of culture.

Marcuse agrees with Freud that only work transforms nature into sufficiency[20] and agrees further that some slight work will always be with us, but he contends that social production has now reached a stage of such easily produced abundance that the horrors of a repressive society can be minimized, creating social conditions that allow the pleasure principle to become dominant. Although Marcuse equivocates in his insistence on a coming utopia in which the pleasure principle will replace the reality principle, conceding that alienating labor may not disappear entirely and rational control over libidinal forces may have to continue, he nonetheless argues that the tendency to reversal can be so effective—especially if one is willing to live with less—that one can legitimately speak of a reordering of social priorities that will permit a new, less repressive, and more humane society than the present one.[21]

It is on this point that Böll agrees with Marcuse. In Böll's "Anecdote on the Decline of the Work Ethic," he praises the lowly fisherman who fishes only when he needs to and relaxes in the sun when he has caught enough fish for the day. The fisherman appears a wise man compared to the German tourist who tries to persuade him to work harder, to buy a boat, to organize a fishing fleet, to open a cannery, to become rich in order to lie in the sun, in other words, to be able to do what he is already doing. Here Böll clearly endorses the pleasure principle over the reality principle through a concept of refusal to overachieve (*Leistungsverweigerung*).

The tourist stands for excessive sublimation. He is a fictional illustration of the surfeit repression that has become integrated into the cultural personality of the West, the personality that Erich Fromm (1900–1980) defined in 1932 as a product of capitalism. According to Fromm, the inhibited personality internalizes self-denial, not as a means to future pleasure but as an end in itself. Such a personality replaces love with the passion for saving, accumulates things beyond any reasonable relationship to satisfaction of needs, performs his or her duty as the highest goal, rationalizes life for the mere sake of orderliness, and relates to his or her fellow human beings without compassion.[22]

Carl Amery condemns precisely these functional values of our society in his book, *Capitulation or the Lesson of German Catholicism*. (See the discussion of Amery's book in the chapter on the war stories, p. 30.) That Amery's secondary values of the milieu correspond to Fromm's characteristics of the human personality under capitalism is not surprising. That they also overlap with psychoanalytic characteristics of the anal personality (characterized by love of order, frugality, acquisition, duty, honor, cleanliness) is, however, more interesting because this theory of the anal personality offers yet another insight into understanding Böll's novel.[23] That Leni has no aversion to the human body, its functions, or its parts, and actually is aesthetically pleased by stools, bodily fluids, human membranes, that she has a totally natural, healthy, and unalienated relationship to herself and to nature, that she has learned from her teacher, the philosopher-scientist Sister Rahel, to examine her excrement to determine the state of her health, that she hangs the walls of her house with anatomical illustrations of the human body, that she paints a wall-size cross section of the human eye, these are all facts that announce in their own way that Leni represents a new, liberated, nonrepressive social possibility.

The anal character, according to Freud, develops at an early age as a result of authoritarian repression that creates the desire to control, to achieve, compete, and succeed. Marcuse acknowledges the existence of such a personality as the one described by Freud but argues that it is culturally, not psychologically formed. In his insistence that personality is a cultural construct, Marcuse follows Marx. He further differs from Freud in asserting that scarcity is not a permanent condition of civilization and, therefore, the hegemony of the reality principle over the pleasure principle need not be permanent. In reference to Freud's metapsychology (what Marcuse calls Freud's interpretation of human historical development), Marcuse says:

> [Freud's] argument . . . is fallacious in so far as it applies to the brute fact of scarcity what actually is the consequence of a specific organization of scarcity and of a specific existential attitude enforced by this organization. The prevalent scarcity has, throughout civilization (although in very different modes), been organized in such a way that it has not been distributed collectively in accordance with individual needs, nor has the procurement of goods for the satisfaction of needs been organized with the objective of best satisfying the developing needs of the individuals. (36)

Instead, Marcuse continues, the distribution of scarcity has been imposed first by violence and later by the rational utilization of power. In Marcuse's own words, "No matter how useful this rationality was for progress of the whole, it remained the rationality of domination, and the gradual conquest of scarcity was inextricably bound up with and shaped by the interest of domination" (36). Marcuse then distinguishes the negative term, *domination,* from the positive concept of *rational exercise of authority.* Domination is always exercised, according to Marcuse, by a particular controlling group in order to sustain and enhance its position of privilege. In other words, this group controls scarcity—which means it distributes society's wealth—to its own advantage. The "rational exercise of authority," however, is a phenomenon necessary in any social order to increase production, distribute goods, and administer things "necessary for the advancement of the whole" (36).

Marcuse then concludes that the various modes of production (capitalist or socialist) affect the various historical forms of the reality principle.

The libido cannot be left to run amok seeking satisfaction of pleasure. Repression is necessary, but different types of societies effect different modes of repression. Repression will be different in scope, manner, and degree according to whether production is for satisfying needs or for profit, whether a socialist or a market economy prevails, whether there is socialist or private property. According to Marcuse, these differences "affect the very content of the reality principle, for every form of the reality principle must be embodied in a system of societal institutions and relations, laws and values which transmit and enforce the required 'modification' of the instincts" (37). After acknowledging the necessity of repressive controls over instincts in every historical situation, Marcuse distinguishes between controls in the interest of domination and those indispensable for civilized human association. He labels the controls for domination "surplus repression" (37) and the latter "basic repression" (35). The prevailing form of the reality principle in excess of reasonableness, which produces "surplus repression," he calls the "performance principle" (*Leistungsprinzip*) (35). Variations of Marcuse's terminology abound in *Group Portrait*.

The reality principle, which has as its purpose increased productivity to meet human needs, has over generations developed into the performance principle, which no longer has as its purpose the satisfaction of human needs but merely domination and the creation of more needs. It does not improve the quality of life—increase freedom—but enslaves people by maintaining the social structures of dominance. Thus, the continued surplus repression of instincts no longer serves a humane purpose. It serves only to exploit. This concrete form of domination—the performance principle—manifests itself in society's laws and institutions, but an intangible form of domination appears also in the mores and values of society. These mores and values are more effective in dominating the individual than is external oppression, because they work internally. These internalized controls extend beyond the realm of the political and the economic and include the sensual. Marcuse insists that with the abundance that society now has, the performance principle can be abrogated and surplus repression can be eliminated, and this abrogation of repression will allow people to live more liberated lives.

In *Group Portrait* Böll presents Marcuse's argument in fictional form. Leni and Lev are models of people who have achieved this liberation from surplus repression. Leni and Lev fight against the economic domination emanating from the Hoysers. Leni shares her house on the basis of need and ability to pay. Lev employs his organizational genius to benefit his fellow sanitation workers, to permit them to labor less for the same results. But besides Leni and Lev there are various other representatives of the "great refusal." Leni's father Hubert Gruyten, a one-time successful builder, designs the so-called "dead-soul-enterprise" during the war: he adds fictional names to his list of employees in order to swindle the government, to help his real employees, and to avenge the death of his son. After the war he rejects the opportunity to rebuild his fortune in favor of remaining a simple laborer. Because of their exceptional behavior, Leni, Lev, and Hubert Gruyten become outsiders—rejected as the "garbage" of society—but they succeed in living decent, productive, and meaningful lives that serve themselves and others. In Leni's model existence, she also finds self-fulfillment in art, satisfying her creative instincts with music, painting, and poetry. In this regard, she liberates her senses through aesthetic experience by creating an order that harmonizes reason and pleasure. Her desire for the sensual pleasures of sound, sight, smell, touch, and taste are gratified by her playing the piano, singing original songs, loving Boris and Mehmet, enjoying the aroma and warmth of her coffee, and delighting in the feel of her breakfast rolls and the crackling sound they make when she chews them. For this reason, the "Au." calls Leni "a genius of sensuality" (*WRE* 5: 33). She is a model of what Marcuse suggests each person can become. In Marcuse's and Böll's utopia, she would no longer be an outsider but a representative individual of a nonrepressive social order.

In the idiom of Marcuse, the "unrepressed development [of the senses] would eroticize the organism to such an extent that it would counteract the desexualization of the organism required by its social utilization as an instrument of labor" (39). Leni has achieved this freedom, not, however, through intellectual reasoning but through intuition. Even in her youth she resisted repression by the school system, the church, and her elders, all of whom tried to desexualize and deeroticize her instincts. The best example of this resistance is her natural contesting of the repressive constraints of her religion teacher. In preparing Leni for her First Communion, the teacher labeled Leni's "spontaneous sexual expressions 'criminal' " (*WRE* 5: 36), and he felt obliged in readying Leni spiritually for the sacrament to repress what was behind her "flaming eyes" and her "sensual mouth" (*WRE* 5: 37). He finally forbade Leni to receive her First Communion because of her failure to suppress her "proletarian-materialistic desires for the sacred host" (*WRE* 5: 37).

Marcuse argues further that in a society governed by the performance principle, wealth, plenty, and abundance do not reduce repression but become the means of more enslavement. Instead of liberating the individual, commodities become the implements of control as they create additional needs.

This phenomenon is also at work in *Group Portrait* as the Hoysers try to induce Leni into giving up her old house by offering her a new apartment, fully modern, efficient, and rent-free with upkeep provided by the owners. They have calculated that a new building on the plot of her dwelling will produce more income than her house, allowing them to be generous in Leni's case. But Leni rejects the Hoysers' attractive economic offer because she does not live by the performance principle, thereby escaping their control. She is fond of her old house and is concerned about her tenants whom the Hoysers would evict without blinking an eye. Her interests are not economic but human. While the wealth of the Hoysers fails to control Leni, it does not fail to enslave them.

In a similar example the Hoysers attempt to control the "Au." When Otto Hoyser accidentally tears the "Au.'s" favorite jacket, the old man immediately tries to buy his way out of the embarrassment. He offers the "Au." a new and better jacket, but the "Au.," like Leni, does not want something new and better, he just wants his coat sewn. He likes his old garment, the way it smells and feels. Furthermore, he attaches memories to it that he wishes to keep alive. Here the "Au.'s" jacket has the same function as Leni's old faded housecoat—the one in which she wants to be buried—her comfortable prewar shoes, and her old books, falling apart from rereading.

Important in these examples is the role memory plays in pleasure. The "Au.'s" jacket and Leni's housecoat, shoes, and books are sources of pleasure, not only because they have served well for many years but because they are associated with pleasurable occurrences. The capability of memory to re-create pleasure characterizes the nonrepressed personality. This phenomenon also explains Leni's ability to experience spontaneous orgasm by associating the touch of her toe on a crack in the pavement with past events.

In *Eros and Civilization* Marcuse maintains that "nothing in the nature of Eros justifies the notion that the 'extension' of the impulses [to obtain pleasure] is confined to the corporeal sphere" (210). This statement expresses an idea long prevalent in Böll's writing. As far back as 1958, in his "Letter to a Young Catholic," Böll wrote, "The separation of love into the physical and the other is assailable, perhaps untenable; there is no purely physical nor purely nonphysical love; both contain some of each other" (*WESR* 1: 265).

Marcuse makes the same observation, "The notion that Eros and Agape may after all be one and the same—not that Eros is Agape but that Agape is Eros—may sound strange after almost two thousand years of theology" (210). It is in this single realm of the two kinds of love—that of the spiritual and the physical—that Leni dwells. Artistic creation is for her an expression of Eros, as is physical love. In the right and true order of things, for which Leni stands, Böll is saying, this harmony of mind and body will prevail.

When Marcuse attacks Freudianism for its "psychoanalytic concept of man with its belief in the basic unchangeability of human nature" (238), he is primarily trying to replace Freud with Marx, for Marx maintained that changing society causes the human personality to change. By demonstrating the possibility of a utopian element in Freudian theory, Marcuse shows how, within Freud's categories of the pleasure principle and the reality principle, one can anticipate the ultimate human triumph over surplus repression in a society that produces enough to eliminate want. Because liberation from scarcity is possible, excess repression can be eliminated. It is this idea of Marcuse's, which harmonizes Freud and Marx, that Böll illustrates fictionally in his utopian possibility represented by Leni and Lev.

Ultimately, therefore, Böll's *Group Portrait* is a revolutionary book. The novel stands starkly against idealist thought that criticizes social evils such as acquisitiveness, the ideology of success, the commodity relations between people, while accepting the basic pattern of society. Böll's novel shows how the social pattern can be changed. Leni and Lev do not leave the reader "with the conviction that the 'higher values' can and should be practiced within the very conditions which betray them" (Marcuse 261). Böll's heroes reject the existing order of society. Werner Hoyser says of Leni, "She exudes destruction and self-destruction" (*WRE* 5: 336). He even calls her a "non-human" (*Unmensch*) because she is indifferent to a "healthy sense of profit and desire for possessions" (*WRE* 5: 336).

Although Leni rejects society intuitively rather than rationally, her way of life nonetheless abrogates the capitalist order just as Werner Hoyser claims. Her actions show clearly that she does not accept the alienation that derives from the commodity relations of a market economy. Although she does not think in Marxist terms of "optimal development of the species" and "total realization of individuality," she nonetheless acts out these possibilities. Böll makes clear that such a life is only possible now for an outsider, but a restructured society would make Leni the norm. If the majority of people lived like Leni, the existing order would be different from what it is today. Hence, Leni and Lev and the "Au." and Sister Klementina and those who share the world view that Leni represents are revolutionary characters. This is why society rejects them, treats them as "garbage." This is why Böll argues with a brand of humor that reverses the order of things, why he tries to create a new iconography, and why he structures his book as a beatification process. Heinrich Herlyn calls Böll's *Weltanschauung* in *Group Portrait* "the victory of humanism over moralism" and labels it the "decisive characteristic of utopian thought" as it exists in Böll's work (38).

Still, there are problems with the iconographic figure of Leni. How can a person who acts intuitively rather than rationally serve as a model? How can someone incapable of articulating the ideas and ideals of liberation, who simply lives out freedom without theory, plan, or rational process, a person who has only feelings as a guide, serve as a model? Is not some element of rationality a prerequisite for change? This contradiction is especially troublesome since Leni is a woman. To what extent is she an extension of the cliché, of the stereotypical emotional, intuitive, feeling, irrational woman? Is liberation ill-served by a woman unconscious of the act of being liberated? Does not human liberation, especially women's liberation, need informed, rational motivation if it is to succeed? Furthermore, does Böll's novel, on the surface at least, come too close to espousing biologism, the belief that the essential social differences between men and women are biological rather than cultural? It is difficult to think of a male Leni, although the collective personality of Boris's gentleness, Lev's "intentional underachievement," and Cousin Erhard's sensitivity form a composite Leni. Would their tenderness, lack of aggression, and new work ethic embodied in a single male character present a problem of reception? Would a male counterpart to Leni, attired in the refinements of sensuality without an attending rationality, be a credible character? Leni, on the other hand, even without rationality, is capable of standing for total human liberation, not just feminine liberation. While these questions may suggest a shortcoming in Böll's vision of the world, they actually reveal more about society—its limits of thinking and imagining set by social stereotyping, sexual ideology, and a masculine-dominated culture—than they do about his artistic fantasy.

Marcuse's theory of repression in *Eros and Civilization* also may help explain why Böll chose to construct a new icon lacking in rationality. In the modern and post-modern world (here "post-modern" refers to the psychic state of society, wrought by advanced technological forms of rationalization, succeeding the mental state, wrought by industrialization), rationality has, according to Marcuse, become the main instrument of societal repression. Today, total rationalization determines the various forms of division of labor, creating unquestionably increased productivity, growth, abundance, and wealth but also unprecedented alienation.

In *Group Portrait* Böll singles out war as the time of ultimate repression by the rational order. In the novel, rationality reaches its insurpassable inhumanity when war creates the conditions under which the normal tempering restraints of decency do not prevail. The novel details the rational use of slave labor and advanced technology to exploit people in work camps and to murder them in death camps. The testimony of characters in the novel actually is quoted material from transcripts of the Nuremberg trials. But Böll introduces additional hidden quotations in the novel from a military service manual of 1939 and a 1937 handbook on the administration of the army. These quotations suggest that for Böll the military is, per se, a model of rationalized oppression even in peacetime.[24]

At the end of the 1960s and the beginning of the 1970s, the movement for social, human, and emotional liberation naturally tended to take the path of irrationalism or anti-rationalism because reason had, in the eyes of many social critics, become so discredited as a tool of domination that it had become suspect as an instrument of freedom. This simple analysis also explains much of the romantic rhetorical sloganeering of the sixties that tends to find its way into *Group Portrait*. Since rationality had, in its various guises as economics, politics, and ideology, played its role in the catastrophies of contemporary history (World War II, the Holocaust, Stalinism, Vietnam), irrationality had become a necessary counterbalance. This irrational counterbalance took the form of liberation of the instincts. Feeling and intuition became more important than thinking. Instincts had to win the battle against oppressive reason before liberation could take place.

In Böll's *Group Portrait*, however, Leni should not be seen entirely as a representative of a libido-dominated new reordering of society, but as a model of the first stage of freedom before the balanced harmony of mind and body can prevail. She is the harbinger of a harmonious ideal, a necessary revolutionary figure in a patriarchal world of reason. Böll himself reinforced this interpretation in an interview with Johannes Poethen when he said of the counterculture of the sixties: it is too easily explained as a "quasi-mythical reaction to an over-rationalized world. . . . I do not believe that the rational and irrational exclude one another. In philosophical and sociological polemics they are seen as antithetical. Basically—and I believe that it is an important task for literature to show this—the two do not exist separately, but in various combinations. . . . In general we are taught to think dualistically, and I think that is dangerous. There is a trinitarian possibility . . . and this combination of the rational and the irrational, that is what I would call 'the third way' " (*WI* 1: 100). It is along the path of this "third way" that *Group Portrait* tries to go.

The Lost Honor of Katharina Blum
(*Die verlorene Ehre der Katharina Blum*)
Background

On 2 June 1967, while the Grand Coalition was still in power and the ex-Nazi Kurt Kiesinger was Federal Chancellor, the Shah of Iran paid a state visit to West Berlin. The police, attempting to control the crowds that had gathered to protest the visit, began beating demonstrators when they started throwing eggs and chanting "Shah murderer." One reporter called the action of the police "the most brutal bludgeoning" in Germany since the Hitler period (Aust 51).

In the course of the melee, a policeman attacked a young man whom he considered one of the leaders of the demonstration. As a crowd gathered around the policeman, he fired his gun, shooting the young man in the head. The demonstrator was Benno Ohnesorg—twenty-six years old, student of romance languages, pacifist, member of the Evangelical student community—participating in his first demonstration. At that moment Ohnesorg became the first martyr of the violent decade that was to follow.

Nine months later, 22 March 1968, partly in response to the shooting of Ohnesorg and partly in protest of the Vietnam War, Andreas Baader, born 1943, son of a Munich historian who had disappeared in Soviet imprisonment, and Gudrun Ensslin, born 1940, daughter of a Lutheran pastor, set fire to a department store in Frankfurt. They were arrested on 2 April 1968. At their trial in October of that year Ensslin stated, "We did it as a protest against the indifference with which we look at the murder of the people in Vietnam" (Aust 69). Because the arson was overtly political, caused no loss of life, produced very little damage, and the perpetrators were without previous arrests, the defendants and their attorneys expected a light sentence of a few months; instead Baader and Ensslin received three years.

On 11 April 1968, while Baader and Ensslin were in prison awaiting their trial for the Frankfurt arson, a twenty-four-year-old worker—with a clipping in his pocket from the radical right-wing *Deutsche Nationalzeitung*, dated 22 March 1968, the day of the arson—went up to a student in Berlin, ascertained that he was Rudi Dutschke, the most prominent young leader in the APO, and shot him in the head. The clipping in his pocket read: "Stop Dutschke now! Or else there will be civil war. The demand of the day is: Stop the left radical revolution now or else Germany will become the Mecca of the dissatisfied from all over the world" (Aust 63). Dutschke recovered from his wound and eventually became a professor of philosophy in Denmark after finding it impossible as a "leftist radical" to obtain a position in West Germany. In 1981 in a poem for the artist Joseph Beuys, entitled "Für Beuys zum 60. In Memoriam Rudi Dutschke" ("For Beuys at 60. In Memoriam Rudi Dutschke"), Böll wrote: "Do not forget, Beuys / the repeatedly German crucified / Rudi Dutschke / he is standing there in the corner / freezing hungering laughing forgotten" (*Wir* 55). This poem was not the only time Böll expressed sympathy for the young radicals of the sixties. In 1984 Böll also wrote a poem "Für Peter-Jürgen Boock" ("For Peter-Jürgen Boock"), protesting Boock's conviction for terrorism and his sentence to three life terms, although he had committed no crime that led to loss of life. His conviction and harsh sentence were based on his association with the Red Army Faction (RAF) and his refusal to testify against his associates. To Böll, Boock's sentence was the continuing legacy of the political irrationality of the Baader-Meinhof era.[25]

The clear connection between the shooting of Dutschke in 1968 and the demagogy of the right-wing press at this time became for Böll a problem of increasing concern and ultimately the basis of the story *The Lost Honor of Katharina Blum*.

While Baader was serving his three-year sentence for the Frankfurt arson, Ulrike Meinhof, an activist social worker, a prominent columnist for the magazine *Konkret* who wrote often on the problems of young girls in reform schools, arranged to interview Baader at the German Central Institute for Social Questions in Berlin. From the beginning, the interview was a ruse to free Baader from prison. Meinhof, Baader, and two accomplices carried out the escape, seriously injuring one of the employees of the institute in the process. The day Meinhof freed Baader, 14 May 1970, became the founding date of the Baader-Meinhof Group, later known as the Red Army Faction.

In Hamburg on 22 October 1971 two policemen, seeing a suspicious young woman, called to her to stop. She ran and as the policemen pursued her, two friends of the woman appeared and shot one of the policemen. The young people turned out to be members of the Baader-Meinhof Group and the policeman, Norbert Schmid, became the first state casualty of domestic terrorism. Two suspects were later arrested for the shooting of Officer Schmid, Gerhard Müller and Irmgard Möller. During their trial, the Hamburg *Morgenpost,* a publication of the Springer Press, ran the headline, "Today in Court: Meinhof's Lover Who Shot a Policeman" (Aust 184). The right-wing press, especially the Springer Press, was growing increasingly demagogic and sensational in its reporting of the events relating to the issue of law and order. The boulevard press, notorious for its yellow journalism, was attributing so many violent crimes to the Baader-Meinhof Group, with little or no evidence to support the accusations, that a climate for lynch justice was prevalent.

On 22 December 1971, exactly two months after the shooting of Officer Schmid, four people in masks robbed a bank in Kaiserslautern. In the process one policeman was shot. The headline of the Christmas Eve *Bild-Zeitung,* the main publication of the Springer Press and West Germany's and Western Europe's most widely read newspaper with a daily circulation of 4.33 million (1989) and a daily readership of about 10 million, ran the headline, "Baader-Meinhof Band Continues to Murder. Bank Robbery: Policeman Killed." At the time the headline appeared, the robbers were unknown; there was no evidence that the criminals were members of the Baader-Meinhof Group, and the policeman who was shot was in the hospital. To Böll, this outrageous headline of intentional misreporting and distortion of information had gone further than any before it in creating a public mood of fear; it was a blatant attempt to discredit all left of center political thought in the country.

On 10 January 1972 Böll published a hurriedly written article in *Der Spiegel,* West Germany's most important weekly news journal, denouncing the Springer Press. The article, entitled, "Will Ulrike Gnade oder freies Geleit?" (Does Ulrike Want Mercy or Safe Conduct?), was not a defense of Ulrike Meinhof or the Baader-Meinhof Group. In fact, Böll stated clearly that they were a group of "desperate theoreticians" (*WESR*

2: 543), and he added: "There can be no doubt about it: Ulrike Meinhof has declared war on this society. She knows what she is doing and what she had done" (*WESR* 2: 543–44). The article was above all an attack on the *Bild-Zeitung,* which he said "is no longer crypto-fascistic, no longer fascistoid, but naked fascism: incitement, lies, garbage" (*WESR* 2: 545).

Böll's intention was to bring reason to an emotional political issue and to suggest mercy and restraint as the basis for a solution to a national crisis. Böll's article could not achieve its goal, due in part to the prevailing anti-leftist climate, but mostly because its angry tone lacked the moderation Böll himself recommended. Nonetheless, it was successful in drawing national attention to the problem of right-wing demagogy in the press. The storm of protest it unleashed in the German media ran for several months.[26] The jurist Dieter Posser, the North-Rhine-Westphalian Minister for Federal Affairs, became Böll's most judicious critic. He felt that Böll had minimized the danger of the Baader-Meinhof Group and found fault with his inappropriate use of archaic legal terms such as "mercy" and "safe conduct." Still Posser agreed, as did other moderate commentators, with Böll's outrage over the reporting practices of the *Bild-Zeitung.* Böll, on the other hand, defended his article against Posser's criticism by denying that he underestimated the danger of terrorism and by claiming that he chose his vocabulary as a "writer," not as a "jurist," and by insisting that a society that had given up the concept of mercy was in danger of giving up its soul.

While the controversy surrounding the *Spiegel* article was still at its height, the new Federal Chancellor Willy Brandt called a meeting of the presidents of all the West German states (*Länder*), and together they agreed (28 January 1972) on the Radical Decrees that granted the individual states the right to bar from public employment anyone suspected of disloyalty to the "free democratic order of West Germany." The decrees immediately became the legal foundation of job discrimination based on social attitudes and political convictions. The misuse of the decrees to fire, blacklist, and not to hire people because of their politics quickly began to undermine the very democracy the decrees were intended to protect. After leaving office in 1974, Brandt publicly regretted his support for the decrees.

Böll's *Spiegel* article is extremely important for two reasons. It and the voluminous commentary that it brought forth comprise the best historical record of the national state of mind during this period of West German history. And as an insight into Böll's personality and oeuvre it is indispensable. The article reveals in an undisguised fashion Böll's passion for justice and his sense of fairness, as well as his deeply felt attachment to the new German democracy[27] which, he realized better than most people, was being endangered more by an irresponsible press than by a small group of petty bourgeois radicals. And above all, the article shows Böll's profound sense of compassion for the hounded people of this world—whether criminal or not. With the Gestapo era a recent memory the author thought his fellow countrymen should have had more sympathy for just such people. Ulrike Meinhof was a woman who had, through her writing, fought for the underprivileged in society and had up to the time of Böll's article committed no documentable crime except the freeing of Andreas Baader. In Böll's view, it was not too late for Meinhof to turn back. His sense of humanity requested mercy for such a tragic figure driven to excess by a disturbed sense of righteousness. In Böll's eyes, Meinhof was a female Michael Kohlhaas.

Despite the obvious similarities of the public events of the Baader-Meinhof affair with the story of Katharina Blum and in spite of a natural desire for literary vindication for the vilification heaped on him by the Springer Press, Böll claimed these conditions did not motivate the writing of the novella. In an interview with Christian Linder, he stated that his intention to write against the practices of yellow journalism existed long before 1972: ''The whole Baader-Meinhof affair has little to do with *Katharina Blum*. A long time ago I asked one of my occasional collaborators to keep an eye on the *Bild-Zeitung* and other boulevard newspapers for striking examples of defamation of known and unknown persons'' (*WI* 1: 390). Böll explained further in an interview with Dieter Zilligen that the story had its origin more in the Brückner affair than it did in his own personal experience with defamation: ''What I actually wanted to present [with *Katharina Blum*] was the frightening role of Prof. Brückner in his connection with the Baader-Meinhof case. He was simply a man who came in touch with members of the Baader-Meinhof Group; he gave them a place to stay, something entirely natural, and was destroyed psychologically because of it. . . . That is the starting point of the problem: not the [Baader-Meinhof] group itself, but people who are treated as lepers'' (quoted from Beth 71–72).[28]

In a letter to *Der Spiegel* in August 1974, one month after the publication of *Katharina Blum*, Brückner actually described his own psychological destruction, which Böll had tried to re-create in *Katharina Blum:*

I saw myself in a situation in which I became a victim, subjected to general disdain. . . . A new reality developed around me. Whenever an article about me appeared in the newspapers, I was deluged day and night by anonymous telephone calls. There were threatening letters. Many people turned away from me on the street. I suddenly saw myself assailed, oppressed, and defamed, and I asked myself: is this me or someone else?

The problem of isolation became immediate. There was publicity about me which was not a result of any good deed or crime. In the fall of 1972, I discovered my likeness in a Sunday newspaper under an article with the title: "Ulrike Makes Her Men Happy in Bed." A new Brückner was being produced whose image no longer corresponded to the image the victim had of himself. Through this negative publicity I was made into a nonperson and at the same time made the object of personal defamation. The distance between the official nonperson and society grew. Every meeting—even with friends and people of my own political persuasion—became an event. The possibility of normal communication with people disappeared. . . . [Brückner ends this letter with a sentence that applies directly to the reporter Tötges in Böll's story.] I met some [journalists] who were capable of anything.[29]

In July of 1974 *Katharina Blum* appeared serialized in *Der Spiegel*. It carried the pointed disclaimer: "Persons and events in this story are freely invented. If descriptions of certain journalistic practices resemble those of the *Bild-Zeitung* they are neither intended nor accidental, but unavoidable."

On 10 November, four months after the publication of *Katharina Blum*, Günter von Drenkmann, highest-ranking judge in West Berlin, went to his door to receive flowers—he had just celebrated his sixty-fourth birthday. After he opened the door, a group of four young people shot him in his hall when he resisted kidnapping. He was the first public figure to be murdered by German terrorists. Drenkmann had never handled a case involving the Baader-Meinhof Group. His jurisdiction was civil, not criminal affairs. He was a liberal jurist and member of the SPD. Later, a group called "2 June," named after the day on which Benno Ohnesorg was killed, claimed responsibility. The imprisoned members of the Baader-Meinhof Group formulated in their jail cell a chilling response to the "execution" of Judge Drenkmann: "We shed no tears for Drenkmann. We are happy about his execution. This action was necessary; it makes clear to every pig judge and cop that he too can at any time be called to account" (Aust 294).

In addition, because Böll had immediately condemned the killing of Drenkmann, the imprisoned terrorists chastised the author and his kind, claiming they were more concerned with the death of a bureaucrat than with the death of a revolutionary. Nevertheless, they used Böll's story of Katharina Blum to justify and explain the Drenkmann-action: "What else did Böll mean with his *Katharina Blum,* if not that the shooting of a representative of the ruling power apparatus is morally justifiable. However, when 'literary violence' becomes material violence, the same Böll goes over to the side of those whose words he has just pilloried as lies" (Aust 294).

Böll's story was from the moment of its publication in the firestorm of public controversy, more misunderstood than understood. Not only did the left misread the book, so did the right. The journalist Matthias Walden accused Böll on Berlin television of having "fertilized the soil of violence."[30] And the CDU minority leader in parliament, Karl Carstens, later president of the Federal Republic (1979–1984), made a speech in Duisburg on 12 December 1974 in which he called upon "the entire populace to distance itself from terrorist activities, especially the poet Heinrich Böll who a few months ago under the pseudonym Katharina Blüm [sic] wrote a book that presents the justification of violence."[31] These statements make clear the difficulty that exists in interpreting a work at the center of heated political controversy.

Because it dealt so openly and militantly with a contemporary crisis, the novella became one of Böll's most popular successes. But this brief work also remains one of Böll's important books because it transcends the social conflict that produced it.

Summary-Structure

The narrator calls his story a "report." In the opening lines he informs the reader of his main sources of information: police transcripts of interrogations; the attorney for Katharina Blum, Hubert Blorna; and the state prosecutor, Peter Hach. Additional sources become obvious in the course of the report. In chapter 2 the narrator compares the structuring of his report to a child's playing with puddles (representing sources) that are tapped and channeled into a single canal that forms the stream of information that makes up the story. Throughout the remainder of his report, he continues to allude to this metaphor of drainage. Since the first two chapters actually cover less than a page each, chapter 3 initiates the story: "One should begin with the brutal facts: on Wednesday, 20 February 1974, on an evening during Mardi Gras, a young woman of twenty-seven leaves her apartment at around 6:45 to go to a party. Four days later . . . on Sunday evening almost at the same time—more exactly, around 7:04, she rings the bell of the police chief Walter Moeding . . . and informs him that this afternoon in her apartment at about 12:15 she shot to death the journalist Werner Tötges. . . . ''

The method and tone of the narration is clearly a continuation of Böll's technique in *Group Portrait:* an objective, even pedantic narrator prosaically tries to get his information straight and to present it in a manner undistorted by emotive language. His intention is to let the facts speak for themselves. This dry, objective language is meant to contrast with the way the events in Katharina's life are reported by the journalist Tötges for his newspaper. The narrator is also careful of his choice of language and frequently calls attention to distinctions between words like *gütig* (good), *gutherzig* (good-hearted), and *nett* (nice) and in the sexual sphere between *zärtlich* (tender) and *zudringlich* (aggressive), thus demonstrating a moral concern for responsible language. On this point the narrator and the author are one.

In 1959 Böll wrote in his speech ''Die Sprache als Hort der Freiheit'' (Language as a Bulwark of Freedom): ''Words set worlds in motion. They can comfort and kill. . . . There are terrible possibilities of robbing a person of his dignity: whipping, torture, the mills of death—but the worst possibility that I can imagine, which would attack my spirit like a disease, would be to be forced to write or speak a sentence that could not stand up in the court of my conscience as a free writer'' (*WESR* 1: 301–5). This early speech gives an insight into why Böll abhorred the journalistic practices depicted in *Katharina Blum*. Most simply put, the novella deals with words that kill and rob people of their dignity and with journalists who have sold out their consciences to political and commercial interests.

Important also in the narrator's method is his focusing the story not on *what* happened, but on *how* and *why* it happened. In this variation of a mystery story, the crime and the murderer are known from the outset. Thus, the real concern of the work is the subtitle of the story, ''How violence originates and where it can lead.'' The social focus of the narrative is further highlighted by the unusually pointed disclaimer that introduces the novella.

The story does not develop chronologically. In fact the events are reported in such a convoluted manner that a perfect chronology is difficult to work out even with the closest reading. Böll himself apparently had difficulty keeping the order of things clear because the book contains a few factual mistakes.[32] In summary the following occurs. During the week of Carnival in Cologne, on Wednesday, 20 February 1974, Katharina Blum attends a party where she meets a young man, Ludwig Götten. They leave the party together and go to her apartment. The following morning, Götten informs Katharina that he is wanted by the police. How much he tells her is not clear. He seems only to mention that he is a deserter. His actual crime, however, is not terrorism as the police suspect, but theft of the regimental cash box, involvement with corrupt officers, and theft of the Porsche that he is driving. Katharina helps him leave the apartment unseen. An hour later, at 10:30 on Thursday morning, the police raid her apartment to arrest Götten. Because of her association with the suspect, the police take her in for interrogation. Thus, she becomes an item in the news that is reported on the front page of an unidentified newspaper, called simply the *News*.

On Friday morning the first edition of the *News* appears denouncing Katharina as a "gun moll" and "terrorist sweetheart." Saturday's *News* continues the denunciations, and Katharina becomes the victim of crank calls, threatening letters, and sexual harassment. On Saturday afternoon she arranges an interview for Sunday morning with the journalist Tötges. In the meantime, the reporter has interviewed Katharina's dying mother and precipitates her death. The Sunday morning edition appears with more denunciations, innuendoes, and distortions. In a fit of despair over her ruined life and reputation, Katharina smashes the interior of her apartment. When Tötges appears at her apartment door at noon on Sunday, he suggests that they have sex before the interview. As he reaches for her dress, Katharina shoots him. Later that evening, she gives herself up without any expression of regret or remorse. She looks forward to being with her beloved Ludwig, who had in the meantime been apprehended.

The novella interweaves several themes that give it a depth beyond the political circumstances that occasioned it: police harassment; demagogic yellow journalism; the cooperation of police and the press in a manner that violates the constitutional spirit of a democratic country, if not the law itself; the vulnerability of innocent people, especially women, in a society hungry for sensation; and finally hidden political and financial interests working behind the scenes to effect a social agenda. All of this material gives Böll's work a basis in reality that relates to problems in most Western democracies and that accounts for its continued popularity.

Analysis

In the political climate of the 1970s, especially in the terrorist years 1972–1977, the tendency in Böll criticism was to deal with *Katharina Blum* as a political novella. The subtitle of the work became its focus. Böll said in an interview with Manfred Durzak that despite the weaknesses of the story line, he was satisfied with the book because of its "direct political effect" (*WI* 1: 344). This "direct political effect" can best be understood by a brief comparison of the novella to its film version. When Volker Schlöndorff and Margarethe von Trotta completed filming the story in 1975, some changes emerged with Böll's approval—all of which emphasized the social-political aspect of the plot and led the author to say the film was actually better than the book (*WI* 1: 388). In the film it is clear that the police and employees of the *News* are all under forty, that they are citizens of the Federal Republic not tainted by a Nazi past and, therefore, represent problems of democratic and not National Socialist origin.[33] In addition, the film presents the events in strict chronological order, simplifying the progression of Katharina's tragedy from its innocent beginnings to its inevitable conclusion, thereby encouraging the identification of the viewer with the heroine. Thus, the film enhances what Böll considered the Aristotelian aspect of the story. In his interview with Durzak he also speaks of Katharina's tragic flaw (*Verschuldung*) and the unalterability of her entanglement in events (*Verstrickung*). From this point of view he calls the work a "classical tragedy" of "mythical material" (*WI* 1: 335).

A further change from the book was the adding of a satiric epilogue in the form of a graveside speech, given presumably by the editor or publisher of the *News*. With a sense of outrage the speaker says:

> The shots which killed Werner Tötges were not only fired at him. They were fired also at the freedom of the press, one of the most valuable commodities (*Güter*) of our young democracy. And by these shots we also, we shocked mourners, have been affected and injured. Who does not feel the wound, who does not feel the pain that goes far beyond just the personal? Who does not feel the breath of terror and the savageness (*Wildheit*) of anarchy? Who does not feel the violence with which our free democratic order has been shaken? This order which is so valuable to all of us. Here private motivation has led to a political assassination. But for us the message is clear: Be careful of beginnings. Be alert, because everything depends on freedom of the press: prosperity, social progress, democracy, pluralism, freedom of opinion. And whoever attacks the *News,* attacks all of us. (Quoted from Buschmann 66)

Although conceived by the directors, this brilliant addition, which summarizes the main ideas of both the film and the book, had Böll's approval.[34] While the speech is laced with ironic commercial language, calling freedom of the press "one of the most valuable commodities" of democracy, it is in its tone and substance actually a parody of commentary that appeared in the *Bild-Zeitung*. In an article about transforming the book into a film, Christel Buschmann quotes an excerpt from *Bild* that is very similar to this graveside speech (69). In its directness, the speech calls attention to the misuse of freedom of the press for financial gain, the reduction of human values to market considerations, the disregard of the rights and dignity of the individual, the violation of the spirit of the West German constitution, and the mutual interest of business and the press to oppose, on grounds of protecting democratic freedoms, any restriction of their right to exploitation. The speaker makes clear to the mourners—all representatives of the establishment—that "this order is valuable to all of us," that is, it should be protected because it permits making profit even from the destruction of an innocent person's human dignity.

Despite his harsh attack on the boulevard press, Böll emphasizes in the book and the film that the practices of the *News* are not the norm. While Katharina is being interrogated, a policewoman brings her fifteen clippings from several newspapers that have reported her story without names and without pictures, treating this minor event in an appropriate manner. But Katharina responds: "Who reads that? Everybody I know reads the *News*" (*WRE* 5: 422). Besides revealing something about Katharina and her circle, this statement points to the power of a single irresponsible newspaper to destroy individuals by labeling them communists and to create an atmosphere of hysteria for reactionary political purposes, and in the case of Katharina Blum to concoct "facts" with impunity because the victim is powerless.

In this respect Katharina's status as a model representative of the capitalist ethic is important because her fate shows that anyone without power is a potential victim when caught in the market mechanisms of a sensational press. Katharina is no Leni-like emissary of *Leistungsverweigerung*. She is an illustrious example of conformity, a proletarian without class consciousness striving to become a petty bourgeois by the accepted means of hard work and clean living. Her friends even call her the "nun." She holds three jobs, lives frugally, and cares for her family. She is "radically helpful" (*WRE* 5: 408), as one of her employers expresses it. And until her entanglement with the law and the *News*, her efforts have paid off. She has recently purchased a car and an apartment. Böll characterized her in an interview as someone who would become an "efficient, somewhat intimidating forty-five-year-old hotel director" (WI 1: 386). Still, the News puts her industriousness in doubt and attributes her success to prostitution and association with criminals. Contrasting with the News's depiction of Katharina is its treatment of the prominent Christian businessman, Sträubleder. When he is brought into the affair as Katharina's mysterious "gentleman caller" (Herrenbesuch), he is kept out of the public eye because of his power and connections.

The most important change from book to film, however, is in the murder scene itself. The book makes clear that Katharina's loss of honor, if understood as her impugned reputation and her destroyed material existence, is not her reason for shooting Tötges. Nor does she shoot Tötges to avenge her mother's death. The murder in the book is an act of self-defense, an attempt to protect her last remaining value, her personal dignity. Böll said of the shooting, "It is almost exclusively erotically determined" (WI 1: 329).

Katharina's defense attorney, Hubert Blorna, tries to make the same point by distinguishing between "thoughts of murder" and "plans for murder" (WRE 5: 465). Thoughts of murder, he says, are natural feelings of hatred that everyone at one time or another experiences. Plans for murder, on the other hand, are criminal actions. Katharina experiences the former but does not engage in the latter. Only after Katharina has made arrangements on Saturday to meet Tötges on Sunday at noon does she receive the invitation from Konrad Beiters, a friend of her aunt, to spend Saturday night alone in his apartment for reasons of privacy and security, and only there—after having set a meeting with Tötges—does Katharina have the opportunity to take Beiters's pistol. Even after she takes the gun, she has no plan to kill Tötges and considers calling off the interview. On Sunday morning before the scheduled meeting she goes to a café that journalists frequent, hoping to see what the person who destroyed her life looks like. After waiting two hours, she says, "I decided, if he were too repulsive, I would not go to the interview, and had I seen him, I would not have gone" (WRE 5: 471). When she returns to her apartment to wait for him she recalls: "The bell rang . . . and then he stood before me. . . . He said, 'Well, my little flower [a pun on her name Blum], what are we going to do now?' I didn't say a word but backed into the room. He followed me and said, 'Why are you looking at me so strangely? I suggest we have a little bang for starters' . . . and then he went for my dress. And I thought: 'If you want a bang, I'll give you one,' and I took the pistol out and shot him" (*WRE* 5: 471).

The sexual assault on Katharina at the end of the novella does not come from out of the blue. Throughout the story Katharina is subjected to sexual harassment. The police commissioner Beizmenne's first words to Katharina when he breaks into her apartment looking for Götten are, "Did he fuck you?" And the *News* uses sexual innuendo: "robber sweetheart" (*Räuberliebchen*) and "gentleman caller" (*Herrenbesuch*) in establishing her in the public's mind as a prostitute. Sexual phone calls and letters drive Katharina from her apartment. Thus, the shooting is related to the image that Tötges and the police have created of Katharina and that Tötges has come to accept himself. He is actually self-deceived and self-victimized by his own reporting—hoist with his own petard.

It is apparent that in the heated climate of the times, Schlöndorff and von Trotta realized that the ending of the book, with its imposition of erotic motivation for the murder, detracted from the political content of the story. Therefore, they suggested to Böll a different ending with a political bias, which the author endorsed as a good idea (*WI* 1: 670).

In his interview with Christian Linder, Böll summarized the ending of the film in this way:

> Schlöndorff has the journalist say to Katharina, "Well, what are you so excited about? I'm not responsible for what happened. Others make the headlines. I just deliver the story. Other people write it up. I don't have anything against you."—You understand? The journalist in the film declares his innocence and suggests—which is, by the way, perfectly logical—that they do a little business—I'm summarizing here in outline form.—"Listen, girl, there's a lot of money in this business for you. You tell your story and you'll get 10,000 marks." I find this conclusion better than the one in the book where guilt, innocence, and honor appear to be . . . integrated. (*WI* 1: 388)[35]

Böll's summary of the conclusion of the film is quite accurate. In the murder scene of the film there is no verbal sexual harassment and no attempted rape. The shooting is motivated by Katharina's total abhorrence of the reporter whose cynicism and commercial values have destroyed her. One of the most important conversations in both film and book has Katharina asking the state prosecutor Peter Hach "if the state—and that is how she put it—could not do something to protect her from this dirt and help restore her honor" (*WRE* 5: 420). Hach merely informs her that as a citizen she has the right to bring a private suit against the *News* (*WRE* 5: 541). Hence, Katharina is fully aware of her isolation, helplessness, and powerlessness in confrontation with the system. It is this feeling that the conclusion of the film enhances by heightening the political and economic aspects of the story and by playing down the sexual.

The violence, then, referred to in the subtitle of the work, that leads to more violence is clearly not just the violent assassination of Katharina's character but also the violence Böll sees in society as part of the normal, daily operation of its political economy—the violence inherent in business as usual, which he called in his 1972 speech before the SPD "the violence that is deposited in the banks" ("Gewalten, die auf der Bank liegen") (*WESR* 2: 605). In other words, *Katharina Blum* calls attention not only to the violence that Böll says "is . . . on the street in bombs, pistols, and stones" (*WESR* 2: 605), but also to "the kind of violence that is deposited in the banks and that is traded on the stock exchange" (*WESR* 2: 605), the violence that "rules our daily lives" and "prevent[s], deform[s], and falsifie[s] human values" (*WESR* 2: 606). Böll is even more explicit about the meaning of the ending of the film in an interview with Viktor Böll. Speaking of the shooting, he said:

> It is provoked . . . by Tötges's drivel. The shooting follows because she [Katharina] recognizes the total commercialization of her situation. . . . Tötges doesn't even have anything against her [Katharina]; on the contrary, he thinks he has done her a favor by making her famous and making it possible for her to earn a lot of money. . . . This moment, the recognition of the total marketability of her problem and of herself, in which she is completely and helplessly caught up, is the cause of the shooting. (*WI* 1: 671)

With the changing political climate, Böll's novella has taken on a new life. The prophecy that Böll's *Katharina Blum* was tied too much to the times to be a work of literature with staying power has not been proven true. Interest in the story is as alive as ever. Like all worthwhile literature, the novella has many facets that can arouse interest. The composer Tilo Medek commented after seeing the Schlöndroff film: "That is the material for a Verdi opera. It shows that true love is still possible."[36] His operatic version of the material premiered in Bielefeld in April 1991, with the American soprano Susan Maclean in the principal role. Currently, the interest in Böll's material focuses on the heroine as a representative of women in a male-dominated society.

Precisely this point of view led the actress Marlo Thomas to make *Katharina Blum* into a television film. Her film, *The Lost Honor of Kathryn Beck,* was shown nationwide on U.S. television in 1984 with Thomas in the title role and Kris Kristofferson playing her lover. Thomas sets the story in the United States but maintains the ending of the German film. She eliminates the sexual motivation for the shooting, making it clear the murder derives from Kathryn's unique situation as a woman, a situation in which a man could never find himself because he could not be victimized in the same way. That the story translates so easily from one milieu to another with little regard for the terrorist theme[37] shows the flexibility of the material and reveals the strength of the work as a tragedy of an innocent person whose flaw is decency.

The Safety Net
(Fürsorgliche Belagerung)
Background

After the publication of *Katharina Blum* in 1974 the problem of domestic terrorism did not abate. On 7 April 1977, while Attorney General Siegfried Buback was being driven to work, two persons on a motorcycle pulled next to his car. The passenger on the motorcycle drew out an automatic weapon and shot Buback, his driver, and his bodyguard. The same day the "Commando Ulrike Meinhof" claimed responsibility for the "execution" of Buback, whom Andreas Baader had called a state terrorist and who Baader's associate, Jan-Carl Raspe, had made responsible for the "murder" of Ulrike Meinhof. (On 8 May 1976 Meinhof had hanged herself in her prison cell.) The killing of Buback's chauffeur and guard also gave new meaning to Meinhof's statement that urban guerrillas "never directed actions against the people . . . only against the imperialist state apparatus" (Aust 350). Three weeks later, on 28 April, the sensational trial of Andreas Baader, Gudrun Ensslin, and Jan-Carl Raspe came to an end. They were sentenced to life in prison (the maximum penalty in West Germany) for murder and for organizing a criminal association.

The murder of Buback was only the beginning of what became West Germany's year of terror. On 30 July, Jürgen Ponto, director of the Dresden Bank, was shot to death in his dining room by three members of the RAF, one of whom was Susanne Albrecht, a young friend of the Ponto family. Ponto was, in fact, the godfather of Albrecht's sister. It was because of this family friendship that Albrecht and her two friends gained entrance into the Ponto home. And a few weeks later, on 5 September, domestic terrorism climaxed with the kidnapping of Hanns Martin Schleyer, president of the Employers' Association of the Federal Association of German Industry. In the process of committing the crime, the kidnappers killed four of Schleyer's police bodyguards. Those who belonged to the circle of possible targets of terrorists were now not only members of government but also bankers, industrialists, and their employees. These two episodes, the murder of Ponto and the kidnapping of Schleyer, provide the immediate background for Böll's *The Safety Net*. The protagonist of the novel, Fritz Tolm, is, like Schleyer, the newly elected president of a national employers' association and beginning a life dictated by total, twenty-four-hour protective *(fürsorglich)* surveillance, denying him any chance of a normal, human existence. And Tolm, also like Ponto, is in greatest danger from a relative who has become a terrorist.

At the time of Ponto's murder, the computer files of the Federal Criminal Office *(Bundeskriminalamt)* listed twelve hundred persons as members of the RAF and six thousand others as sympathizers to whom the active members could turn for help. The president of the Federal Criminal Office drew the pessimistic conclusion that it was impossible to keep tabs on so many people and at the same time protect possible targets of attack. He judged, therefore, that no one was any longer safe:

> It is not a question of a few people; it is a massive problem. Twelve hundred dangerous people in the Federal Republic simply can't be watched, and no one under such conditions can escape danger. Everyone knows that the observation of one person requires about twenty officers. We do not have 1200 times twenty people in the whole German criminal police force. That shows the importance of a permanent, routine, dragnet observation of these people in the form of computerized surveillance. (Aust 452)

In regard to Susanne Albrecht,[38] the president asserted that the police did not know that the Albrecht and the Ponto families were related and reasoned: "Even if we had known, what could we have done? Should we warn the associates of all these 1200—some of whom are highly placed persons—about the people they go around with? . . . And if I did, I would hear no end of reproaches" (Aust 452).

This public fear, which reached a state of near national paranoia, is the background of Böll's novel. The questions the novel deals with are: how can a democracy cope with terrorism without becoming a police state—the kind of state suggested by the federal police president's reference to "permanent, routine, dragnet observation . . . in the forms of computerized surveillance"? How is a normal life possible in a state of fear? Is the stifling protection of the state worse than the danger it attempts to avert? In *The Safety Net* Böll presents this problem of terrorism from the perspective of Fritz Tolm, a kind, decent representative of the establishment, who, because of his position, is a prime symbolic target for the terrorists.

Even before his kidnapping, Hanns Martin Schleyer had already been placed in the category of "security risk 1." He was always routinely accompanied by officers of the state police of Baden-Württemberg. His office in Cologne, his apartment in Cologne, and his house in Stuttgart were under constant protection. He had been given instructions by the police on what to check before going to bed, on getting up, and on going for a walk; various alarms had been installed around his house. This is the manner in which Fritz Tolm and his family live in *The Safety Net*. But despite all the police precautions, Schleyer was kidnapped. This point is the one Böll's novel tries to emphasize: total security is not only impossible, it is also a contradiction of freedom.

The final terrible achievement of Baader and Meinhof after seven years of urban warfare—from the founding of the RAF in 1970 to their deaths in 1976 and 1977—is what Böll depicts in *The Safety Net*.[39] Böll's novel shows that terrorists exacerbated many of the repressive aspects of the state that they had fought against: universal surveillance by technological means, the creation of new national and international police organizations, searches and seizures reminiscent of the Third Reich, harsh new criminal laws, inhumane conditions for prisoners, in general, oppression in the name of security by an omnipresent state. From the perspective of Fritz Tolm, his friends, family, associates, and the police, Böll presents the psychological state of West German society at the end of the 1970s.

Structure

The structure of *The Safety Net* (1979) manifests several similarities to previous works. Like most of Böll's novels since *And Never Said a Word*, it covers the period immediately prior to its publication, in this instance, three days in the late 1970s. Like *Group Portrait* it has over a hundred characters, promoting the translator of the novel, Leila Vennewitz (as she did with *Group Portrait*) to preface the novel with a list of personae to make the story easier to follow. Like *Billiards*, it shifts point of view with each chapter, and like *The Clown, Billiards,* and *And Never Said a Word,* it contracts narrative time as it expands narrated time. The recollections of Fritz Tolm go back to the war years, making it possible for Böll to treat forty years of German history in a period of about seventy-two hours. Again like most other works by Böll, the locales of the novel are Cologne and its surrounding farms and villages. In narrative strategy the novel also returns to the modernist methods of the 1950s and breaks with the post-modernist techniques of a researching narrator used in *Group Portrait* and *Katharina Blum*.

Böll divides his twenty-one chapters into the points of view of twelve characters. Chapters 1, 3, 9, and 12 reveal the perspective of Fritz Tolm; chapter 2 that of his daughter Sabine; chapter 4 that of Helga Hendler, the wife of Sabine's lover; chapters 5 and 18 present the point of view of Hubert Hendler, Helga's husband; chapters 6, 10, and 16 that of Rolf Tolm, Fritz's son; chapters 7, 14, and 17 that of Holzpuke, the head of Fritz Tolm's security; chapter 8 presents the point of view of Erna Breuer, a neighbor of Sabine; chapter 11 that of Bleibl, an industrialist and ex-Nazi; the point of view of chapter 13 is unclear; chapter 15 reveals the perspective of Käthe Tolm, Fritz's wife; chapter 19 that of the terrorist Veronica, Rolf's wife and Fritz's daughter-in-law; chapter 20 that of Katharina, Rolf's lover; and chapter 21 concludes the novel with the dual perspective of Fritz and Käthe Tolm.

The tempo of the novel begins very slowly and increases with each chapter until the pace in the final pages is breathtaking, with so many actions and decisions that the reader's credulity is severely tested. The pace of the novel becomes clear when one looks at the number of pages Böll assigns each chapter. Chapter 1 is a rambling narrative monologue of sixty-three pages; chapter 2 in the same style receives forty-nine pages; chapter 3, forty-five pages. The middle chapters average about fifteen pages each. And the final five chapters are only three to five pages long. This rhythm creates a narrative momentum that drives the story relentlessly forward but has the disadvantage of having three-quarters of the text cover the first day and of forcing all the action to the end. While this structure is typical of a suspense story, in this book, there are, in addition to the main plot of the assassination attempt on Fritz Tolm, so many subplots all coming to simultaneous conclusions that chance rather than inevitability dominates. This structure is obviously Böll's plan, but the accidentalness of so many concluding events undermines the political content of the novel.

Summary

Through recollections of Fritz and Käthe Tolm, the reader learns that at the end of the World War II, Fritz Tolm, the son of a poor school teacher, inherited a defunct village newspaper and a printing press. Because his past was free of Nazi associations, the occupying British forces provided him with a publishing license, sufficient paper, and experienced employees to revive an independent newspaper dedicated to the ideals of democracy. Success comes to Tolm without effort, and in time he buys up one local newspaper after another until he heads a small publishing empire. On the day the novel opens, he has just been elected president of an industrial association. Tolm is now a regional press tsar, but, nonetheless, in the manner of a typical Böll hero, he lacks ambition and radiates a tired humanity filled with self-doubt and capitalist melancholy. Nevertheless, he accepts resignedly the presidency and the danger the office represents, for he knows that in a short time his empire will be taken over or forced into bankruptcy by Zummerling, an even bigger publisher. Tolm's lack of interest in his work has already led to his relinquishing the daily affairs of his business. He prefers to pursue his interest in architecture and his hobby of bird-watching. He has over the years acquired a "liberal" image that now has a life of its own. He says of himself, "I was and remain a clever boy, but I lack the power to act" (*FB* 146). He lives in times that he characterizes as the "age of nice monsters" (*FB* 151), and he freely acknowledges that he and Zummerling are two of the monsters that make up the age. He is adept at the main skill expected of a president of the association. He can convincingly spout the bromides of cooperation between management and labor that allay the economic fears of the public. In this respect Tolm is reminiscent of Hans Schnier's father, the millionaire coal magnate, who appears so moderate and gentle on television that he is thrown into television debates as a visual representative of the humaneness of capitalism. Indeed, it is this aspect of Tolm's personality that makes him an ideal choice for the presidency of the national industrial association.

Fritz and Käthe Tolm have three children, Herbert, a student of philosophy and an environmental activist living in an alternative commune in a rundown building owned by his father; Sabine, a "beautiful princess" with true religious piety, married to a porno-addicted playboy millionaire who exploits industrial workers in the Third World; and Rolf, married to Veronica but now in the fourth year of living with Katharina Schröter. Rolf and Katharina live in a village near Cologne in a parish cottage provided by the local priest, Pastor Roickler. Although Rolf has a degree in finance, he is unemployable because of his conviction for taking part in a demonstration against the Zummerling Press that resulted in property damage and also because of his eight-year marriage to the terrorist Veronica Zelger, now in hiding with her lover Heinrich Bewerloh. Rolf is the father of two children, Holger I, whose mother is Veronica, and Holger II, whose mother is Katharina. While Holger I has been taken by his mother and Bewerloh to "somewhere in the Near East"; Holger II lives with Rolf and Katharina. Throughout the novel, the name "Holger" functions as a provocation because it calls to mind the militant RAF member Holger Meins, who in 1974 starved himself to death while in prison. Rolf and Katharina now lead an idyllic life, supporting themselves by gardening and helping neighbors with child care.

The terrorist Heinrich Bewerloh is an old friend of Rolf's and the Tolm family. He had a one-time relationship with Sabine when they were both young and has had his university education financed by Fritz Tolm. Bewerloh and Veronica are now known by the police to be plotting the assassination of a public figure, and Fritz Tolm is judged to be their prime target.

The Tolms, their friends, relatives, associates, and the police make up the characters of the novel. They are brought together for a period of seventy-two hours, which begins with the day of Fritz Tolm's election. On the morning of this same day his daughter Sabine, six months pregnant, leaves her husband to return to Tolmshoven, the Tolm estate. Her husband, however, is not the father of the child she is carrying. That man is Hubert Hendler, one of the policemen assigned to guard her. Still on the same day, Sabine leaves Tolmshoven to live with her brother Rolf and Katharina in their two-room cottage in the nearby village of Hubreichen. She arrives as Pastor Roickler decides to leave the priesthood and live with his girl friend, Anna.

On the second day Fritz Tolm receives news of the suicide of Kortschede, one of his "few true friends" (*FB* 338), who was passed over as association president because of his homosexual relationship with a young man suspected of being a terrorist. Kortschede has had his share of misfortune. His daughter committed suicide when she discovered that her fashionable leftist lover was merely interested in her money. She scrawled a lipstick farewell note on her hotel mirror proclaiming the most important message of the novel, "Socialism will still be victorious" (*FB* 387).

Kortschede has addressed a final letter to Fritz Tolm that contains economically dangerous "dark prophecies about the environment, atomic energy, the growth rate, banks, and industry" (*FB* 375), as well as about "lobbies, bribes, and the future" (*FB* 395). His pessimism and depression over the state of affairs in West Germany in the late seventies is the cause of his suicide. The letter is considered so explosive because of its dark prophecies about the economy that the police have for the time being withheld it from Tolm.

On this second day Holger I arrives alone at the Frankfurt airport from Istanbul. He is taken to his grandfather. On this afternoon Tolm also receives news of Bewerloh's suicide in Istanbul. Tolm demands that the body be brought back to Germany for burial by threatening to reveal the contents of Kortschede's letter, which he now has received from the police. On learning that Sabine has left her husband, the policeman Hubert Hendler leaves his wife to live with Sabine.

On the third day the funerals of Kortschede and Bewerloh take place. Veronica, Rolf's wife and Bewerloh's mistress, returns from Istanbul and gives herself up at the Dutch border. She also warns that her son Holger I has a "bomb in his brain" (*FB* 404). Her warning about her son, however, comes too late, for Holger has already set fire to the Tolm estate. Nonetheless, Fritz and Käthe Tolm are unharmed because they are attending the funeral of Bewerloh instead of the funeral of Kortschede. The decision to attend with their children the funeral of a terrorist who had once been their friend is a symbolic rejection of their association with power and corruption and an affirmation of the simple life of their son Rolf and of the environmental and social concerns of their son Herbert. As Fritz and Käthe see the smoke from their burning estate, Fritz says to Käthe: "You know that I have always loved you. And there is something else you must know [repeating Verna Kortschede's last words] . . . that socialism must come, must be victorious . . . " (*FB* 414). They have no regrets about the burning of Tolmshoven, their medieval estate, because it is about to be lost anyway to the coal interests that plan to exploit the vast coal reserves under their mansion. The sinking of the land would destroy the house in any case. The novel ends like *Billiards,* with all the Tolms reconciled and the main characters resolved to begin a new life. Even the Tolms' acceptance of the destruction of Tolmshoven has similarities to the Fähmels' acceptance of the destruction of Saint Anthony's Abbey. The reconciliation of both families to the losses of architectural masterpieces indicates an affirmation of human values over material ones. The novel ends with Käthe's question, "Is anyone hurt or in danger?" (*FB* 415). When she receives the answer no, she replies, "Then I've heard of worse things" (*FB* 415), and Fritz laughs.

Analysis

Although there are clear references to time scattered throughout the novel, it remains extremely difficult to determine the exact extent of the narrative time; nonetheless, it is no more than three days, albeit three days incredibly packed with events. The arrangements for the release of Bewerloh's body and for both his and Kortschede's funeral, as well as the planning of the terrorist attack at Kortschede's funeral, are only some of the examples. It is not just a question of too much happening in such a short time, it becomes a question of the physical possibility of its happening at all in the time limits of the novel. Along with the demands of working it all out, the novel puts an enormous strain on the reader's ability to suspend belief.

Despite this criticism the novel is well executed. Through what Helmut Heißenbüttel calls *Rollenprosa* (characterization through language) and through language itself, Böll reveals much of what is morally questionable in West German society. This social analysis begins with the semantic contrast in the title between the military term *Belagerung* (siege) and the modifying adjective *fürsorglich* (caring, caring for, helpful, helping). Böll stated in an interview with Robert Stauffer: "I very consciously chose the title *Fürsorliche Belagerung* in order to liberate the concept *Belagerung* from the pure atmosphere of threat. Such a title does not come about by chance; it is well thought out. The choice of the adjective *fürsorglich* was most difficult because I wanted to establish some ironic distance from the word *Belagerung*" (Stauffer 26). The title might well be translated as "Protective Siege."

Unfortunately, the English title *The Safety Net* directs the reader's attention away from both the author's method and his intent. It is, however, important to acknowledge that in his introduction to the novel Böll himself used the word *Sicherheitsnetz* (security net or safety net) to describe the elaborate surveillance measures taken by the police.[40] Still, the phrase "safety net" in American usage calls to mind the social safety net of welfare payments, unemployment insurance, medicare coverage—matters that have very little to do with the novel.

Böll's attempt to look at West German society through semantics, suggested by the contrast in the title, revolves foremost around the words *Bewachung, bewacht/Überwachung, überwacht,* all derived from the root *wachen* (to watch). *Bewachung* and *bewacht* refer to watching people in order to protect them and *Überwachung* and *überwacht* to watching people in order to spy on them. Böll actually had personal experience with this dual function of observation. In the above-mentioned interview with Robert Stauffer, Böll relates a humorous episode as a guest in a foreign embassy in Bonn. He had to be accompanied to the toilet by a security officer who had to lower the shades before he could enter the rest room because, as the officer explained, the window offered a perfect view from the neighboring roofs, and one could not be too certain who was out there (Stauffer 28). Also, when Aleksandr Solzhenitsyn was exiled from the Soviet Union in 1974, his first residence in the West was with Böll. For days his house was surrounded by police and reporters, making the most ordinary private action a public event. Also, in 1977, on Böll's sixtieth birthday, prominent politicians visited him with an entourage of security. In addition, Böll and his sons were suspected of being RAF sympathizers, which also led to surveillance of him and his family.[41]

The English language has some difficulty expressing graciously the distinction between *Bewachung* and *Überwachung,* but to Böll, linguistic experimentation is at the heart of the novel's method of social analysis. Böll's own words provide the best explanation of what he is doing in the novel. In his 1976 interview with René Wintzen, during the time he was working on *The Safety Net,*[42] Böll said:

> I believe that every writer, no matter whether he is French, Russian, or Swedish approaches problems, conflicts, complications through his interest in language. The starting point is not one's so-called commitment [*Engagement*], rather it is language, and with language one deals with whatever the subject matter is: state or society. . . . I do not believe that the primary thing is what one attacks. The primary thing is the language and the wish to present a specific problem, a specific thing, a person, his or her entanglements, difficulties, and possible guilt. I do not see the starting point as morality—as it might appear. A lot is just play. . . . And since I'm not capable of writing the historical or utopian novel— and don't care to—I find myself getting involved again and again with the problems of today, which I reveal in language. . . . Naturally there are times when one consciously attacks something political, a special development, where morality is the starting point and language is secondary. But most of the time the starting point is the language itself. *(WI 1: 507)*

In an interview with Dieter Zillingen Böll explained the main theme of *The Safety Net* as the problem of *Bewachung-Überwachung:*

A person watched over, someone watched for his own security, becomes at the same time a prisoner. That is what I wanted to demonstrate. I wanted to show also the imprisonment of the spied on, a group to which one of his [Fritz Tolm's] sons belongs, and that of the watched over, the group to which he [Fritz Tolm] belongs, and also how the watching transforms the two groups. I see that as one of the most important phenomena and problems of our time, not just in the Federal Republic, but internationally as well. People are simply destroyed by surveillance. (Zillingen 16)

In the same interview Böll added, "The question, who is worse off, the watched or the watched over, is the basic theme of the novel" (Zillingen 17). In his interview with Robert Stauffer, Böll also relates the German security problem to the Holocaust in that both have their origin in German perfectionism, the desire to do to the ultimate limit whatever is done, to carry things out to their perfect conclusion.[43] "There is something terrible," he said, "in the speed with which this over-organized perfection occurred. There is something terrible in the attempted perfection of our security system. I perceive it as a danger rather than as a protection because these security measures produce fear and tension which can become dangerous" (Stauffer 28).

In this introduction to the novel, Böll expressed the topic of the novel slightly differently, "The problems and conflicts of the characters in this novel develop out of their desire for and their idea of security, of a totally external security that does not exist" ("Einführung in die *FB*" 74). In this introduction Böll divides the personnel of the novel into four categories: the watched over, the spied on, the watchers, and the *Sicherheitsgeschädigte*—those whose lives are harmed by the security measures. The first group comprises the businessmen and the politicians who are potential victims of the terrorists; the second, those suspected of terrorism, and those associated with the suspects; the third group, the police and security agents; and the fourth group, those in the other three groups along with their friends and associates who have their family, professional, or private lives damaged by surveillance. Böll explains the moral crux of the novel by asking two questions, "Does providing protection create more security or more insecurity, and how many people suffer merely by getting caught in the security net" ("Einführung in die *FB*" 74).

At one point in the novel, after Tolm has pondered the effect security has had on the marriages of his daughter Sabine and his son Rolf, he is forced to conclude, "I no longer try to convince myself that there is any kind of security at all, internal or external" (*FB* 164). With this statement the novel expands the meaning of security to include the emotional as well as the physical realm. Stephen Smith (see his "Schizos Vernissage . . . ") and Bernd Balzer (see his "Ausfall in die Sorglosigkeit . . . ") have both pointed out that the tension between helping and harming suggested in the title goes far beyond just the political problem of *Bewachung-Überwachung;* the novel treats also the problem of limiting the freedom of others, infringing on their rights, restricting their development regardless of whether the harm comes from good or bad intentions, from caring for them or controlling them, from love or suspicion. Too much security even distances one from truly humane existential concerns. Pastor Roickler, for example, leaves the "protection" of the church not just to live with his girl friend Anna and to escape living the lie of celibacy but also to find the freedom denied him by his comfortable, protected existence.

Sabine also claims the right to satisfy her repressed emotional life denied her in a protective marriage to a generous but unsatisfying husband. Erna Breuer chooses to leave her husband who has given her a secure good life with a house, a garden, and a pool but who cannot give her the internal security that comes from tenderness. In the novel the rubric "caring" *(fürsorglich)* specifically covers the providing of internal as well as external security.

The many unsuccessful marriages in the novel are all the result of an insufficiency of one or the other type of security. As such, marriage functions in the novel as a metaphor for the state of the nation, and the state of the nation serves as a paradigm of human relations. The relationship of husband and wife is included in the conflict implied in the meaning of the title "besieging with care." Sabine and Erna are besieged with care that is too often merely external. It is not by chance that old Tolm ends the novel by combining his declaration of love for Käthe with the hope that socialism will triumph because the idea of socialism in the novel stands for the realization of the proper balance between providing care and protection, that is, satisfying a person's internal and external needs. The novel makes the problems of marriage and the problems of the nation one. Both at the personal and at the collective level, happiness depends on whether external and internal needs are met.

Nowhere in the novel is the providing of merely external security successful. Although Tolm's life is saved at the end of the novel, it is not because of the security measures of the police. When Veronica returns, she could easily carry out her attack, but she simply chooses to give herself up because she is incapable of murder. When Holger I torches Tolmshoven, security is unable to prevent it. The marriages that fail do so in the midst of material security because they are unable to provide internal security. Not only the Fischers' and the Breuers' marriages suffer this fate but four of Bleibl's marriages also end in divorce, and Rolf and Veronica's ends in separation. The new union of Erna Breuer and Peter Schubler seems doomed because of a lack of external security. Schubler is prevented by Erna's husband from finding adequate employment, so he cannot provide Erna the minimum external security that she needs. On the other hand, the relationship between Rolf and Katharina succeeds because each has modest external needs and they offer each other internal security. The novel leaves open what kind of arrangement will develop from the affair between Sabine and Hubert Hendler after Hubert leaves his wife, whom he still loves, but the novel suggests the possibility of a *solution à trois*.[44] The only marriage tested by time, Fritz and Käthe's, has survived thirty-five years because they have learned to sustain each other both physically and emotionally.

That the problem of marriage is even more central to the novel than the important question of surveillance is easily recognized from the structure of the book. The only terrorist whose consciousness Böll presents is Veronica's, and she is allotted merely five pages of the entire novel after she has ceased to be a terrorist. The presentations of the consciousnesses of Sabine, Erna Breuer, Hubert and Helga Hendler, and Bleibl cover half the book. In these pages it is marriage that is on their minds. When one considers also the number of pages related to marriage in the interior monologues of Fritz and Käthe, as well as of Rolf and Katharina, it is clear that personal human relations in the context of the family are more important within the novel than the direct political aspect of security.

The Safety Net presents West Germany as a deeply troubled land. In his *Frankfurter Vorlesungen* of 1966 Böll asked, "Why is it that no one writes a happy novel about this flourishing land?" (*WESR* 2: 60). In the sixties the answer was clearly that West Germany was still dealing with the Nazi past. In the seventies the phenomenon of terrorism prevented the happy novel, but terrorism was only the surface manifestation of deeper social problems. The RAF terrorists saw remnants of fascist values in West Germany and argued that they were nurtured by the restoration of capitalism after the war and were perpetuated by old Nazis in government and business. *The Safety Net*, through the actions of the majority of Fritz Tolm's contemporaries, illustrates this point of view. In 1979 Böll still was convinced that a happy novel about West Germany would be a lie. Although he rejected the terrorists' solution, his essays of this period encourage political leaders to take notice of the validity of some of criticisms of the terrorists. His *Safety Net* reveals how much he agreed with the radicals. The difference in the novel between Fritz Tolm's activist children and Bewerloh is only their methods. The book is striking also in that it shows how prosperity often does not solve social problems, but creates them; material plenty does not comfort the grieving soul but merely agonizes the psyche.

The novel abounds in suicides: Kortschede's, his daughter's, Bewerloh's, that of the son of the farmer Schwergen, who is described as "a nice young man, loved, a good dancer," who hangs himself, as the novel emphasizes, "without apparent reason . . . with no motives to be discovered" (*FB* 225). And there are murders, too, not just those planned by the terrorists that are never carried out, or the one committed by Bleibl during the Nazi period, but the unexplained murder of Frau Halster in the idyllic village of Hubreichen, committed by her husband Jupp, "a fellow with an economically successful, well organized farm with pictures of the Madonna on his wall . . . well-off, well thought of, a silent man who treated his workers so well that his generosity was legendary" (*FB* 226). All these dissolved unions, suicides, and murders are surrounded in the novel by an atmosphere of insecurity.

The Safety Net in its weighing of the dangers of security and insecurity becomes Böll's most philosophical novel. By exploring and exposing through language the moral, religious, political, and economic aspects of caring, the novel probes the metaphysics of security and insecurity. Under such conditions it is not surprising that the most frequently occurring word in the novel is *fear (Angst)*. It appears 107 times on sixty-three pages.[45] In keeping with the implication of the theme announced in the title, the word *fear* appears consistently in the idioms "fear of" *(Angst vor)* and "fear for" *(Angst um)*. The word appears 9 times on the first two pages in contrast to the words "worry/worried about" *(Sorge/besorgt um)*. Fritz Tolm says on page 2, "Worry had been suppressed; now there was no more fear of anything, just fear for—for Sabine, also for Herbert."

The people in the novel are fraught with fears, not just for their lives, but of a loss of security of various kinds. Tolm fears increased power in the hands of a few industrialists like Bleibl and Herbtholer. Rolf, Herbert, and their friends fear unemployment in the form of *Berufsverbot*. Besides economic fears, there is the ideological fear that the media will be concentrated in the hands of a few press tsars like Zummerling and Amplanger. Parents fear a developing generation gap. Neighbors fear the loss of friendship because of intolerance. Spouses fear losing a loved one to divorce or separation. And there is above all the fear of surveillance. The motif "chaos and disintegration everywhere" ("Ringsum Chaos und Auflösung") indicates the atmosphere of terror that does not come from urban guerrillas alone but is endemic in the system.

The West German society depicted in the novel lacks a spirit of community, destroys neighborhoods, and, despite its material abundance, produces fear best of all. The novel elevates two concepts fallen into disrepute since their exploitation and misuse by fascist propaganda in the Hitler years: *Gemeinschaft* and *Heimat*. To Böll these two concepts, correctly understood, need to be revived, for they are essential for internal and external security and, hence, form the basis of Böllian socialism. But Böll is no idealist suggesting an escape to the village of Hubreichen. Rolf and Katharina, who live there, know the idyll in their beflowered cottage is only temporary. "We can't grow tomatoes forever," Rolf says (*FB* 233). And Rolf wants most of all to practice his profession in banking and finance. All the Tolms are aware that the idyll in Hubreichen, like the "paradise in the tombs" in *Group Portrait*, must come to an end, that reality must dominate, and they realize that it is essential that social critics like Rolf and communists like Katharina and environmentalists like Herbert and wise and tolerant people like Fritz and Käthe become active in shaping a better, more humane West German society. Now that East and West Germany have united, the novel can be read as a plea for a caring (*fürsorglich*), united Germany that will dispel the palpable fear existing in the former GDR in matters of material security.

The frequency of the word *fear,* is matched in the novel only by the frequency of the word *nice (nett)*. *Nice* occurs in the novel 104 times on seventy-four pages.[46] The repetition of this word and its various synonyms, such as *dear (lieb)* and *sweet (süß)*, has led Wolfram Schütte in his review (see "Lauter nette Menschen") to call Böll's language in *The Safety Net* "trivial" and "kitsch" and has caused Marcel Reich-Ranicki in his review (see "Nette Kapitalisten und nette Terroristen") to write with sarcasm: "Erna Breuer is a 'nice, dear, pretty woman,' Amplanger is 'nice, educated, and clever,' Plotzkehler is a 'nice and energetic teacher,' Karl is a 'very, very nice fellow,' Claudia is 'a nice girl,' Roickler is 'a nice pastor,' Sabine Fischer is 'a nice woman,' Holger I is 'a nice young boy,' Peter is 'a very nice young man,' the young Zummerling is 'really nice,' the

Köhlers are 'nice, simple people,' and the Bangors are 'nice, she nicer than he.' That's what I call nice prose.'' Reich-Ranicki could have added that even Bewerloh is called a ''bomb of niceness'' (*FB* 152). Both Schütte and Reich-Ranicki focus on one of the most important aspects of the novel but misunderstand what Böll is doing with his language. To conclude, as they do, that Böll has suddenly lost his sense of style after forty years of writing and not to try to discover the function of Böll's repetitive language, limited vocabulary, and simple characterizations is to relinquish one's critical faculty and to dwell merely on the surface of the text.

Böll indicates what he is doing when he has Rolf and Katharina say of Pastor Roickler that he is ''really nice and humane'' after he helps them settle in Hubreichen, and then has them both add ''there are also nice and humane capitalists, even nice communists, nice liberals, and they themselves are in their way nice too'' (*FB* 54). This passage underlines with the single adjective, *nice*, one important aspect of Böll's social criticism. It points out that in liberal, pluralistic society the way to succeed, to get on, to get ahead, whether it is on the right or the left or in the political center, is to be *nice*. Niceness oils the machinery of success. In a free society niceness is the prerequisite for achieving one's ends. Böll's criticism is the same as that made fifty years ago by Robert Maynard Hutchins when Hutchins was president of the University of Chicago. At that time he recognized that the bourgeois function of the American university was the teaching of niceness. He characterized higher education as the ''place where nice boys and girls have a nice time under the supervision of nice men and women in a nice environment.''[47] The novel makes clear that whether one is an industrialist or a press tsar, a terrorist or a chief of police, a radical activist or a conservative farmer, one needs to be perceived as nice. The unwritten motto of the ''free democratic basic order'' of the Federal Republic is ''appear nice.'' Contemporary usage has developed variations on this theme to make necessary subtle distinctions between *nice, very nice, really nice, (nett, recht nett, echt nett, wirklich nett, sehr nett).* Bourgeois society is only nice on the surface, Böll implies. Every corruption, betrayal, buy-out, and sell-out is done nicely. All negotiating, all bargaining, all human intercourse requires a pleasant façade. It is the best way to get the better of the competition, to dominate the enemy. Every act, good or evil, generous or self-seeking, is accomplished better with niceness. The novel makes clear that whether one is planning a business takeover, a terrorist attack, a divorce, a marriage, a separation, or a desertion, whether one is creating employment or increasing unemployment, whether one deals in private or public affairs, amicability is the best weapon and the best defense. If the manifested niceness is real so much the better. The novel claims the power for niceness that Karl Marx once attributed to money. It can help the lame to walk, the blind to see, and enable the weak to become strong. The novel shows a smile is more effective than a gun. This point is the one intended by Böll's language. That is why there are just "nice" and "truly nice" people in the novel, whether Bewerloh or the Tolms.

Certainly the authentic alternative to niceness is not rudeness nor meanness, but honesty. Being nice is a very nice thing, indeed, but Böll's novel points out that the language of today to describe the good and the bad often is the same. Böll calls attention to the purpose of his idiom and sums up his intention when he has Fritz Tolm declare how nice Bewerloh is and then adds: "The concepts 'nice' and 'niceness' sa[y] nothing, not the slightest thing about what a person is capable of. One ought not to trust nice people too much" (*FB* 52).

In his *Frankfurter Vorlesungen* Böll said, "As author . . . I do not fear educated interpretations of [of my work] from opponents nor from my supporters—I fear attempts at interpretation that approach the text without prerequisites when the text has prerequisites" (*WESR* 2: 46). In the case of *The Safety Net,* the prerequisites are not only economic, political, and religious but linguistic as well.

It has been mentioned above that the structure of *The Safety Net* resembles that of *Billiards,* but the similarity goes even deeper than just the handling of time and point of view. The ending of *The Safety Net* also exhibits a variation of the conclusion of *Billiards.* As the Fähmels on the fateful day of Heinrich Fähmel's eightieth birthday decide to alter their lives, so too do the Tolms in the few hours following Fritz Tolm's election to the presidency of the association. Fritz and Käthe Tolm choose to shift their allegiance from the establishment to their children. They do so by attending Bewerloh's funeral instead of Kortschede's. With this act, Fritz rejects what the presidency of the association stands for, and he and Käthe demonstrate solidarity with the critics of society rather than with its supporters. Their children too make important decisions. Rolf and Katharina conclude their idyll in Hubreichen and hope to enter the professions they have trained for. Herbert cancels the demonstration he has planned to block all the roads into the city to protest air pollution because his mother has persuaded him it may cost the lives of people who need emergency transportation. Sabine opts for a new life with Hubert Hendler. And Veronica gives herself up to the police. For the Tolms these momentous changes are sealed in a symbolic fire, for when Holger I burns down Tolmshoven there can be no return to their old way of life.

The conclusions of *Billiards* and *The Safety Net* differ, however, in one major respect, reflecting a significant change in Böll's political position from 1959 to 1979. The Fähmels retreat into a private sphere, but the Tolms enter the world of active opposition to the status quo.

The Safety Net is an uncomfortable book, for it represents the beginning of a more intense interest by Böll in the need for social change in prosperous West Germany. Böll's socialism, which manifested itself for the first time as a clear commitment in *Group Portrait,* has become in *The Safety Net* less utopian and more realistic.

Women in a River Landscape
(Frauen vor Flußlandschaft)
Background

In 1967, in an interview with Marcel Reich-Ranicki, Böll labeled himself a "verhinderter Kommunist" (*WI* 1: 62), that is, that he was not a communist but would have been one had historical circumstances been different between the wars at the time he was growing into political awareness, that is, had the Stalinists not betrayed socialism and the Nazis not persecuted communists. But more specifically Böll expressed his sympathy for communism in his 1961 essay on Karl Marx, in which he portrays the founder of scientific socialism and the father of dialectical materialism as a great humanist (*WESR* 1: 395–413).

Despite this pro-Marxist attitude, however, Böll's protagonists have been socialists or communists only in a naive and unaffiliated way that derives as much from their religious convictions as it does from their moral-political understanding. And although the author himself reflected long on politics, his socialism was also more intuitive than ideological. The characters Leni and her son Lev in *Group Portrait with Lady* (1971) illustrate this kind of natural communism. In fact, Böll models Leni after his mother, whom he once described as the only true Catholic leftist he ever knew ("Interview mit mir selbst" 10). This statement reinforces the idea that Böll's concept of socialism was, indeed, quasi-religious, for his mother was a loyal, though freethinking, Catholic who voted regularly for the Catholic Center party.

Böll's last novel, *Women in a River Landscape* (1985), exploits even further this relationship to socialism found in his previous works. Although on the surface more a humanist than a leftist apologetic, it nonetheless offers a devastating socialist criticism of West Germany. As the title suggests, the novel is first about women and the role they play in the nation's capital on the Rhine. But by exploring the relationships women have to their husbands and lovers, Böll reveals the ethical-moral void in West German political and economic life. Thus, the novel is not obtrusively ideological but presents a subtext that is clearly Christian-Marxist or Christian-socialist.

In the year 1753 the Academy of Dijon proposed a topic for a competition that read, "What is the origin of inequality among men, and is it authorized by natural law?" In his contribution to this competition Rousseau explained social inequality with the famous sentence, "The first person who enclosed a piece of land and said: 'This is mine' and found people stupid enough to believe it, was the true founder of bourgeois society" (535). Immediately after these words, Rousseau warned his readers, "You are lost if you forget that the fruits of the earth belong to all and that the earth belongs to no one" (535). But already by 1767 Simon Nicolas Henri Linquet in his *Theory of Civil Law or Fundamental Principles of Society* could remark, "The spirit of the law is property."[48] The perception in Linquet's sentence that Marx quotes in *Das Kapital* and the insight in Rousseau's statement on the relation of ownership to power and inequality are the ideas that inform Böll's last novel.

While Böll's *Group Portrait with Lady* demonstrates through its heroine, Leni Pfeiffer, and her son, Lev, the possibility of a profitless and classless society, his *Women in a River Landscape* exposes the social forces that prevent this socialist ideal from developing. *Women in a River Landscape* is based on the principle that an understanding of bourgeois democracy is impossible without a comprehension of the interplay among economics, politics, law, and culture. To claim to understand one independently of the others is a metaphysical delusion. The novel begins by showing that the possession of property translates into power over those with less property and ends by revealing that without change in property relations, the issues of inequality, class justice, and pseudo-democracy become permanent social phenomena. Although the hero, Ernst Grobsch, commits himself to social change, there is not the slightest indication that he and his few friends can be successful in reforming from within West German political and economic life. This suppressed knowledge that they are expending effort in a hopeless but noble cause produces the melody of resignation that runs through the novel. It is this prevailing social pessimism that more than anything else accounts for the melancholy that dominates the work, especially in the suffering psyches of the female characters. While the proletarian Grobsch opts for struggle, his decision to do so in a major bourgeois party undercuts the hope his decision offers because in reality all the major parties are committed to the existing system. Thus, the novel is fraught with an insoluble contradiction. It tries to indicate that change is possible but leaves the reader with a sense of futility. Nevertheless, behind this un-Marxian pessimism can be discerned the bedrock theory of Marxist economic determinism: that no matter how varied the structure of bourgeois democracy becomes, no matter how independently interest groups develop, no matter how deeply embedded in the constitution the separation of powers is, as long as there are no or few restrictions on the acquisition of property, the class that controls society's economy will dominate its politics, law, and culture.

The West German liberal society Böll presents in the novel is actually best characterized not as democracy but as oligarchy in its classical sense as defined by Plato in the *Republic,* Book VIII. Here Socrates is asked, "And what manner of government do you term oligarchy?" Socrates responds: "A government resting on a valuation of property, in which the rich have power and the poor man is deprived of it. . . . And in proportion as riches and rich men are honored in the state, virtue and the virtuous are dishonored."[49]

In the novel Böll makes his most effective criticism of West German democracy semantically, by distinguishing between *regieren* and *herrschen*. These two words mean much the same in English, namely, "to rule." *Regieren,* however, means to rule through a system of government, through political means; it is related to the word *regime*. In the text Böll uses it to mean rule through elected officials; therefore, his words *Regierer* and *Regierende* refer to representatives in elected office. *Herrschen,* on the other hand, derives from the word *Herr* (lord); in Böll's text it means to rule by means of class standing, to exert power and authority through position. Hence, his words *Herrscher* and *Herrschende* always imply those who govern but are not elected. In West Germany the *Herrscher* are the people (in all cases men) behind the scenes who, on the basis of their economic power, determine political power. The *Regierer* (again all men) are those who execute authority for the *Herrscher* in a legal system. The *Herrscher* are the bankers, capitalists, industrialists or, in another word from the text, the *Geldadel* (*FF* 81), the nobility of money. The *Regierer* are the politicians who manage the political corporation, administer the business of democracy, the people whom the *Herrscher* maintain in office as long as they are effective and efficient in the execution of their assigned tasks. The English version of the novel usually renders *regieren* as "to rule" and *herrschen* as "to control"—a reasonable solution to a ticklish problem of translation.

Contained in this simplified view of society is then another class that must be *regiert* and *beherrscht,* that is, ruled and controlled. Böll gives this class the expected label "proletarian" (*FF* 91). This group has little or no influence, and besides being ruled and controlled is manipulated, dominated, and exploited. Böll's tripartite social structure is only slightly more nuanced than Marx's bipartite division into bourgeoisie and proletariat.

In 1985, while working on the novel, Böll published an essay entitled "Die ungehaltene Rede vor dem deutschen Bundestag" (An Ungiven Speech before Parliament) (*Fähigkeit* 39–53). He organized this address under four headings: "The dignity of the person is inviolate," "All people are equal before the law," "Property has its obligations," and "The politically persecuted have the right to asylum." What gives these topics burning relevance is that they are all quotations from the Basic Law of the Federal Republic. This ungiven speech can serve as an introduction to the novel. Böll speaks here in a definitive way of the difference between *herrschen* and *regieren*. In reference to the Flick scandal, in which an executive of the Flick conglomerate paid bribes to all three major parties— Christian Democrats, Social Democrats, and Free Democrats—in return for favorable tax legislation, Böll said: "This executive is a *Herr,* a proven *Herrscher.* That such a person does not bother about *regieren* is well documented. If he were offered a minister's post he would probably laugh" (*Fähigkeit* 45–46). On the basis of the outcome of the scandal—no prison sentences and slight fines for those involved—Böll concluded: "All people are equal before the law? Obviously not!" (*Fähigkeit* 46). Böll reasoned that this perversion of democracy and justice derived from property. It was inevitable, he concluded, that property led to power and that this power led to its abuse. To highlight this corruption of bourgeois idealism Böll quoted Article 14 of the West German constitution, which proclaims, "Property has obligations; its use should serve the common good." Then he followed with a bitter formulation of the practical meaning of this passage, "It [property] obliges the owner to only one thing: to the acquisition of more and more property" (*Fähigkeit* 47–48). The ideas in this speech and this final restatement of Marx's law of capital accumulation, along with the ideas of Linquet and Rousseau, are what make up the ideological positions of *Women in a River Landscape,* and Böll incorporated these positions into the novel, often with the identical language he used in his ungiven speech.

Structure

Böll calls *Women in a River Landscape* a novel in dialogues and soliloquies. It can be described as an experiment in dramatic form. Since the novel consists of only the spoken word, except for comments amounting to stage directions, it resembles a play of great length, divided, however, not into acts, but into twelve chapters. The motto introducing this dramatic novel is a poem from Goethe's *West-östlicher Divan,* which announces with a certain amount of irony the major theme of the work.

Wanderers Gemütsruhe
(Wanderer's Peace of Mind)

Übers Niederträchtige
Niemand sich beklage;
Denn es ist das Mächtige,
Was man dir auch sage.

In dem Schlechten waltet es
Sich zu Hochgewinne,
Und mit Rechtem schaltet es
Ganz nach seinem Sinne.

In paraphrase the poem reads: Let no one complain about baseness *(das Niederträchtige),* for no matter what they tell you it is the power in the land. In an evil person (or in bad times) [*dem Schlechten*] it leads to great profits, and with the law (or with the just person) [*dem Rechten*] it does as it pleases. Following the motto, Böll adds prefatory remarks that describe the major characters and explain their relationships to each other.

The advantage of this form is the freedom it gives Böll to work completely in the idiom spoken by people with whom he is most familiar: the educated middle class, intellectuals, politicians, entrepreneurs. Even when representatives of the working class appear, they are always depicted as intelligent and keenly observant. No one represents the uneducated, stunted, and deprived proletariat. Thus, Böll works in the novel with a level of language that is essentially his own, and he has no need to imitate an idiom foreign to him. The disadvantage of this dramatic form is the limitation it puts on the author's narrative talent. The lack of narration forces Böll to inform the reader entirely through conversations. Characters, therefore, tell each other facts that they surely already know. This unnaturalness is most obvious in conversations between Erika and Hermann Wubler, who have been married for thirty-six years and speak of events in their past as if for the first time. Also, the novel is characterized by lengthy monologues that occur with no immediate motivation. But one such soliloquy, Ernst Grobsch's twenty-three-page speech, comprising the whole of chapter 6, produces the artistic high point of the novel. Standing alone as a self-contained first-person narrative, this monologue is reminiscent of Böll's best early short stories. In this confessional form that Böll practically invented as a genre in the 1950s, Grobsch not only exposes the corruption of his mentor, Minister Plukanski, for whom he works as speech writer and assistant, and lays bare the opportunistic ruthlessness of their party but also reveals his own too-eager willingness to compromise his social ideals for a political career.

The temporal structure of the novel is like that of several other previous works. The present time of the novel covers a period of a little more than three days, during which the major characters make momentous decisions to change their lives and during which Böll presents a political tableau of the entire postwar period.

Chapters 1 to 6 cover the preparations made by various characters to attend a high mass commemorating the death of the founder of their party and the events that are to follow in the evening celebrating the anniversary of the party. Chapters 7 to 10 cover the following day, as Minister Plukanski's death becomes known; the party announces his successor, Fritz Blaukrämer; and the new minister celebrates his political promotion with a party despite the suicide of his wife that morning in a mental institution and the death of his predecessor. Chapter 11 covers the morning after Blaukrämer's party, as Erika Wubler and various friends of old Heinrich von Kreyl meet in Erika's living room to advise the old man about the offer of the party to have him replace the retiring president of the republic. The time in chapter 12 is indefinite but covers the period between Heinrich's rejection of the offer and the acceptance of the position by his rival, the ambitious Dimpler.

It is only natural that this dramatic novel would be adapted for performance. Hans Krogmann and Christian Linder have converted the material into a radio play running an hour and forty minutes, which premiered 17

December 1986 on Bavarian (BR) and West German Radio (WDR), and Volker Schlöndorff has prepared a stage version that ran successfully in Munich in February 1988.

Summary

The novel opens with a breakfast scene on the terrace of the Wubler villa overlooking the Rhine. Erika Wubler refuses to dress for the high mass to commemorate the death of Erftler-Blum, the founder of the currently ruling political party. Although Böll never mentions the party by name, it is clearly modeled after the CDU, as Erftler-Blum is after Konrad Adenauer. Erika has overheard conversations of the previous night between her husband Hermann and other leading members of the party, who are plotting face-saving strategies to cover up political failures and corruption. Erika has heard similar conversations before, but this time she simply refuses to support her husband again. She tells him that she will not attend this political-religious affair nor the celebration planned for that evening. Her decision forces her husband to take stock of his life too.

The Wublers' friend, old Count Heinrich von Kreyl, while attending the mass, experiences a sense of emptiness in the church, in himself, and in the people in the pews. Because of this epiphany and advice from close friends, he refuses the presidency of the nation to avoid becoming a mere figurehead for a corrupt party. He understands the motivation of the previous president, who resigned because he, like Erika Wubler, "can't take all the garbage any more" (*FF* 239). On this day Hans Plukanski must also be replaced as minister because his crimes in Poland during the war have just been disclosed by the Polish government. Plukanski's past has always been known within the party, but now he is no longer "sustainable." The ruthless phone call in which he is informed that he is "out" and Fritz Blaukrämer is "in" causes his death from a heart attack. Ernst Grobsch, a young member of parliament and Plukanski's assistant who is with the minister when he dies, is forced to reassess his political career and party membership. He decides to reclaim his lost ideals and elects to change parties. Free of his former affiliation, he now hires as his assistant Karl von Kreyl, the unemployed, young radical son of Count Heinrich. Karl accepts the position as an opportunity to put his idealism to work for a politician in whom he has confidence. Thus, in a brief time the positive characters in the novel decide to change their lives in order to work politically "to lessen the garbage," as Grobsch expresses it, "because this is the only state we have" (*FF* 239).

While the men have power and wield it without mercy in matters of state and for personal gain, the novel is not primarily concerned with this aspect of bourgeois society. The world of power politics is simply the given milieu of the novel. More important to Böll is the effect this oligarchical, bourgeois society has on those who are not *Herrscher* and *Regierer,* those without power, specifically the wives and girl friends of the power elite. As the title of the novel states, the book is about the lives of women in the political landscape of Bonn: about the moralist Erika Wubler, who refuses to go along with her husband's politics any longer; about the suffering Elisabeth Blaukrämer, who commits suicide when her husband becomes minister; about the independent and intellectual Eva Plint, who decides to live with Ernst Grobsch after leaving her husband Karl von Kreyl; about the working student Katharina Richter, who lives with Karl von Kreyl and studies economics so she can help the poor; and about the angry and impatient waitress, Lore Schmitz, who caters the parties of the rich and wants immediate political change. These are the figures who are behind the public actors of the novel. In them Böll reveals the suffering and the conscience of the nation. While men determine the society in which they live, these women have to bear the nation's burdens with little chance to effect change.

Analysis

In *Women in a River Landscape* Ernst Grobsch, who is described as a "prole with the face of a sociologist" (*FF* 124), a brilliant member of parliament who has risen from the bottom, makes this comment about the fall of Minister Plukanski:

> It was impossible to keep Plukanski any longer. And Blaukrämer [Plukanski's successor] will also one day stumble and fall. But the gentlemen who do not rule, but only control, they will never stumble and fall. Even [President] Heulbuck will one day fall [and maybe go to jail], but [the bankers] Florian, Kapspeter, Bransen, Krengel, and Blöhmscher will never, never see a prison from the inside. They can be maintained forever, they represent the divine right of money. . . . They don't rule, so they can never fall, they remain pure like those who in past times used to rule by the grace of God.'' (*FF* 125–26)

Although Grobsch is the main spokesman for the author, this view of society manifests itself in the utterances of other characters as well. The young lawyer, Karl von Kreyl, a social dropout, characterizes the rule of the mysterious Paul Chundt with words that sound like Louis XIV's summation of absolutism, "L'état, c'est moi." Karl's version is: "The state is Chundt, and Chundt is the state" (*FF* 77). It is this disillusionment with the legal system that alienates Karl from society. However, besides believing Chundt is above the law (*FF* 92), he also thinks that the democratic free press is in collusion with the *Herrscher*. "Scandals are never cleared up in this country," he says. "Deep inside [this society] sits a false god to whom sacrifice must be made and to whom sacrifice is made" (*FF* 192). The false god to whom Karl refers is the trinity of money, power, and politics. The novel is filled with this kind of mystification of evil which, while it veils the inner workings of the system, nonetheless makes Böll's point that mystification is the essence of the system's *modus operandi*.

In another passage Grobsch implies that the true function of democracy is the perversion of its stated purpose; politicians, he contends, are not in office to serve the people but to manage them and advance the *Herrscher:* "We the politicians do the dirty work so they, the *Herrscher,* need not get their hands dirty. They never think of the blood, the sweat, and the shit from which their money is made" (*FF* 120–21). Grobsch is not talking here of the efforts of the working class that produce the nation's wealth but of the merciless political struggles the politicians engage in to maintain the system.

The biography of the new minister, Blaukrämer, makes clear how concentration of responsibility is one way democratic power is preserved. Besides being minister, Blaukrämer is also "a state representative, a county representative, a state advisor, a member of his party's executive committee, an advisor to the state police, is on the board of directors of a savings institution, of a health insurance organization, and a state hospital" (*FF* 223). This conglomeration of conflicting interests and interlocking executive positions keeps the vassal Blaukrämer discreetly at the nexus of money and power in order better to serve himself and society's *Herrscher.*

Of the *Herrscher,* the least visible but most powerful is the man known only by his nickname Schwamm (meaning "sponge") because he absorbs money and power. The mere mention of his name causes fear. He can make or break any deal, triumph over any opponent, and finance revolutions in the Third World (*FF* 225–26). He is beyond mere interest in money. Chundt explains: "More important to him is that people obey. From the politicians he expects loyalty" (*FF* 227).

Although his criticism is based on humanist Christian concepts of social justice, Böll's analysis of society is uncompromisingly Marxist. Five important social assumptions are at the foundation of his vision of West

Germany. First, it makes little difference which of the three major bourgeois parties is in power, the Social Democrats, the Christian Democrats, or the Free Democrats; the tripartite division of society *(Herrscher, Regierer, Proletariat)* will remain the same because all of the ruling parties tolerate the existing class structure, and none has the intention of changing the system. Still, moderate reform is possible; this possibility is reason enough for Grobsch to change his party affiliation. The novel concretizes Böll's comments in his 1976 interview with Marcel Reich-Ranicki about the major West German parties: "In 1965 one could still put hope in the SPD, but that is no longer possible. In a country in which there is no longer a left, only left wings of three predominately national liberal parties, it is senseless, a waste of time to get engaged politically" *(WI* 1: 60). Böll's activity in the 1970s for the SPD was only to assist Willy Brandt's Ost-Politik, but his support of the newly formed Greens in the 1980s was based on his conviction that they offered a new social philosophy and on his desire to further their position on peace and the environment. In the novel the party to which Grobsch switches is unnamed, but it is most likely the Greens.

Second, the *Herrscher,* as Grobsch says, will "never see the inside of a prison" because they need never transgress the law. The point here is that of Brecht's thought-provoking query: Why rob a bank when you can found one? Their social power rests on the right of property and is, therefore, legal. Krengel's explanation of the takeover of his family banks is an example in the text. "Rumors ruin a bank like ours," Krengel says. "The rumor got around that we could not pay our depositors, and as more and more customers began to demand their money, soon the demand for withdrawals was too great. . . . Kapspeter finally got what he wanted. I capitulated, and he took over our bank just as he had taken over others for a tenth of their real value. All legal" *(FF* 248–49). Krengel calls this process of takeovers the "Europeanization" and "Americanization" of practice, but he also sees it as similar to the "Aryanization process" of a previous generation, when such takeovers also had a legal foundation *(FF* 250). And he observes further that the old Nazis are still around. Pleitsch, for instance, he says, has changed his name to Plonius and has become a democrat. With no attempt to hide his resentment, Krengel sums up the situation, "He [Plonius] is a democrat now, acts in accordance with the law, and even his conversion is legitimate" *(FF* 251).

Third, the legal system is class justice. When the "nobility of money" and its servants, for reasons of profit or power, transgress the law, they "never see the inside of a jail" or do so for only a short time because they have the money and connections that give them legal advantages. In the novel, the Bingerle affair is the best example. After a brief confinement in prison for accepting bribes (reminiscent of the Flick affair), Bingerle is released because he knows too much and possesses incriminating documents against Chundt. He is immediately reinstated in the political system and becomes secretary to the new Minister Blaukrämer. The waitress Lore Schmitz comments bitterly on this social phenomenon:

> I read the newspaper, I watch TV and listen to the radio. And when one of them is caught who doesn't even need to do anything wrong—those people with their hundreds of thousands and millions—and when I read how one day they are dying and the next day they appear in court beaming with a suntan and claim their innocence, and I see how they appear before committees beaming, gracious, laughing, do you expect me to obey the law and believe in justice? I've never broken the law, never even committed a misdemeanor out of fear of getting caught. We can't appear in court beaming like winners, we're condemned before the sentence is read. (*FF* 237)

Another example of class justice is Blaukrämer's manipulation of the hearing to decide his wife's pension and reparations as a victim of fascism. Elisabeth Blaukrämer neither wants nor needs the money and knows the claim is based on lies. Therefore, her husband finds it necessary to thwart her attempt to hinder his greed by having her opposition interpreted as that of a mentally ill woman and by placing her in a mental hospital. Her characterization of the rigged hearing, nonetheless, shows its true nature: it was "a real joke, a regular peasant farce" (*FF* 171).

Fourth, the *Herrscher* as a class will remain in control of society as long as they possess the controlling mechanisms of society, especially the sources of wealth, the means of production, the banks, and the media. In existing circumstances, they control not only the people who manage the business of democracy but also indirectly the people the politicians govern. Grobsch makes the point: "I would like to run a TV and radio station. Next to the banks that's where the real power is. Then I could really get into politics" (*FF* 146). Other statements in the text express the idea that the real purpose of the media is to manipulate the public. Hermann Wubler talks of his "consolidating the media" after the war (*FF* 59), Chundt admits to orchestrating the Bingerle affair through the "newspapers, embassies, news agencies, and editors" (*FF* 207), and Wubler warns a friend not to forget that "the newspapers and media obey Chundt" (*FF* 207). In the novel, the principle behind controlling the media is the belief that the communication industry can make any truth into a lie and any lie into a truth to suit the political needs of the moment. Chundt's proof of the effectiveness of his own methods is his assertion, "Don't forget everything that Elisabeth [Blaukrämer] said was true," but nobody believed her (*FF* 184).

Also implied in Böll's vision of society is that the media derive their power from "freedom of the press" and "objective" reporting. According to the novel, if the media were not "free" and "objective," no one would believe them; they would simply lose their power to manipulate. The text makes clear that the appearance of neutrality and independence is the primary prerequisite for this kind of system of control to work. Chundt praises Wubler for his farsightedness at the end of the war by means of a rhetorical question, "Who would have thought that these miserable little provincial newspapers could ever have become important, who would have thought that this foolish flickering picture on TV could ever have amounted to anything?" (*FF* 222).

A good explanation of what Böll is saying in the novel about the media can be found in Michael Parenti's book, *Inventing Reality.* Parenti points out that those who control or who can manipulate the media are also those who determine the national agenda. What the public does not see or hear is no issue; in a political sense, what the media do not report does not exist. To control the media means to control the political discourse; it does not mean one has to determine every word and picture that goes over the air waves. Whether one believes or disbelieves the information presented does not matter. Those who present the issues determine how the issues are addressed, whether those issues are drugs, unemployment, white-collar crime, or violence in the streets, success or failure of the economy, foreign aid, involvement of federal intelligence agencies at home or abroad, corruption in government, influence of lobbies, briberies and swindles on the stock market, those who determine the range of discourse set the limits within which solutions to social problems must be found. If a specific approach, that is, a socialist approach, to the issues can be kept out of the discussion, then the eventual actions can never incorporate this approach in the solution. This summary is the bourgeois method of social control in a democracy portrayed in Böll's *Women in a River Landscape.* That this method is undemocratic, in fact, is antidemocratic, but not perceived as such, is one of the points of the novel. Böll also makes clear that one of the roles of the media in bourgeois democracies is to maintain this deception. When he has Grobsch say, "I would like to control a TV and radio station . . . that's where the real power is" (*FF* 146), he is acknowledging just this function of the media.

This method of "defining the scope of respectable political discourse" (ix), as Parenti calls it, is a main critical point in the novel. In other words, in *Women in a River Landscape* the media channels the public discussion in ways that support the existing political and economic system. Although Böll's novel does not treat life outside of West Germany, the book contends that the manipulated media of a "free" society achieve results essentially the same as those in a society with direct censorship. Gorbsch's comment on the power of television and radio implies also that he is fully aware that the national agenda is set by the media not just in news programs but in entertainment programs as well. Grobsch recognizes that the ideology of the ruling class infiltrates all aspects of public life. In fact, the hidden ideological values in an entertainment program are often the most successful method of setting the desired national agenda because it occurs subliminally.

The fifth social assumption in Böll's novel is that bourgeois democracy tolerates diversity in politics, differences in religion, and variety in culture as long as such tolerance does not endanger society's property relations. This is illustrated in *Women in a River Landscape* by the politicians who come and go while the ruling *Herrscher* remain. The conclusion to be drawn is that such a society is fundamentally undemocratic and must be changed. The cause of this perversion of democracy, according to the novel, is the threefold class structure of society. The novel makes clear that as along as people like Schwamm and Chundt have the right to accumulate profit and appropriate power, or as the text puts its, "to suck up and absorb money" (*FF* 14), the *Herrscher* will continue to exert control forever.

In the few days in which the events of the novel take place, some of the people in the circle around Erika and Hermann Wubler come to the same conclusion. But very few of the newly enlightened are led by this insight to work for social reform; most of them, in fact, fall prey to resignation. Erika Wubler retreats from political involvement with an attitude of detachment, "I've had enough, I've had enough" (*FF* 224). Her husband, Hermann, continues in politics much as before, although he now recognizes the interconnectedness of his good life with the realities in the world: "Every piece of bread I eat I take from someone else, someone I don't know. The milk that I drink I owe the grain that in another part of the world would be bread, porridge, or flat cakes. Not even the wine we drink belongs to us—the fertilizer that it requires could grow food somewhere else. . . . Although I know what I'm doing, I don't know all the consequences of my actions'' (*FF* 224–25).[50] And the humane old Count Heinrich von Kreyl refuses the presidency because he would rather retire than cooperate any more with a system he now sees as unjust.

Of the politicians who come to awareness in these fateful days, only Ernst Grobsch, the man whose name drives from *grob* (coarse) and suggests proletarian seriousness, this compromised but talented man of the people, pleads with the old count to accept the presidency and offer internal resistance. ''This is the only state we have,'' he says, ''there is no other and none better. It has made us, and we have made it. . . . You must accept the garbage and try to reduce it. . . . I would like to have a country in which Lore [Schmitz] here could recognize that it is beautiful to obey the law even if others commit crimes and get by with them. I want to make it clear that it is our law and not theirs. You, Count, have to start carrying away some of the garbage'' (*FF* 239–40).

Although Karl, the son of the old count, advises his father to retire because of his age and health, he himself, nonetheless, comes to the same conclusion as Grobsch that it is time to work for change. He rises above his passivity, gives up his symbolic gestures of protest (dismantling the grand pianos of the rich), and takes a position as Grobsch's assistant. He explains his decision with the militant formulation that he wants to see to it that ''the *Herrscher* don't stay our lords forever'' (*FF* 240).

For only one person, the conditions in West Germany are bad enough to induce emigration. Hilde Krengel, the daughter of the banker, chooses to go to the Third World. She ''would rather die in Nicaragua than live here'' (*FF* 192). At the end of the novel she flies to Central America, hoping to use her expertise in agricultural economics for the good of the Nicaraguan people. Katharina Richter, who lives with Karl, also considers emigration but decides to stay. Karl explains that ''her Cuba and her Nicaragua are here'' (*FF* 253). She believes that the knowledge she has acquired from her dissertation on the banking system and its methods of ''maximizing profits from the third world'' (*FF* 48) can be used for economic reform at home. Eva Plint, who lives with Grobsch, does not share his proletarian optimism, but she supports his effort of reform because ''it is here that I live. I would like to go somewhere else, but I couldn't live anywhere else'' (*FF* 31).

The problem for the critic is to discern the ideological stance of the novel and to determine what social action the book advocates. Böll's life and works, especially his essays, make clear that Grobsch comes closest to the author's own position, namely, that it is a citizen's obligation to recognize the ideal of social justice and to work for its realization. The book is torn, however, by a contradiction that impedes the activation of the reader. The dominant tone of the novel is a combination of sadness, melancholy, and resignation that argues against the suggested struggle for change. There is no indication in the work that the "eternal" rule of the *Herrscher* can be defeated from within or reformed out of existence. The efforts of men of good will, such as Grobsch and Karl von Kreyl, and of intelligent women, such as Eva Plint and Katharina Richter, to alter the structure of West German society seems unlikely to be powerful enough to dispel the aura of despair that emanates from the system and its corruption. The most sensitive characters (all women of the war generation) commit suicide: Frau von Kreyl throws herself into the Rhine, Elisabeth Blaukrämer hangs herself, and Frau Krengel simply dies by succumbing physically and psychically to the corruption around her. Other positive figures drop out. The novel presents no real strategy for changing West German society from within, although it leaves no doubt that the hoped for solution is some form of socialism. In the novel each example of corruption and perversion of democracy derives from a misuse of power that comes from wealth based on property. The book is unyielding in its revelation that the political principle behind bourgeois democracy is that whoever owns the republic controls it.

The two major acts of protest in the novel reinforce this idea. The fifteen-year-old American Jeremias Arglos, whose name means "simple" or "guileless," and who, in fact, plays the role of a naive prophet, refuses to sell a valuable piece of property overlooking the Rhine which he inherited from his relatives who died in the Holocaust. He is offered five million and then ten million marks for the land, but he wants the ruined villa to stand as a memorial for the dead. For Jeremias and Grobsch, who acts as his lawyer, property exists not as a means to wealth and power, but as an opportunity to serve a humane purpose.

The second example is Karl von Kreyl's piano protests. In a conversation with his father in which he tries to explain his motivation for the destruction of the symbols of culture, he utters the most important hidden quotation in the novel, Böll's favorite sentence from the West German constitution. "Property creates obligations," he says, "The piano was mine . . . and seven years ago I was obliged to destroy it" (*FF* 67). He smashed his famous grand piano on which Beethoven had played after he had learned that his friend Konrad Fluh had been mistakenly shot as a terrorist. For Karl the offering of his piano was "a kind of private, quiet, divine service, a holy and sacrificial act, a ritual" (*FF* 69). The description is clearly a reference to the mass, which is also called a holy sacrifice because it commemorates Christ's sacrifice of himself for the sins of the world. Böll recalls this attitude through Karl's methodic ritualistic behavior. In Karl's society the holiest of holies that can be sacrificed is property. His symbolic gesture is the heart and soul of the novel. He calls his action an "anti-materialistic sign" (*FF* 194), a protest against the accumulation of property that no longer has any relationship to the satisfaction of human needs. The banker Krengel, whose daughter emigrates to Nicaragua, understands Karl's intention and calls his act "a heavenly protest . . . against luxury, hunger, thirst, war, and every misery and every form of materialism" (*FF* 191). Karl's destruction of his own piano, as well as his later dismantling of other privately owned famous pianos on which great composers have played, also has a second meaning. It is a protest against the connection of art and money through which valued objects and culture itself become the possession of the *Herrscher*. His symbolic destruction points to Marx's idea that the basis of value is not property per se, but human labor, or as Karl expresses the concept of his protest, it shows "the connection between music, pianos, and money—money understood as metaphysical material—transformed back into that from which it came: tears, work, sweat, blood" (*FF* 195). These symbolic protests against private property run as leitmotifs through the novel and form a frame for the dramatic structure. In the very first dialogue of the novel, between Erika Wubler and Katharina Richter, and in the very last conversation, between old Count Heinrich, his son, and the banker Krengel, the mysterious dismantling of pianos around Bonn is the topic of discussion.

On the final day of the novel, the day of decision, Karl gives up his symbolic protests (*FF* 252) and decides to work with Grobsch to fulfill the constitutional stipulation that property should serve the common good. He is attracted to Grobsch because he sees him as "proper, sharp, cynical, but not corrupt" and refers to him as "the new nobility, proletarian" (*FF* 91). Grobsch expresses his personal transformation by proclaiming a commitment to a more democratic Germany: "I am going to see to it that those who are not elected no longer rule. I have a lot to do, and I want to get to work" (*FF* 127).

Of all the German reviewers of *Women in a River Landscape,* only Dieter Lattmann, a novelist and former Social Democratic member of parliament, emphasized the political aspect of the novel. He remarked, "The aesthetic critique of the novel seems to me of secondary importance, considering the pattern of politics that Böll reveals'' (197). Still, Lattmann faults the book for its lack of realism: "In general what we have here has little to do with authenticity. . . . Böll simply does not treat real, existing democracy'' (200). Lattmann is referring to the complexities of Western democracy that Böll neglects—party rivalry, honest elections, a functioning parliament, labor unions, and the fact that there are some elected officials who honestly represent the people. Lattmann's list certainly could be extended. For example, Böll could have done more to show that Western democracy defines itself purely in terms of political democracy and not in terms of economic democracy; Böll could have revealed that Western democracy does not concern itself with granting workers a democratic voice in economic affairs or in the business decisions of corporations that most affect their lives.

For Lattmann the content of the novel poses the question: What is realism? It is a question that long interested Böll, in fact, he tried to answer it in his theoretical essay "Der Zeitgenosse und die Wirklichkeit," 1953 (Contemporary Man and Reality). Here Böll argues that literature presents reality by going beyond superficial factuality. According to Böll: "Reality is never a gift. It demands our active, not our passive attention. . . . Reality always lies beyond the actual" (*WESR* 1: 73). Böll's final novel exemplifies this theory. It ignores the democratic veneer of party rivalry, unions, the election process, and the like—those "actualities" that Lattmann complains are missing—and explores the deeper social mechanisms at the heart of liberal democracy. Reality is, as Böll says, never immediately visible. To find it, one must practice creative imagining, one must use one's critical faculty and rational fantasy in harmony. In *Women in a River Landscape*, Böll succeeds in combining the two to reveal the truth about liberal democracy.

Despite the modified Marxist vision of society in his last novel, Böll was, in his life and work, never an ideologue. In a review of Wladimir Bukowski's *Dieser stechende Schmerz der Freiheit* (This Piercing Pain of Freedom), in which Böll deals with the rightist emigrants from Eastern Europe who refuse to recognize any failures in the Western brands of democracy, justice, and economics, Böll quotes a moderate passage from the conservative Bukowski with which he does agree: "In the final analysis nobody knows what socialism is. There are as many socialisms as there are socialists, and it disturbs me that so many people in the world believe they can solve all problems with a simple restructuring of society" (*EZ* 223).

Böll's later works, especially after *Group Portrait* (1971), illustrate his intuitive socialism or naive communism. This moral imperative in Böll's work derives ultimately from a religious impulse. For the Catholic Böll, who once said, "I have only two themes: love and religion" (*WI* 1: 68), the biblical story of creation had a simple social meaning: because men and women were created in the image of God, they had imposed on them the imperative to love the creator and to love each other as much as they loved themselves. Böll did not believe that capitalism could provide the basic conditions in which human beings could realize this obligation. Instead, he believed that socialism, as the beginning of a classless and profitless society, could at least initiate the prerequisites for working toward this goal.

NOTES

1. The idea for this comprehensive approach to interpreting Böll's thematic comes from private correspondence with Arpád Bernáth, a Hungarian scholar of Böll.

2. Two examples of this Böllian iconization of anarchy (one from *And Never Said a Word*, 1953, and one from his last novel *Frauen vor Flußlandschaft*, 1985 [*Women in a River Landscape*]) show the consistency through the years of this tendency in Böll's work. Käte says, "I knew I loved Fred when I realized how much he hated laws" (*WRE* 2: 154), and Lore Schmitz draws her existential wisdom from exposure to social corruption reported by the media: "I watch TV, I listen to the radio. And then you expect me to keep the law and believe in order" (*FF* 237).

3. When this statement of Käte's in this 1953 novel is compared to that of Eva Plint's as she cares for a sick friend in Böll's last novel *Frauen vor Flußlandschaft*, 1985 *(Women in a River Landscape):* "Naturally I prayed, said a litany for you. That also helped you" (116), then the durability of this theme of prayer in Böll's work becomes obvious.

4. The character of Gäseler and the social problem of forgetting the war, or more specifically, of forgetting the unpleasant, embarrassing, or criminal aspects of the Hitler years, is the continuation of the theme that in *Das Vermächtnis (A Soldier's Legacy)* was centered in the person of Schnecker.

5. See Alexander and Margarete Mitscherlich, *Die Unfähigkeit zu trauern*. Böll's indebtedness to the Mitscherlichs is clear in the title of his last collection of essays, *Die Fähigkeit zu trauern, Schriften und Reden 1983–1985*. See also Margarete Mitscherlich, *Erinnerungsarbeit zur Psychoanalyse der Unfähigkeit zu trauern*. However, this theme of the repression of sadness is present in Böll's work long before its appearance in the definitive study by the Mitscherlichs.

6. Now the question of the East German Stalinist past is a major moral question in German *Vergangenheitsbewätigung*.

7. The historians' debate began in the eighties with a new approach to the study of the Nazi period. These new studies are characterized by a departure from a concern with the origins of fascism, the rise of Nazism, the causes of World War II, and the probing questions of guilt and responsibility. The new research deals with life in the *Heimat* and daily existence during the Hitler period. The debate centers on the legitimacy of research, that in theory is intended to illuminate all aspects of the Hitler period, but in practice often tends to emphasize the normalness of existence through the thirties and the sufferings of Germans during the war.

The routine of life in small towns, the misery in the cities during the war, and the suffering of Germans in the East as the Russians advanced comes to the fore. The Holocaust and other crimes of Nazism are put at the edge of concern and appear as just another example of man's inhumanity to man, no worse than the crimes of Stalin and the Turkish treatment of the Armenians during the period of the First World War. The Holocaust becomes merely one more example of people finding a scapegoat for economic-political problems. These aspects of the new history are observable in statements by politicians, in television programming, in the *Zeitgeist* of the eighties and nineties in Germany and Austria, and even in the United States.

Also demonstrative of the change in the atmosphere of the eighties is the debate that surrounded the October 1985 production of Rainer Werner Faßbinder's play, *Der Müll, die Stadt und der Tod* (Garbage, the City and Death) in Frankfurt. The main character is a despicable Jew. Regardless of one's concept of freedom of expression, the ferocious debate it caused revealed altered attitudes in Germany. This theater scandal was covered widely in the press at the time and for months to follow. See James Markham's report in the *New York Times* 31 Oct. 1985 and Hans Schueler's report in *Die Zeit,* North American Edition, 12 Dec. 1986: 5.

For background on the historians' debate see Konrad H. Jarausch, "Removing the Nazi Stain? The Quarrel of the German Historians," *German Studies Review* 11.2 (May 1988): 285–302. This article explains the origin of the debate, shows its cultural-political ramifications, and demonstrates its implication for understanding contemporary German history. Jarausch concludes that the debate raises fundamental issues that will "provide chronic discussion for years to come" (289).

8. The concept of "late birth" for Kohl's generation needs close analysis. This generation, which was between the ages eleven and eighteen years at the end of the war, was not mature enough to have shared responsibility for National Socialism, but it was the generation that grew up entirely under Nazism and experienced its primary socialization during that regime. That group was most subjected to Nazi schools and propaganda; it did not know a previous nonfascist system and was most isolated from varied opinion. This generation may be "innocent," but the question must be asked if it can be unaffected or uninvolved.

9. See Nägele 135–40 for a summary of this criticism.

10. A corrective is necessary regarding this quotation from Demetz. Actually the minister is not parading below but is on the balcony next to Johanna, and the "lambs" in the novel commit no violent acts. Johanna, Robert, and Ferdi, the positive figures who attempt assassinations, are not the lambs of the novel but the "shepherds" who try to protect the lambs. These confusions indicate the difficulties a reader has in following the details of the story. For an excellent presentation and analysis of the chronology of events and the structure of the novel see Therese Poser, "Heinrich Böll: *Billard um halbzehn.*"

11. Besides this novel, Böll's polemical writing from this period can help the reader to understand the author's political position. In essays published before *Billiards,* he opposed reinstatement of fascists and militarists in the Adenauer government, opposed the rearmament of Germany, the institution of the *Bundeswehr* with its compulsory service, and West Germany's inclusion in NATO's nuclear shield. His "Brief an einen jungen Katholiken," 1958 (Letter to a Young Catholic), addressing some of these issues is one of the most effective moral political essays of the 1950s.

12. The English translation renders the word *Frau* in this context as "woman" and thereby makes the marriage aspect of this seduction scene less obvious than in German.

13. This episode, in fact, resembles one in Böll's own life in which his mother was saved from the Gestapo by a local party member who refused to act on a report of her anti-Hitler remarks.

14. Because of this Erfurt episode in *The Clown,* it is the only novel by Böll that was never published or distributed in East Germany.

15. Quoted from Balzer, et al., *Die deutschsprachige Literatur in der BRD* 299.

16. Important to notice in this interview of 1971 and elsewhere in Böll's discussions of *Group Portrait* is that his vocabulary—his key words and phrases—is the idiom of the 1960s. An analysis of Böll's choice of words in the interviews relating to this novel would reveal as well as any other means how closely this novel is related to the romantic, anti-technological, political environment and *Zeitgeist* of the decade between 1963 and 1973 known as the Sixties.

17. *Die Zeit*, North American edition, 10 Aug. 1971: 10.

18. From *Group Portrait* one can conclude that Böll believed that the West's deification of *Leistung* and economic growth produced great wealth without improving the quality of life. For Böll, the quality of existence depends less on material abundance than it does on an absence of stress, worry, and anxiety from economic uncertainty. For this reason, Böll probably would have seen the collapse of the functional but less competitive East German economy brought on by unification as a tragedy not completely compensated for with more freedom. *Group Portrait* strongly suggests that West Germany had something important to learn from East Germany—a lesson missed in the speed of unification.

19. In an interview with Karin Struck, Böll admitted to reading Freud, "But I believe, when one reads Freud, it becomes clear that he has brought many scientists to his ideas by means of his novelistic treatment of certain problems" (*WI* 1: 280). In addition to this casual reference, there are various references to psychoanalysis in *Group Portrait*. The gardener Grundtsch says of Pelzer, "It was psychoanalytically very interesting what was going on with Walter Pelzer" (*WRE* 5: 203). The Exalted Personage, who uses his influence during the war to try and save Boris, says of Lev, "Psychoanalytically expressed, the boy has a dangerous mother-complex and a father-trauma" (*WRE* 5: 293). The prison psychologist in his report on Lev writes: "L. B. G. has in fact overcome much, but also repressed a lot" (*WRE* 5: 364). These references are taken from Herlyn 137, n. 49.

20. Two important questions will not be addressed here: Must work always be alienating labor? And is it not possible for work to be satisfying and, therefore, a pleasure?

21. Also ignored here will be the important question assumed in Marcuse's revision of Marx, which implies that utopian change can come about gradually under capitalism without a radical altering of property relations. The problems in this note and in the one above simply go too far beyond the task here of understanding Böll.

22. Originally from Erich Fromm, "Die psychoanalytische Charakterologie und ihre Bedeutung für die Sozialpsychologie," *Zeitschrift für Sozialforschung* 1 (1932): 269, taken from Heinrich Herlyn 22. I am indebted to Herlyn for the direction of my analysis of *Group Portrait*.

23. Fromm explains the development of the anal personality in his article, "Die psychoanalytische Charakterologie." It is the personality of the person who has repressed original pleasure in the release of his or her stool and has replaced it with the pleasure of control. Since the stool is the body's first production and possession, control of it in the form of retention manifests itself in the adult personality as a love of possessions, savings, accumulation, wealth. As the personality develops, the infant learns to reject its waste and retain what it truly values. The infant's love of its excrement is replaced by the adult's love of money. (This summary of Fromm's explanation is taken from Herlyn 22.)

24. These sources, as well as the origin of the hidden quotations in the novel, were revealed by Böll in an interview with Manfred Durzak: they are Reibert, *Der Dienstunterricht im Heer*, Neubearbeitung von Dr. Allmendinger, Major (Berlin: Mittler, 1939); *Wehrmachtsverwaltungsvorschrift*, 2. Entwurf, III. Teil, Truppenunterkunft (Berlin: Mittler, 1937). See Durzak, "Bölls epische Summe" 179–80.

25. For a translation of the poem and an analysis of Böll's protest of Boock's sentence see Conard, "The Poems of Heinrich Böll Since 1972," 14 and note on p. 19.

26. See Grützbach for a selection of representative articles for and against Böll's *Spiegel* article.

27. The opening sentence of Böll's essay, "Die Würde des Menschen ist unantastbar," 1972 (The Dignity of the Human Being Is Inviolable) reads; "The Basic Law of the Federal Republic of Germany is probably the best possible constitution that a state in the twentieth century could give itself" (*WESR* 2: 575). In this same essay, Böll chastises the *Bild-Zeitung* for publishing at the time of Baader's arrest a sensational photograph of him lying naked on a stretcher. The photo raised for Böll also the issue of cooperation between the *Bild-Zeitung* and the police because, Böll believed, the picture could only have come from police files. Further evidence of possible illegal or unethical cooperation between *Bild* and the police occurred on 7 February 1975, when *Bild* reported in its morning edition that the police raided the house of Böll's son looking for arms and terrorists. The raid, which turned up nothing, actually took place after the report appeared in *Bild*, between two and four o'clock in the afternoon of 7 February. (For details see *WI* 1: 744.)

28. Peter Brückner was chairman of the psychology department at the Technical University in Hannover. In 1972, because of his rumored association with the Baader-Meinhof Group, he was suspended under the Radical Decrees from his university duties and subjected to considerable calumny in the press.

29. "Betroffen, belastet, diffamiert," *Der Spiegel* 19 August 1974: 7.

30. Walden based his charge not on *Katharina Blum* but on a speech Böll made in Wuppertal in 1966 in which he said: "There where the state could and should be, I see only the rotting remains of power. And these obviously precious remnants of rot are defended with rat-like rage" (*WESR* 2: 229). Böll immediately brought suit for damages, feeling something had to be done to stop the unwarranted attacks on him. Böll lost his case in the first court but won an appeal in 1976 (see Böll's statement at the time, *WESR* 3: 208ff.), lost again in 1978 on Walden's appeal, and finally won the case before the Supreme Court in 1981. Walden and the Berlin television station, Sender Freies Berlin, that had broadcast Walden's defamation of Böll, had to pay damages of 40,000 marks. (See Reid, *Heinrich Böll: A German for His Time* 165 and V. Böll, *Heinrich Böll . . . gebunden an Zeit* 65–66.)

31. Quoted from Schröter 107. The artist Klaus Staeck used this quotation, which makes clear Carstens had never read the book, for a satiric poster attacking the growing national hysteria that was beginning to limit freedom of expression. For further information on the political reception of *Katharina Blum* see Reid, *Heinrich Böll: A German for His Time* 180–89.

32. For example, when the narrator refers to Katharina's reading the first article about herself in the *News* on Thursday morning (*WRE* 5: 465), he actually means Friday because Katharina's arrest and first interrogation only occurred on Thursday after the appearance of the Thursday edition of the *News*. On Friday, during Katharina's second interrogation, the text reads: She took "both issues of the *News*" (*WRE* 5: 420) out of her handbag. Two issues could not have appeared by this time. (See Beth 91, note 66, for more details.) Also, Moelding is referred to as "chief commissioner" (*Kriminaloberkommissar, WRE* 5: 386) when, in fact, he is the assistant to Commissioner *(Kriminalhauptkommissar)* Beizmenne. (See Beth 90, note 35, for more details.) Furthermore, the suspicion of the police that Katharina was also the murderer of the *News* photographer Adolph Schönner, killed Tuesday (26 February), seems an inconsistency since Katharina was in custody from Sunday (24 February) on, the time she gave herself up to Moelding. (See Nägele 76 for further details.) Such mistakes have led Joachim Kaiser in his review for the *Süddeutsche Zeitung* (10–11 Aug. 1974: 76) to conclude that readers no longer scrutinize Böll's manuscripts before publication.

33. See Böll's comments on this aspect of the film and book in "Sieben Fragen an Volker Schlöndorff und Margarethe von Trotta," *Die Zeit*, North American edition, 17 Oct. 1975: 15.

34. In an interview with Viktor Böll ("Die Verfilmung der *Katharina Blum*"), 1976, in V. Böll, *Heinrich Böll als Filmautor*, Böll said, "Margarethe von Trotta wrote the film script. I looked at it and made notes" (*WI* 1: 668).

35. In the film Tötges actually says: "Now you're 'in.' I've made you famous. Now you can get a piece of the big money." Also in the film some of Katharina's friends share this point of view. After they collect clippings of Katharina, one of them says: Katharina is "now famous just like a film star."

36. *Scala* 10 (1984): 22. For a review of Medek's opera see Eckhard Roelcke, "Mief und Moral," *Die Zeit*, North American Edition, 3 May 1991: 16.

37. In Thomas's film Kristofferson is suspected of being a bank robber, and the Weather Underground is mentioned on one occasion.

38. In June 1990 and in the weeks prior to German unification several wanted members of the RAF were arrested in East Germany living with new identities provided by the state. One of these was Susanne Albrecht. The East German government gave the RAF members asylum on the condition that they renounce terrorism and lead normal lives. Police officials in the West maintain some of those given asylum continued their terrorist activities while living in East Germany. The eastern authorities who authorized the asylum also were motivated by their conclusion that a fair trial for suspected terrorists was impossible in West Germany. See "RAF-Aussteiger: Wie die Wasserfälle," *Der Spiegel* 13 Aug. 1990: 56–57, "Dann sind bald alle tot: Die RAF-Aussteigerin Sigrid Sternebeck über ihren Weg in den Untergrund und über die Endstation DDR," *Der Spiegel* 13 Aug. 1990: 57–67, "Ich bitte um Vergebung: Interview mit dem Aussteiger Baptist Rolf Friedrick über sein Leben mit dem RAF," *Der Spiegel* 20 Aug. 1990: 52–62, "Die mit den Hüten: Die inhaftierten RAF-Aussteiger aus der DDR belasten sich gegenseitig, die Ermittler erfahren 'immer mehr,' " *Der Spiegel* 20 Aug. 1990: 62–63; see also the interview with Kurt Rebemann, West German Attorney General in the 1970s, *Die Zeit*, North American Edition, 31 Aug. 1990: 19, and the interview with the former RAF member arrested in East Germany, Werner Lotze, *Die Zeit*, North American Edition, 30 Nov. 1990: 7. On 4 June 1991 Albrecht was sentenced to twelve years imprisonment for her role in the Ponto murder and in the attempted assassination of General Alexander Haig in June 1979.

39. On 19 October 1977, Andreas Baader, Gudrun Ensslin, and Jan-Carl Raspe were found shot to death in their cells. The official verdict was suicide, but that verdict was not universally accepted (see Aust 581–92). In April 1991 at her trial in Stuttgart, Susanne Albrecht testified that she was informed in Baghdad by fellow terrorist Brigitte Mohnhaupt that the trio had planned a collective suicide to look like a police murder. See *Kölner Stadt-Anzeiger*, 27–28 April 1991: 1.

40. See Heinrich Böll, "Einführung in die *Fürsorgliche Belagerung*" 74.

41. It is not surprising that the book is dedicated to his three sons, who at least in a loose sense are the models for Tolm's three sons in the novel. Nor is it surprising that Tolm is Böll's age and that each had been married for about thirty-five years.

42. Böll stated after the publication of *Fürsorgliche Belagerung* that he had worked on the novel for four years. See "Besuch bei Böll," *Stern* 19 Sept. 1979: 50.

43. In a private conversation in May 1985, a few weeks before Böll's death, I, my wife, who is English, and Böll were talking about the Holocaust. Böll said he did not believe the Holocaust could have occurred anywhere but Germany, not in America or in England, given even the same degree of racism and anti-Semitism. He also said the main difference was not the political systems nor the strong and weak traditions of democracy, although the differing political institutions were important. Böll thought the German concept of perfectionism was the key to understanding how a civilized nation like the Germans could execute the Holocaust. It was a matter of carrying out an idea and a task derived from it to its consistent, logical, absolute conclusion. It is this same fanaticism at work in the German security system that he attacks in *The Safety Net*. In an aside to Stauffer, Böll revealed this deeper impulse for writing the novel: "The most perfect thing we have had in our German history was the concentration camps, and after I dealt with that, one can say as I worked with it: how people were

delivered up, with what perfection this net was spread all over Europe—German occupied Europe—and after I saw the first films and pictures of the concentration camps and read about the whole organization, I developed a certain aversion to perfectionism. That was really the most perfect thing ever in German history, and my fear of perfectness or perfection may have something to do with it [*The Safety Net*]'' (Stauffer 29).

44. See Bernd Balzer's treatment of this aspect of the novel and its relationship to the story of Count von Gleichen and Goethe's drama *Stella* ("Ausfall in die Sorglosigkeit . . . " 69–80).

45. See Viktor Böll, "Sicherheitsgeschädigt" 86, note 11.

46. See Viktor Böll, "Sicherheitsgeschädigt" 86, note 15a.

47. Quoted from James Heft, "What's the Point? America is Searching for a Sense of Purpose to Its Educational System," *Dimension*, University of Dayton (Winter 1989–90): 8.

48. Cited in Karl Marx, *Das Kapital I* (Frankfurt a/M: Ulstein, 1969): 565, note 74.

49. *Republic*, trans. B. Jowett, in *Plato*, ed. Louise Ropes Loumis (New York: Walter J. Black, 1942): 437–38.

50. The point Böll is making here through Hermann Wubler is that using grain to feed cattle to produce dairy products or meat yields less food than the grain itself. In terms of feeding the most people, it is more practical for poor countries to grow grain for domestic consumption than it is for them to develop a cattle or dairy industry. Poor countries, however, often choose to use farmland for the production of export goods—meat or dairy products— than to use the land to produce food for local consumption. Raising cattle for export creates, however, higher profits for the landowner and raises hard currency that enables the import of goods from the developed world. The statement by Hermann Wubler also suggests that even the grain German farmers use in the dairy industry could better be used for feeding the Third World.

CONCLUSION

German unification can only serve to make Böll's work more relevant. What he has written about the Federal Republic of Germany in his novels, stories, and essays, as well as in his other writings, will continue to be important reading material in the era of the new Germany. The united nation, whether under Christian or Social Democratic leadership, is unlikely to develop differently from the way West Germany has already evolved. Böll's art mirrored late Western twentieth-century society, and it will continue to reflect accurately the new Germany of the emerging twenty-first century. Böll's life's work will now have a double value. It will be a record of West German history and a permanent remainder of how much the new Germany will be like the old. It will show how the early postwar years have made Germany what it is now and how the liberal democratic capitalist values, with all their strengths and weaknesses, continue to form the new nation. Reading Böll's work in the future will be like reading a prophecy of the destiny of a united Germany, especially its problems with social justice. As we wait out the end of this century, it will be interesting to see if another German writer will develop into the chronicler of the next German era, if he or she will become, like Böll, both an artist of the people and conscience of the nation.

BIBLIOGRAPHY

Böll's Works
in English Translation

Absent without Leave and Other Stories. Trans. Leila Vennewitz. New York: McGraw-Hill, 1965.

Acquainted with The Night. Trans. Richard Graves. New York: Holt, 1954.

Adam and The Train: Two Novels. Trans. Leila Vennewitz. New York: McGraw-Hill, 1970.

Adam, Where Art Thou?. Trans. Mervyn Savill. New York: Criterion Books, 1955.

And Never Said a Word. Trans. Leila Vennewitz. New York: McGraw-Hill, 1978.

Billiards at Half-past Nine. Trans. Patrick Bowles. London: Weidenfeld & Nicolson, 1961; New York: McGraw-Hill, 1963.

The Bread of Those Early Years. Trans. Leila Vennewitz. New York: McGraw-Hill, 1976.

The Casualty. Trans. Leila Vennewitz. New York: Farrar, Straus, Giroux, 1986.

Children Are Civilians Too. Trans. Leila Vennewitz. New York: McGraw-Hill, 1970.

The Clown. Trans. Leila Vennewitz. New York: McGraw-Hill, 1965.

Eighteen Stories. Trans. Leila Vennewitz. New York: McGraw-Hill, 1966.

End of a Mission. Trans. Leila Vennewitz. New York: McGraw-Hill, 1968.

Group Portrait with Lady. Trans. Leila Vennewitz. New York: McGraw-Hill, 1973.

Irish Journal. Trans. Leila Vennewitz. New York: McGraw-Hill, 1967.

The Lost Honor of Katharina Blum. Trans. Leila Vennewitz. New York: McGraw-Hill, 1975.

Missing Persons and Other Essays. Trans. Leila Vennewitz. New York: McGraw-Hill, 1977.

"Poetry to 1972." Trans. Robert C. Conard in collaboration with Ralph Ley. *University of Dayton Review* 13.1 (Winter 1976): 23–44.

"Poetry from 1972 to 1984." Trans. Robert C. Conard in collaboration with Ralph Ley. *University of Dayton Review* 17.2 (Summer 1985): 5–14.

The Safety Net. Trans. Leila Vennewitz. New York: Knopf, 1982.
A Soldier's Legacy. Trans. Leila Vennewitz. New York: Knopf, 1985.
The Stories of Heinrich Böll. Trans. Leila Vennewitz. New York: Knopf, 1986.
Tomorrow and Yesterday. Trans. Mervyn Savill. New York: Criterion Books, 1957.
The Train Was on Time. Trans. Richard Graves. New York: Criterion books, 1956.
        Trans. Leila Vennewitz. New York: McGraw-Hill, 1970.
Traveller, If You Come to Spa. Trans. Mervyn Savill. London: Arco, 1956.
The Unguarded House. Trans. Mervyn Savill. London: Arco, 1957.
What's to Become of the Boy? Or, Something to Do with Books. Trans. Leila Vennewitz. New York: Knopf, 1984.
Women in a River Landscape. Trans. David McLintock. New York: Knopf, 1988.

Works by Heinrich Böll
Cited in Text

Bild, Bonn, Boenisch. Bornheim-Merten: Lamuv, 1984.
Das Heinrich Böll Lesebuch. Munich: Deutscher Taschenbuch Verlag, 1982.
Das Vermächtnis. Bornheim-Merten: Lamuv, 1982.
Die Fähigkeit zu trauern: Schriften und Reden 1983–1985. Bornheim-Merten: Lamuv, 1986.
Die Verwundung und andere frühe Erzählungen. Bornheim-Merten: Lamuv, 1983.
Du fährst zu oft nach Heidelberg. Bornheim-Merten: Lamuv, 1979.
"Einführung in die *Fürsorgliche Belagerung.*" *Text + Kritik* 33. Ed. Heinz Ludwig Arnold. Munich: Text + Kritik, 1982: 74–75.
Ein- und Zusprüche. Schriften, Reden und Prosa 1981–1983. Cologne: Kiepenheuer & Witsch, 1984.
Frauen vor Flußlandschaft. Cologne: Kiepenheuer & Witsch, 1985.
Fürsorgliche Belagerung. Cologne: Kiepenheuer & Witsch, 1979.
Gesammelte Erzählungen 1-2. Cologne: Kiepernheuer & Witsch, 1981.
"Interview mit mir selbst." *Mensch, Gesellschaft, Kirche bei Heinrich Böll.* Ed. Albrecht Beckel. Osnabrück: A. Fromm, 1966.
Querschnitte aus Interviews, Aufsätze und Reden. Eds. Viktor Böll and Renate Matthaei. Cologne: Kiepenheuer & Witsch, 1977.
Rom auf den ersten Blick: Reisen, Städte, Landschaften. Bornheim-Merten: Lamuv, 1987.
"Sicherheitsgeschädigt." Interview with Robert Stauffer. *Materialien zur Interpretation von Heinrich Bölls "Fürsorgliche Belagerung."* Cologne: Kiepenheuer & Witsch, 1981: 23–36.
"Über *Fürsorgliche Belagerung.*" Interview with Dieter Zillingen. *Materialien zur Interpretation von Heinrich Bölls "Fürsorgliche Belagerung".* Cologne: Kiepenheuer & Witsch, 1981: 13–22.

Vermintes Gelände: Essayistische Schriften 1977–1981. Cologne: Kiepenheuer & Witsch, 1982.

Was soll aus dem Jungen bloß werden? Oder irgendwas mit Büchern. Bornheim-Merten: Lamuv, 1981.

Werke: Essayistische Schriften und Reden 1–3. Cologne: Kiepenheuer & Witsch, 1979.

Werke: Hörspiele, Theaterstücke, Drehbücher, Gedichte 1. Cologne: Kiepenheuer & Witsch, 1979.

Werke: Interviews 1. Cologne: Kiepenheuer & Witsch, 1979.

Werke: Romane und Erzählungen 1–5. Cologne: Kiepenheuer & Witsch, 1977.

Wir kommen weit her. Gedichte. Mit Collagen von Klaus Staeck, Nachwort von Lew Kopelew. Göttingen: Steidl, 1986.

Other Works Cited

Adorno, Theodor W. *Prisms.* Trans. Samuel and Shierry Weber. Cambridge: MIT Press, 1981.

Agee, Joel. "Lieutenant Schelling, How He Died." Rev. of *A Soldier's Legacy,* by Heinrich Böll. *New York Times Book Review* 23 June 1985: 9.

Amery, Carl. *Die Kapitulation oder deutscher Katholizismus heute.* Hamburg: Rowohlt, 1963. Trans. Edward Quinn as *Capitulation: The Lesson of German Catholicism.* New York: Herder and Herder, 1967. This book was strongly influenced by Böll's "Brief an einen jungen Katholiken" and in turn this book's concept of "milieu catholicism" influenced Böll's attitude to the German Catholic Church.

Arendt, Hannah. *Eichmann in Jerusalem: A Report on the Banality of Evil.* New York: Viking, 1963.

Armster, Charlotte. "Katharina Blum: Violence and Exploitation of Sexuality." *Women in German Yearbook* 4. Eds. Marianne Burkhard and Jeanette Clausen. Lanham: UP of America, 1988: 83–95. An analysis of *Katharina Blum* from a feminist perspective

Aust, Stefan. *Der Baader-Meinhof Komplex.* Hamburg: Hoffmann Campe, 1986. A thorough treatment of the Baader-Meinhof Group. Provides the historical background necessary for understanding Böll's works dealing with terrorism.

Baker, Donna. "Nazism and the Petit Bourgeois Protagonist: The Novels of Grass, Böll, and Mann." *New German Critique* 5 (Spring 1975): 77–105. Argues that the middle-class values of the protagonists in the novels of Grass, Böll, and Mann tend to lead these characters to passivity rather than to activism in their approach to the solution of social problems.

Balzer, Bernd. "Ausfall in die Sorglosigkeit? Heinrich Bölls *Fürsorgliche Belagerung.*" *Materialien zur Interpretation von Heinrich Bölls "Fürsorgliche Belagerung."* Cologne: Kiepenheuer & Witsch, 1981. 37–88.

Balzer, Bernd, Horst Denkler, Hartmut Eggert, Günter Holtz. *Die deutschsprachige Literatur in der Bundesrepublik Deutschland: Vorgeschichte und Entwicklungstendenzen.* Munich: Iudium, 1988. This book does a good job placing contemporary German literature in historical context.

Bance, Alan. "Germany." *The Second World War in Fiction.* Ed. Holger Klein with John Flower and Eric Homberg. London: MacMillan, 1984. 88–132. Bance relies heavily on Böll's war stories for his analysis of the Second World War.

Basmajian, Hamida. *Metaphors of Evil: Contemporary German Literature and the Shadow of Nazism.* Iowa City: U of Iowa P, 1979.

Beck, Evelyn T. "A Feminist Critique of Böll's *Ansichten eines Clowns.*" *University of Dayton Review* 12.2 (Spring 1976): 19–24. Beck sees the clown, Hans Schnier, as a negative figure for his exploitation of Marie and Marie as victim of male domination.

Beckel, Albrecht. *Mensch, Gesellschaft, Kirche bei Heinrich Böll, mit einem Beitrag von Heinrich Böll: "Interview mit mir selbst."* Osnabrück: A. Fromm, 1966. This important essay by Böll is available only in this book.

Bergson, Henri. *Le rire: Essai sur la signification du comique.* 143rd ed. Paris: Presses universitaires de France, 1961. Trans. Cloudesly Brereton and Fred Rothwell as *Laughter.* New York: MacMillan, 1912. Bergson's theory of humor applies well to Böll's satires.

Bernáth, Arpád. "Heinrich Bölls historische Romane als Interpretationen von Handlungsmodellen. Eine Untersuchung der Werke *Der Zug war pünktlich* und *Wo warst du, Adam.*" *Studia Poetica* (Publication of the University of Szeged, Hungary) 3 (1980): 307–70.

Bernhard, Hans Joachim. *Die Romane Heinrich Bölls. Gesellschaftskritik und Gemeinschaftsutopie.* 2nd ed. Berlin: Rütten & Loening, 1973. This book is still the best analysis of Böll's work from an East German, Marxist perspective.

Beth, Hanno, ed. *Heinrich Böll: Eine Einführung in das Gesamtwerk in Einzelinterpretationen.* 2nd ed. Königstein/Ts: Scriptor, 1980.

Bienek, Horst. *Werkstattgespräche mit Schriftstellern.* 2nd ed. Munich: Hanser, 1962. This collection of interviews with German writers contains one of the most important interviews Böll has ever given.

Böll, Viktor. "Sicherheitstgeschädigt: Personal und Leser." *Text + Kritik* 33. Ed. Heinz Ludwig Arnold. Munich: Text + Kritik, 1982: 76–88.

Böll, Viktor, and Ivonne Jürgensen, eds. *Heinrich Böll als Filmautor.* Cologne: Stadt Köln Stadtbücherei, 1982. The only book available on the films made from Böll's works.

Böll, Viktor, and Gabriele Ricke, eds. *Heinrich Böll . . . gebunden an Zeit und Zeitgenossenschaft. . . .* Cologne: Stadt Köln Stadtbücherei, 1988.

Buschmann, Christel. "Da machen wir nicht mit, Herr Staatssekretär. . . ." *Heinrich Böll als Filmautor.* Eds. Viktor Böll and Ivonne Jürgensen. Cologne: Stadt Köln Stadtbücherei, 1982. 66–68.

Cernyak-Spatz, Susan E. *German Holocaust Literature*. New York: Peter Lang, 1985.

Conard, Robert C. *Heinrich Böll*. Twayne World Author Series. Boston: G. K. Hall, 1981.

————. "Heinrich Böll's 'Nicht nur zur Weihnachtszeit': A Satire for All Ages." *Germanic Review* 59 (1984): 97–103.

————. "Notes to the Poems of Heinrich Böll since 1972." *University of Dayton Review* 17.2 (Summer 1985): 15–21.

————, trans. "The Poems of Heinrich Böll since 1972," in collaboration with Ralph Ley. *University of Dayton Review* 17.2 (Summer 1985): 5–14.

————. "The Relationship of Heinrich Böll's Satire 'The Thrower-away' to Jonathan Swift's 'A Modest Proposal.'" *The Michigan Academican* 10 (Summer 1977): 37–46.

Demetz, Peter. *Postwar German Literature*. New York: Pegasus, 1970, 185–98.

Deschner, Margarete. "Böll's 'Lady': A New Eve." *University of Dayton Review* 11.2 (1974): 11–23.

Durzak, Manfred. "Heinrich Bölls epische Summe? Zur Analyse und Wirkung seines Romans *Gruppenbild mit Dame.*" *Basis: Jahrbuch für deutsche Gegenwartsliteratur* 13. Frankfurt a/M: Athenäum, 1972. 174–97. This essay is important because it reveals the sources of the military quotations and material Böll uses in his novel.

————. *Der deutsche Roman der Gegenwart*. Stuttgart: Kohlhammer, 1971: 19–106.

Eco, Umberto. *The Name of the Rose*. Trans. William Weaver. San Diego: Harcourt, 1983.

Ezarahi, Sidra Dekoven. *By Words Alone: The Holocaust in Literature*. Chicago: U of Chicago P, 1980.

Fischer, Fritz. *From Kaiserreich to Third Reich: Elements of Continuity in German History, 1871–1945*. Trans. and introduced by Roger Fletcher. London: Allen & Unwin, 1986.

Fraenkel, Ernst. "Historical Obstacles to Parliamentary Government in Germany." *The Path to Dictatorship 1918–1933*. Trans. John Conway. Garden City, NY: Doubleday, 1966: 19–31.

Friedrichsmeyer, Erhard. *Die satirische Kurzprosa Heinrich Bölls*. UNC Studies in Germanic Languages and Literature 97. Chapel Hill: U of North Carolina P, 1981. The only existing thorough treatment of Böll's satires.

Golden, Leon. "Aristotle on Comedy." *Journal of Aesthetics and Art Criticism* 42 (1984): 283–90.

————. "Eco's Reconstruction of Aristotle's Theory of Comedy in *The Name of the Rose.*" *Classical and Modern Literature* 6.4 (1986): 239–49.

Grothmann, Wilhelm H. "Zur Struktur des Humors in Heinrich Bölls *Gruppenbild mit Dame*". *German Quarterly* 50.2 (1977): 150–60.

Grützbach, Frank, ed. *Heinrich Böll: Freies Geleit für Ulrike Meinhof. Ein Artikel und seine Folgen.* Cologne: Kiepenheuer & Witsch, 1972. Historically, this book is important because it documents the enormous social impact of Böll's Meinhof essay.

Haase, Horst. "Charakter und Funktion der zentralen Symbolik in Heinrich Bölls Roman *Billard um halbzehn.*" *Weimarer Beiträge* 10 (1964): 219–26.

Herlyn, Heinrich. *Heinrich Böll und Herbert Marcuse. Literatur als Utopie.* Lampertheim: Kübler, 1979. An excellent study of Böll's use of the concept of *Leistungsverweigerung* as a principle of a humane world.

Hoffmann, Gabriele. *Heinrich Böll.* Bornheim-Merten: Lamuv, 1986. This biography was commissioned by the Böll family shortly after Böll's death. Although written in a journalistic style, it contains an abundance of information on Böll's life not available elsewhere.

Huber, Lothar. "Zur satirischen Methode in den Werken Heinrich Bölls." *Sprachkunst* 15.1 (1984): 50–67.

Jarausch, Konrad H. "Removing the Nazi Stain? The Quarrel of the German Historians." *German Studies Review* 11.2 (1988): 285–302. A thorough account of the historians' debate, showing its importance in understanding contemporary Germany now and for years to come.

Jeziorkowski, Klaus. *Rhythmus und Figur: Zur Technik der epischen Konstruktion in Heinrich Bölls "Der Wegwerfer" und "Billard um halbzehn".* Bad Homburg: Gehlen, 1968. Ignoring the political and sociological aspects of Böll's work, Jeziorkowski reveals important aesthetic structures in *Billiards* and in "The Thrower-Away."

Kalow, Gert. "Heinrich Böll." *Christliche Dichter der Gegenwart.* Ed. Hermann Friedmann and Otto Mann. Heidelberg: Rothe, 1955. 426–35.

Kurz, Paul Konrad. "Heinrich Böll: Die Denunziation des Krieges und der Katholiken." *Stimmen der Zeit* 96 (1971): 17–30.

Kuschel, Karl-Josef. "The Christianity of Heinrich Böll." Trans. Arlene Swindler. *Cross Currents* 36.1 (Spring 1989): 21–36. Although this essay is not cited in the text, it is such a clear analysis of the Christian values in Böll's life and work that it is worth listing here.

Langer, Lawrence. *The Holocaust and the Literary Imagination.* New Haven: Yale UP, 1975.

———. *Versions of Survival: The Holocaust and the Human Spirit.* Albany: State U of New York P, 1982.

Lattmann, Dieter. Rev. of *Frauen vor Flußlandschaft,* by Heinrich Böll. *Die Horen* 30.3 (1985): 197–200. More than any other reviewer of *Frauen,* Lattmann sees the political importance of the work.

Ley, Ralph, ed. *Böll für Zeitgenossen: Ein kulturgeschichtliches Lesebuch.* New York: Harper & Row, 1970. Unfortunately, this excellent reader is now out of print. The importance of the book comes from its perceptive introductions to the various chosen readings.

————. "Compassion, Catholicism, and Communism: Reflections on Böll's *Gruppenbild mit Dame.*" *University of Dayton Review* 10.2 (1973): 25–39.

Marcuse, Herbert. *Eros and Civilization: A Philosophical Inquiry into Freud.* Boston: Beacon Press, 1955, 1966. An essential book in understanding Böll's view of contemporary western society.

Martin, Werner. *Heinrich Böll: Eine Bibliographie seiner Werke.* Hildesheim: Olms, 1975. An excellent bibliography up to 1975.

Mitscherlich, Alexander and Margarete. *Die Unfähigkeit zu trauern.* Munich: Piper, 1967, 18th ed. 1986. A very important book to help understand Böll's attitude toward postwar Germany.

Mitscherlich, Margarete. *Erinnerungsarbeit zur Psychoanalyse der Unfähigkeit zu trauern.* Frankfurt: S. Fischer, 1987.

Nägele, Rainer. *Heinrich Böll: Einführung in das Werk und in die Forschung.* Frankfurt a/M: Athenäum Fischer Taschenbuch Verlag, 1976. This *Forschungsbericht,* summary of current scholarship, is extremely thorough up to the mid 1970s and rich in insights.

Parenti, Michael. *Inventing Reality: The Politics of the Mass Media.* New York: St. Martin's, 1986. This analysis of the practices of the western media provides a point of view helpful in understanding Böll's own criticism of the media.

Poser, Therese. "Heinrich Böll: *Billard um halbzehn*" *Möglichkeiten des modernen deutschen Romans.* 2nd ed. Ed. Rolf Geissler. Frankfurt a/M: Diesterweg, 1965. 232–55.

Price, Martin. *Swift's Rhetorical Art: A Study in Structure and Meaning.* London: Archon Books, 1963.

Reich-Ranicki, Marcel. *Deutsche Literatur in West und Ost.* Munich: Piper Verlag, 1963. 120–42.

————. "Nette Kapitalisten und nette Terroristen." Rev. of *Fürsorgliche Belagerung. Frankfurter Allgemeine Zeitung* 4 Aug. 1979.

Reid, James Henderson. *Heinrich Böll: A German for His Time.* Oxford: Oswald Wolff, 1988. Reid places Böll's life and works in the context of his times.

————. *Heinrich Böll: Withdrawal and Re-emergence.* London: Oswald Wolff, 1973.

Rosenthal, Erwin Theodor. "Böll in Brasilien." *Böll: Untersuchungen zum Werk.* Ed. Manfred Jurgensen. Bern: Francke Verlag, 1975. 147–52. Rosenthal explains why Böll's work is popular in Brazil, a country seemingly very different from West Germany.

Rousseau, Jean-Jacques. "Discour sur l'origine de l'inégalité parmi les hommes." *The Age of Enlightenment: An Anthology of Eighteenth Century French Literature.* 2nd ed. Eds. Otis E. Fellows and Norman L. Torrey. Englewood Cliffs: Prentice Hall, 1971. 525–42.

Ryan, Judith. *The Uncompleted Past: Postwar German Novels and the Third Reich*. Detroit: Wayne State UP, 1983. 81–94.

Schiller, Friedrich. *Complete Works of Friedrich Schiller*. 8 vols. New York: Collier & Sons, 1902.

Schlöndorff, Volker, and Margarethe von Trotta, dirs. *Die verlorene Ehre der Katharina Blum*. Paramount/Orion/WDR/Biskop-Film, 1975. Böll commented that this film was better than his book.

Schöter, Klaus. *Heinrich Böll in Selbstzeugnissen und Bilddokumenten*. Reinbek bei Hamburg: Rowolt, 1982.

Schütte, Wolfram. "Lauter nette Menschen." Rev. of *Fürsorgliche Belagerung*. *Frankfurter Rundschau* 4 August 1979.

Schwab-Felisch, Hans. "Der Böll der frühen Jahre." *In Sachen Böll*. 3rd ed. Ed. Marcel Reich-Ranicki. Cologne: Kiepenheuer & Witsch, 1970. 213–23.

Smith, Stephen. "Schizos Vernissage und die Treue der Liebe." *Heinrich Böll: Eine Einführung in das Gesamtwerk*. Ed. Hanno Beth. Königstein: Skriptor, 1980. 97–128.

Sokel, Walter. "Perspektive und Dualismus." *In Sachen Böll*. 3rd ed. Ed. Marcel Reich-Ranicki. Cologne: Kiepenheuer & Witsch, 1970. 333–44.

Stauffer, Robert. "Sicherheitsgeschädigt." Interview with Heinrich Böll. *Materialien zur Interpretation von Heinrich Bölls "Fürsorgliche Belagerung"*. Cologne: Kiepenheuer & Witsch, 1981. 23–36.

Stern, Fritz. "Introduction." *The Path to Dictatorship 1918–1933*. Trans. John Conway. Garden City, NY: Doubleday, 1966. vii–xxii.

Swift, Jonathan. "A Modest Proposal." *Gulliver's Travels and Other Writings*. Ed. Louis A. Landa. Boston: Houghton Mifflin, 1960. 439–47.

Thomas, Marlo, actress. *The Lost Honor of Kathryn Beck*. Dir. Simon Langton. 1984. Thomas produced this film as well as starred in it. Despite singificant changes, it maintains the spirit of Böll's novella.

Vogt, Jochen. *Heinrich Böll*. Munich: C. H. Beck, 1978.

Wintzen, René. "Heinrich Böll, l'homme et l'oeuvre." *Allemagnes d'aujourd'hui*, Nouvelle série 107 (Jan.-Mar. 1989): 79–96. Wintzen succeeds in succinctly summarizing Böll's life and works and points out why Böll is important for French readers.

Zillingen, Dieter. "Über *Fürsorgliche Belagerung*." Interview with Heinrich Böll. *Materialien zur Interpretation von Heinrich Bölls "Fürsorgliche Belagerung"* Cologne: Kiepenheuer & Witsch, 1981. 13–22.

Ziolkowski, Theodore. "Heinrich Böll: Conscience and Craft." *Books Abroad* 34 (1960): 213–22. An excellent explanation of the combination in Böll's work of morality and commitment.

———. "The Author as *Advocatus Dei* in Heinrich Böll's *Group Portrait with Lady*." *University of Dayton Review* 12.2 (1976): 7–18. This article is the best explanation of Böll's narrative strategy in the novel.

Index